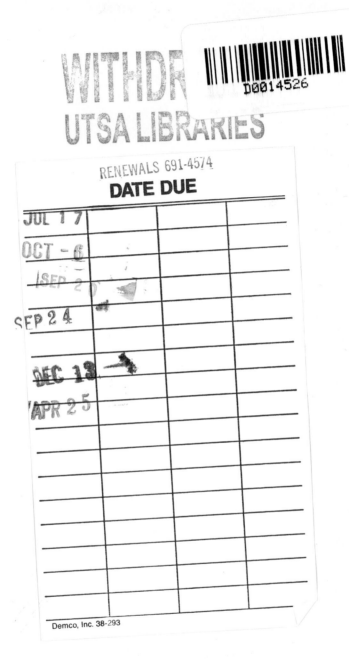

THE PRESIDENCY AND THE MANAGEMENT OF NATIONAL SECURITY

THE
PRESIDENCY
AND THE
MANAGEMENT
OF
NATIONAL
SECURITY

Carnes Lord

THE FREE PRESS
A Division of Macmillan, Inc.
NEW YORK

Collier Macmillan Publishers
LONDON

The Free Press
A Division of Macmillan, Inc.
866 Third Avenue, New York, N.Y. 10022

Collier Macmillan Canada, Inc.

Printed in the United States of America

printing number

1 2 3 4 5 6 7 8 9 10

Library of Congress Cataloging-in-Publication Data

Lord, Carnes.
    The presidency and the management of national security / Carnes Lord.
        p.   cm.
    Bibliography: p.
    Includes index.
    ISBN 0–02–919341–9
    1. United States—National security—Decision making.   2. National Security Council (U.S.)   3. Presidents—United States.   I. Title.
UA23.L7   1988
353.0089—dc19   88–21248
                                                                                    CIP

A version of the Introduction appeared originally under the title "Executive Power and Our Security" in *The National Interest* (Spring 1987), pp. 3–13. Reprinted by permission.

Chapter 4 appeared originally in slightly different form in *Comparative Strategy*, vol. 6, no. 3 (1987), pp. 241–79, Crane, Russak & Company, Inc., New York, NY 10017. Reprinted by permission.

For Meredith

Contents

Preface

THIS STUDY of national security decision making and the contemporary American presidency is not a memoir, though it is informed by recent White House experience; neither is it a conventionally academic work, though I believe it shows a reasonable deference to accepted canons of scholarship. My primary intention has been to provide an analysis that will be of practical benefit to those who may in the future find themselves at the helm of national security affairs in Washington.

Some, though recognizing the need for a study of this kind, may find my approach overly theoretical in relation to its declared purpose and audience. To such readers, I would observe that much of what is wrong with the management of national security in the United States today has to do precisely with the inadequacy of the conceptual framework and basic assumptions supporting it. Above all, there has been a singular failure in both the academic and policy literature on this subject to connect national security decision making with broader issues concerning the nature of the federal bureaucracy and the proper role of the presidential office.

The subject broached here is a large one, and much of the terrain is hidden from ordinary view. I therefore owe a considerable debt to former and present American officials who have shared with me their experience of and reflections on the decision-making process in the White House and the national security agencies. I have learned a great deal over the years from William R. Bode, Seth Cropsey, Kenneth E. deGraffenreid, Manfred Eimer, Charles H. Fairbanks, Jr., Douglas J. Feith, David C. Jordan, Gary J. Schmitt, Abram N. Shulsky, Michael Uhlmann, and Paul Wolfowitz. Thanks are due in addition to Norman A. Bailey, James Ceaser, Richard B. Foster, Walter A. Jajko, Charles Kupperman, Rodney B. McDaniel, John M. Poindexter, Richard G. Stilwell, and Gus Weiss, who read the manuscript in whole or part and provided useful comments. Of course, none of those named necessarily endorses the positions I have adopted. Mention should also be made of the late Richard Beal, from whom I learned some of the arguments advanced here. His pioneering efforts in the areas of national-level information management and crisis planning deserve to be honored and sustained.

It is difficult to write dispassionately of a period and events in which one has been an engaged participant. I have made every effort to compose this study *sine ira et studio.* In doing so, I may have disappointed or offended some; on the other hand, I have gone to considerable lengths not to capitalize on former associations or to settle scores. Even where harsh judgments proved unavoidable, I remained mindful throughout of the unbelievable pressures and difficulties with which responsible officials of the federal government must daily contend as they try to carry out what is frequently an unrewarding and sometimes a personally ruinous service to their country.

Finally, I would like to acknowledge the generous support provided for this undertaking by the Lynde and Harry Bradley Foundation.

This book is dedicated to Meredith Irvin Lord, as a token of my love.

Carnes Lord
Alexandria, Virginia

THE PRESIDENCY AND THE MANAGEMENT OF NATIONAL SECURITY

Introduction

IN CALCULATING the fundamental strength of a nation in the face of strategic challenges, little attention is generally given to organizational factors. Yet history shows that these factors can have a major impact on the conduct of diplomacy and on military planning and operations. In the United States, questions relating to the organization of the government for national security tend to acquire political salience at irregular intervals and in unpredictable combinations. The controversy ignited in the fall of 1986 by the exposure of White House involvement in the clandestine sale of arms to the Khomeini regime in Iran and its link to support for the Nicaraguan Contras has given renewed prominence to the issue of the role of the President's National Security Adviser and the National Security Council (NSC) staff in the conduct of U.S. foreign and national security policy. Typically, the focus of public discussion has been the narrow issue of the propriety of an operational role for the NSC staff in sensitive diplomatic and intelligence matters. Yet the question of the role and functions of the NSC is a more fundamental one, involving as it does such basic issues as the nature and interrelationships of the various instruments of national power and the position of the presidency in the American political system. A debate on these larger matters is long overdue, and is essential if the achievements and shortcomings of the Reagan years are to be seen in their proper perspective.

There can be little question but that the Iran-Contra scandal and its handling by the White House produced a "crisis of confidence in the manner in which national security decisions are made and the role played by the NSC staff," to borrow the words of the Tower

Commission, the special review board that was appointed by the President in late 1986 to investigate the incident.[1] Although the commission's inquiry did not result in a call for major overhaul of the White House decision-making structure, it did raise serious questions about the use or abuse of the existing structure by national security officials in the White House and the agencies, as well as about the President's personal approach to managing the national security decision process as a whole.

These developments were doubly shocking because they were largely unanticipated. By common account, the Reagan presidency had been the most successful since at least that of Dwight D. Eisenhower, restoring a nearly lost faith in the presidency as an institution and in the ability of presidents to accomplish their political agenda. President Reagan had used his leverage over agency budgets to curb runaway growth in federal expenditures; in spite of a failure to redeem early pledges to abolish entire agencies, he made it profoundly unfashionable in all political quarters to promote particular domestic policies through the instrumentality of an expanding and increasingly autonomous public sector. Furthermore, the Reagan White House evidently learned the lessons of earlier Republican administrations, and moved aggressively to expand the number of politically certified executive appointees throughout the bureaucracy.[2]

In the national security area, the situation was rather different, but the overall picture had been of a White House certain of its purpose and in command of the necessary levers. When the administration entered office, it looked on the national security agencies as liberated allies rather than occupied enemy territory. Substantial increases in funding and personnel were sought for the military and the intelligence community, and an effort was made to secure their political rehabilitation after a decade or more of adversarial treatment by the Congress, the press, and (in the Carter years) the executive branch itself. Outward harmony between the national security bureaucracy and the President's executives had since prevailed. In terms of actual performance, there had been, prior to the Iran fiasco, no obvious foreign policy disasters, and (in Grenada in October 1983) a visible military success. And a relatively orderly interagency machinery for the development of national security policy was put in place, suppressing at least the more visible manifestations of the bureaucratic struggles that contributed to the incoherence afflicting key areas of American policy during the Carter era.

In spite of all this, however, it is clear that the Reagan presidency has not in any fundamental sense cured the ills that have plagued the U.S. national security establishment since at least World War II. Unfortunately, the Iran-Contra episode helped to obscure as much as to highlight the basic weaknesses in the management of national security under the Reagan administration. For the very fact that the Reagan NSC staff had expanded its operational involvement in sensitive areas, far from indicating a return to the Kissinger era of White House dominance of foreign policy, pointed rather to the opposite problem—the inability of the White House to ensure effective implementation of its policies by the national security bureaucracy. To be sure, part of the impetus for NSC involvement derived from a desire to circumvent congressional constraints on administration action. But it also reflected in significant part a lack of presidential confidence in the ability of the State Department and the Central Intelligence Agency to carry out a controversial policy with loyalty, discretion, and competence.

A closer look at the administration's performance in major areas of national security policy reveals persisting problems and few unambiguous achievements. In a great many cases, these failings are symptomatic not of a commanding and reckless White House, but rather one that never firmly grasped the reins of a rogue bureaucracy.

The administration's persisting difficulty in coping effectively with terrorism or its sponsors in spite of an early commitment to do so is one case in point. Another is the remarkable bureaucratic foot dragging that until recently had severely limited U.S. assistance to anticommunist insurgencies as called for under a "doctrine" personally identified with the President. Another is the series of disasters of recent years in the area of counterintelligence and security, of which the latest episode is the Moscow embassy scandal.[3]

In one of the most critical sectors of national security policy, arms control, bureaucratic disarray persisted throughout most of the administration. Fundamental disagreements between the departments of State and Defense over approaches to U.S.–Soviet arms control questions led to a situation marked by paralysis of normal interagency procedures and spasmodic and ad hoc decision making at the top. That the administration lacked a coherent strategy linking arms control to U.S. defense planning was evident in the aftermath of the Reykjavik summit in October 1986, as the Joint Chiefs of Staff (JCS) joined the NATO defense ministers in questioning the President's proposal to eliminate all U.S. and Soviet nuclear-armed ballistic missiles within ten years. It later became clear that the

JCS had not had an opportunity to analyze the military implications of the administration positions presented at Reykjavik.

Furthermore, in spite of significant improvements in the nation's military posture since 1980, the systemic weaknesses of the U.S. defense establishment have in recent years drawn cogent commentary and calls for reform from observers across the political spectrum. Even the Grenada action suffered, in the view of many critics, from interservice competition, command and communications failures, and inept planning. Widely acknowledged inadequacies in the areas of resource allocation, defense procurement, and strategic direction of the armed forces have recently led to congressional action to strengthen the JCS chairman and staff and to efforts to reform the defense acquisition process, improve strategic and resource planning, and improve the organization and management of capabilities for low intensity conflict. It is scarcely to the administration's credit that many of these reforms have been merely tolerated when not actively opposed by the Department of Defense and the White House.

Former National Security Adviser Zbigniew Brzezinski has argued that this unsatisfactory record reflects an overall failure of the Reagan administration to develop a "grand design" for dealing with the major foreign policy challenges facing it. According to him,

> [t]his condition is due in part to the president's own style of leadership and in part to the continuing dilution of effective executive control over foreign policy in the American system as a whole. The president has not imposed a systematic top-down decision-making system either on the executive branch as a whole or on his associates. . . . Today, the decision-making process at the very top is institutionally more fragmented than at any point since World War II.[4]

Henry Kissinger, former Secretary of State as well as National Security Adviser, has echoed this analysis. Speaking specifically of the arms control policy process, Kissinger traced the current state of affairs to

> the long-standing failure of the machinery for developing national strategy. Negotiating positions emerge from interdepartmental contests that focus on defending entrenched positions rather than defining national goals. Relations between the State and Defense departments, rarely cordial in any administration, are at their nadir.[5]

It should be recalled that the first Reagan administration came into power pledged to return to "cabinet government" after a decade of intermittent controversy over the relationship of the National Security Adviser and the Secretary of State. Unlike other recent presidents who made such a promise, Reagan by and large kept it. He remained committed to a system involving relatively autonomous cabinet departments and a White House staff of circumscribed authority. This has been particularly evident in the national security area, where the departments of State and Defense and the Central Intelligence Agency all evolved into baronies headed by strong and long-tenured presidential appointees, while a succession of National Security Advisers (six in eight years) had to operate under a variety of personal handicaps and in a White House environment of indifference or positive hostility.

In spite of the animus against bureaucracy in the nation at large, there is a tendency both in and outside Washington to accept at face value the claims of the various national security agencies to perform their tasks with professional competence and political neutrality. The question of the President's relation to the federal bureaucracy is still widely viewed in terms of the distinction between "politics" and "administration" deriving from textbook theories of public administration. Implicit in this distinction are a number of dubious or false assumptions—that the perspective of the President is purely one of political posture or ideology; that the staff and appointees of the President are similarly "political" rather than "substantive" or genuinely expert in any operational sense; and that the substance of the issues with which bureaucracies deal is somehow neutral or apolitical and hence susceptible to routinized administrative handling. Taken to its extreme, such a view tends to deny any real legitimacy to presidential involvement in agency operations or, indeed, in substantive policy making.

Although this view has little standing in contemporary theories of the policy process,[6] it continues to enjoy favor within the bureaucracy itself, if only in half-conscious versions. This is especially the case in the national security bureaucracy. The military, with its special relationship to the President in his capacity as commander-in-chief as well as its unique operational requirements and highly specialized professional skills, not surprisingly remains highly sensitive to civilian encroachment on what are felt to be its prerogatives. The intelligence community tends to see itself as the nation's repository of objective knowledge of the world, a sort of national university, untainted by association with the administration in power. And the State Department—more precisely, the Foreign Service—continues to regard itself as an elite professional corps that is uniquely qualified to manage the nation's foreign relations.

It should not be necessary to make the elementary point that the President, as the nation's highest elected official, has not only the right but the duty to ensure that the policies with which he has identified himself are fully reflected in the operations of the executive branch of the government. The form of government of the United States is democracy—not bureaucracy, technocracy, or meritocracy. To the extent that presidential involvement in the operations of the executive branch agencies proves incompetent or unlawful, it is up to the Congress or the courts to restrain it. In our constitutional scheme, there is no basis for federal agencies acting autonomously in derogation of the power of the President. Unfortunately, the realities of contemporary American politics are quite otherwise.

Failure to impose a presidential perspective on the federal bureaucracy would perhaps not be so worrisome if the bureaucracy were capable by itself of operating in a rational and effective manner. If that were the case, the imprint of presidential policy would be unnecessary at best and undesirable at worst—the price that has to be paid for the political legitimacy that a President elected by the nation as a whole bestows on the operations of government. The proper relationship of the President to the bureaucracy would then be one of complete detachment from substantive policy making, with political control exercised solely through the power of appointment to senior positions in the departments.

Yet few serious observers of the Washington scene would attempt to defend such a view. That bureaucratic behavior is driven by fundamental pathologies is the universal experience of those who have worked in and studied modern American government. Given this fact, it is natural to ask whether or to what extent the pathologies of bureaucracy can be treated by presidential action, since the President is uniquely positioned and empowered to affect what happens in the agencies that formally report to him. Most observers would readily admit that presidential involvement plays an important—indeed, an essential—role in the direction, coordination, and control of the agencies of government.

That so little attention has been paid to the general issue of the proper scope of presidential power and action during the Reagan years is surprising only at first sight. Contemporary American conservatism remains profoundly ambivalent concerning the presidency as an institution as well as the role of the federal government. For many years, presidential power was viewed on all sides as the chosen instrument for the implementation of the liberal agenda in American politics. Even the ostensibly conservative Richard Nixon failed to employ the presidency in the service of conservative domestic or foreign policies; and the abuses of presidential power committed in his name were at least as repugnant to many conservatives as they were to liberals. Ronald Reagan has clearly remained sensitive to the legacy of the "imperial presidency," and deliberately avoided both the appearance and the reality of an activist and commanding presidential role; and conservatives have not attempted to challenge this stance. At the same time, liberals have long ceased viewing the presidency as their institution of choice. Congress, the media, the courts, and the bureaucracy have all proven more promising vehicles for the advancement of liberal policies.[7]

Ironically, the Reagan presidency has contributed at least as much by its successes as by its failures to the prolongation of the crisis of presidential leadership which began with Watergate. Because liberals and conservatives alike have for their own reasons been satisfied with a limited presidency, and because that limited presidency has (at least until recently) proven highly effective in a political sense, few incentives existed on any side to reopen the question of the powers and role of the presidential office. But there is little reason to expect this situation to persist under Reagan's successor. For conservatives, the question will arise whether the conservative agenda can make any further headway under a Republican President lacking Reagan's broad personal appeal without the presidency itself being made institutionally stronger. For Democrats, recovery of the presidency would pose new opportunities; with a Senate that is heavily even if not predominantly Republican, an activist President might be required so as to capitalize fully on those opportunities. When consideration is given to current trends in the judicial branch as well, it is entirely conceivable that liberals will once again come to look favorably on measures to augment the power of the presidency.

A comprehensive treatment of the presidency today would have to devote considerable attention to recent developments in presidential-congressional relations. There is no doubt that Congress is afflicted by pathologies at least as disabling as those of the executive branch. Overlapping and unclear committee jurisdictions, lack of overall discipline and leadership, proliferation of staffs, mishandling of sensitive information, micromanagement, wholly unrealistic reporting requirements, and an incomprehensible and chaotic budget process are widely acknowledged problems.[8] Less often remarked but equally troubling is the growing tendency for members of Congress to assume essentially executive roles in critical foreign and defense policy areas such as nuclear force planning and arms control, and to ignore traditional constraints on independent dealing with foreign governments. It is almost certainly fair to say that the imbalance in the executive-legislative relationship that resulted from Watergate has not only not been corrected, but in important areas has worsened substantially.

Also of considerable relevance for understanding the limitations on presidential power today is the role of the national media. "Decision, activity, secrecy, and dispatch"—such were the terms chosen by Alexander Hamilton to illustrate the characteristics of executive "energy." The bureaucracy and the Congress create problems in all of these areas, but secrecy is surely most threatened from the quarter of the media. Through the power they have asserted over the communication of information derived from or concerning the federal government, the media have become willy-nilly an important player in national politics. The extent to which this development has constrained and distorted policy making within the executive branch itself is insufficiently understood. Again, the remarkable success of Ronald Reagan in dealing with the media has only served to conceal an intractable problem that challenges in a fundamental way the authority and effectiveness of the presidency as an institution.[9]

Nevertheless, the gravity of the challenge to the presidency posed by Congress and the media can easily be overstated. What is truly fatal to presidential power is not so much Congress and the media by themselves, but Congress and the media in alliance with elements within the federal bureaucracy. This is particularly the case in the national security area, where the bureaucracy has a monopoly on the relevant information and undisputed responsibility for the development of policy. When important elements within the national security bureaucracy are out of step with the President's views, they are excellently positioned to thwart him simply by premature or partial disclosure of sensitive information to similarly minded congressional and media contacts.

It will be said that such leaks are inevitable under any circumstances. Yet the porousness of the American bureaucracy is unique in the world, and the situation today is almost certainly worse than it was ten years ago, and much worse than it was prior to Watergate. Furthermore, it is generally agreed that leaks tend to come from relatively high levels within agencies. This suggests a serious breakdown in the effectiveness of presidential control over political appointees as well as the senior career bureaucracy.

Some initial comments concerning the general approach and conclusions of this inquiry may be in order.

Many studies of bureaucratic politics suffer from an overly theoretical or formalistic approach which can be traced to characteristic deficiencies in contemporary American social science. The underlying assumption of such studies is that organizational behavior can be analyzed in terms of universal laws that are insensitive to the goals particular organizations serve and the kinds of political and cultural settings in which they operate. A twofold distortion results from this. On the one hand, bureaucracies tend to be assimilated both to one another and to other large organizations such as business corporations, thereby obscuring both the very different functions and operational codes of key bureaucracies (particularly military and security bureaucracies) and the essentially political context in which such bureaucracies exist. On the other hand, bureaucracies tend to be analyzed in isolation from the larger political system and political culture of which they form a part.[10]

A preoccupation with formalistic organization charts is a common failing in many studies of the U.S. national security bureaucracy, and justifies to some degree the dismissive attitude toward organizational questions that is frequently encountered among knowledgeable observers of executive branch behavior. The usual objection is that "people" are more important than "organization." There is a sense in which this is undoubtedly true. The problem, however, is not only that "good people" can be rendered neutral or even actively dangerous by dysfunctional forms of organization, but also that "good people" as such are rarely available. Practically speaking, all bureaucratic managers, and in particular the President, tend to be faced with difficult choices between loyal and/or capable outsiders lacking relevant knowledge and bureaucratic skills, and experienced bureaucrats who are able to operate effectively but for objectives that may not coincide with those of their political superiors. The real question is how to structure organizational constraints and incentives so as to enable outsiders and careerists alike to function as loyal and effective officers of the President.[11]

A bureaucracy is not merely a formal set of relationships between organizational subunits, but a complex web of formal and informal operating procedures and personnel management practices. It is a mistake to dismiss the importance of formal organizational charts, but it is also necessary to recognize that the shifting around of boxes on such charts is not likely to achieve much unless accompanied by changes in standard operating procedures, including concrete penalties and incentives designed to affect individual behavior. Personnel systems, to the extent that they remain under agency control, tend to be the purest expressions of bureaucratic parochialism.[12] Attacking systemic problems in personnel management can be among the most effective ways to alter bureaucratic behavior over the long term—that is to say, to affect bureaucratic culture as distinguished from bureaucratic organization in a narrow sense.

Bureaucratic culture is not, however, simply a function of the characteristics of specific bureaucracies. It is shaped in fundamental though often subtle ways by the larger society. The American bureaucracy behaves as it does in very considerable measure because it is staffed and run by Americans. Whatever the difficulties with the idea of national character or style or the notion of political culture,[13] the relevant phenomena are observable and widely acknowledged. First, Americans, as a profoundly democratic or egalitarian people, tend to reach decisions by consensus, exercising leadership through persuasion rather than command. Second, because of this collective style of decision making, responsibility is diffused, and there is a tendency to avoid holding individuals accountable for failure. Third, partly for the reason just given and partly out of a sense of compassion that has independent cultural roots, Americans tend to shy away from the administration of punishment. Fourth, Americans tend to be pragmatic, viewing problems in isolation and as susceptible to technical solutions. Fifth, Americans tend to be oriented toward the present and the immediate future, lacking both historical memory and long-term horizons. Sixth, Americans have a marked tendency to view peace as the normal state of things and war or conflict as unnatural and wrong.

In order to appreciate the distinctiveness of the American style, it is sufficient to draw the contrast with the Soviet (or Russian) style, which is sharply different in every one of these respects. But many cultures are closer to the Soviet than to the American model.

Whatever view one may take of the moral worth of these American traits, it is clear that in practical terms they involve many liabilities. In particular, they handicap the American government in its efforts to understand and deal with the chief foreign threat to the security of the United States.[14]

The implications of this analysis for understanding the operating characteristics of the U.S. national security bureaucracy will be explored later on. But one point should be stressed at the outset. Because of their pragmatism and orientation toward the present, Americans tend to be poor at strategy, which requires holistic thinking and attention to the consequences of action over time. It is not surprising, therefore, that U.S. national security policy has rarely been underpinned by genuine strategic planning. In the American context, "policy" is most often the outcome of deliberation on specific and highly limited issues as they arise, rather than a systematic body of doctrine deriving from an overall analysis of the current international situation and a comprehensive strategy for dealing with it. This astrategic orientation is strongly reinforced by a bureaucratic culture that lacks centralized direction and control, since the weight of organizational incentives works against an integrative approach that is seen as providing unwelcome control over agency operations to other agencies or to a central planning staff.

It is the thesis of the present study that the organization and management of national security affairs in the United States has been, and remains, fundamentally unsatisfactory, and that the time has come to rethink in a systematic way the role of the presidency in the national security policy process. This is not intended as a reflection on the individuals who have served as political appointees in senior positions in the national security agencies during the Reagan years. Neither is it meant as an indictment of the professional integrity or competence of those who have made careers in the national security bureaucracy. The inability of senior political appointees to exercise full control of their agencies, and their tendency to adopt and champion agency perspectives, is altogether in the nature of things. The resistance of the bureaucracy to effective political control cannot be traced simply to motives of careerism or political disloyalty to a particular administration; as just indicated, it reflects deeper organizational and cultural realities.

One should not be either very optimistic or unduly pessimistic concerning the prospects for fundamental change in the way the United States presently manages its national security affairs. On the one hand, too much can be made of the power of the permanent government. There is much a President can do if he is serious about the prerogatives of his office. As will be argued at length below, the apparent intractability of the problem of bureaucracy derives in very considerable measure from theories or assumptions concerning presidential governance that can be shown to be questionable. I shall attempt to make the case that the disadvantages under which the President currently labors in his relationship with the national security bureaucracy could be substantially alleviated by a strengthened White House staff structure and enhanced White House control over the process of interagency policy development and implementation. The core of such a reform, a revamping of the National Security Council staff and system, is a measure that would not represent a radical departure from historical precedent or current political realities.

To be fully effective, however, reform of the NSC would need to be accompanied by changes in the organization and operations of the national security agencies. Furthermore, changes would be needed in the way the President himself handles his relationship with the agencies and the political executives who run them. For these reasons, it is important not to underestimate the cultural and political obstacles to reform of a fundamental sort. In a longer perspective, what is needed above all is a recovery of the Hamiltonian conception of the presidency as an institution uniquely capable of decision, activity, secrecy, and dispatch. Such an understanding of the presidency would necessarily involve a thorough rethinking of the relationship of the presidency as an institution to the Congress. It would also involve a rethinking—in full awareness of the operative cultural inhibitions—of the methods of presidential management of organizations and individuals. In the second place, American officials and the bureaucracies that serve them need to acquire a strategic outlook and strategic competence befitting the American role in the contemporary world.

This study does not attempt to do more than provide a preliminary analysis in support of the larger argument sketched here. It is limited almost exclusively to national security decision making; its principal focus is the National Security Council staff and system rather than the bureaucracy as such; and it does not pursue in a systematic way the complex and necessarily speculative dimension of bureaucratic culture.

In the first chapter, a general account is given of the nature of the federal bureaucracy, the nature and history of the office of the President, and the theoretical problem of presidential governance. The second chapter offers a discussion of the nature of national security and an overview of the national security bureaucracy and its pathologies. The third chapter presents a detailed analytical review of the history of the National Security Council, its staff, and the system of interagency policy development associated with it, from its beginnings in the 1940s to the present. In the fourth chapter, a comprehensive analysis is provided of the functions and role of the National Security Adviser and the NSC staff. I attempt to show that the NSC has been widely misunderstood primarily because of a lack of appreciation of its central function, which is or should be national-level strategic planning. At the same time, emphasis is given to a variety of operational roles which necessarily or properly fall within NSC's scope. The fifth chapter develops the implications of this analysis for the functioning of the NSC as an organization, including questions of staffing, internal organization and procedures, and external relationships to offices and entities in the White House as well as to the Congress. In the final chapter, the NSC's relationship to the national security bureaucracy is examined, and suggestions made for changes in the interagency system, in the organization and culture of the agencies, and in the President's general approach to the management of national security issues.

Reforming the operations of the national government is not a partisan issue. Congress has demonstrated as much in its bipartisan effort over the last several years to strengthen the role of the Joint Chiefs of Staff, as well as in recent legislation designed to encourage national-level strategic planning. Strengthening the presidency as an institution may bring short-term benefits to one or another of our political parties. But all should be able to agree that a strong presidency is vital for maintaining control of bureaucracies—the military and the intelligence services—whose autonomy has traditionally been a cause for concern in modern constitutional democracies, and for directing their employment with a single mind and will. More generally, responsible observers of all political stripes have to acknowledge that a strong presidency is essential over the longer term for maintaining the affection of allies, the respect of adversaries, and the support of the American public for measures which are never popular even when they are recognized as necessary.

Chapter 1

The Presidency and the Problem of Bureaucracy

THE CONSTITUTION OF THE UNITED STATES says virtually nothing about the relationship between the President and the executive departments of the government. In the early years of the Republic, presidential control over the departments was uncertain at best. Indeed, the issue of whether the President had sole authority to remove appointees became a major constitutional controversy in the 1790s, resolved by the narrowest of margins in the Senate. Only with Andrew Jackson did a President fully assert his authority to hire and fire federal officials. Only with Theodore Roosevelt and Woodrow Wilson did presidents regularly avail themselves of their constitutional empowerment to propose legislation to Congress, thus initiating the use of the federal bureaucracy for the development of presidential "policy" as distinct from the performance of routine administrative tasks. White House coordination of agency budget requests began only in the 1920s. With the rapid proliferation of federal agencies under the presidency of Franklin Delano Roosevelt in response to the economic crisis of the 1930s, the bureaucracy in its modern form was born.

It very quickly became evident that the expansion of the bureaucracy had created a qualitatively new form of federal governance, and one requiring a new conception of the role of the presidency itself. The increased scale of government, the increase in the number of activities in which government was now involved, and the growing impact of government on American society as a whole demanded that the President take on new responsibilities as chief administrator of the nation.[1]

While bureaucratization seems to be an inexorable tendency in

modern organizations of all kinds, there are at least three basic characteristics that distinguish the federal bureaucracy from other large
organizations, especially private organizations such as business corporations. First and most fundamentally, control of the bureaucracy
by its chief executive—the President—is highly attenuated. Second,
the bureaucracy lacks clear operational goals. Third, it lacks measures
of effective performance. Because they complicate or frustrate bureaucratic accountability, the latter two characteristics further exacerbate the problem of presidential control.[2]

In theory (and to a large degree in the popular understanding),
the goals of the bureaucracy are established through the policies
laid down by the President and the Congress, whether in the form
of legislation, executive order, or declaration (resolutions, speeches,
and the like). The President then ensures the execution of policy
through his control over the appointment of executive officials at
various levels throughout the bureaucracy. In practice, the situation
is considerably more complicated.

The most obvious complication is in the form of the Congress.
As just indicated, the Congress participates jointly with the President
in the development of the policies that constitute the formal goals
of bureaucratic activity. In addition, Congress exercises an extensive
if variable control over key aspects of agency operations, particularly
funding, organization, and personnel policies. The loyalties of the
bureaucracy are as a result inherently divided. Even in the absence
of conflict between the President and Congress over questions of
policy, Congress has substantial political incentives for interfering
in agency operations. Where such conflict does occur, Congress
has many resources. Especially with the recent growth in congressional bureaucracy, interested members of Congress may have available to them, in their own or their committee staffs or in congressional
service agencies, as much or more expertise in substantive policy
areas as senior political appointees of an agency itself. Furthermore,
Congress is capable of exerting considerable leverage over the career
bureaucracy through its statutory power relative to the civil service
personnel system, as well as through informal channels of political
patronage. The proliferation of congressional staffs has also permitted
a level of scrutiny of agency budgets that can and frequently does
become indistinguishable from operational management.[3]

Moreover, Congress is not without allies in its struggle with the
executive branch agencies. The media and a variety of organizations
in the private sector generally stand ready to aid and abet congres-

sional challenges to agency actions. Most agencies have more or less powerful private sector constituencies that can act to some degree as independent sources of policy formulation, and at the same time pervasively affect bureaucratic behavior through shaping professional loyalties and career hopes beyond the bureaucracy. The defense industry is of course the classic case, but in more recent years public interest groups of various sorts have come to play a similar role across a broad range of policy areas. The result of all this is that the bureaucracy as a whole tends to be highly permeable and subject to outside influence. Quite unlike the situation in private industry, for example, it is difficult if not impossible for the President or those personally loyal to him to control communication between the executive branch agencies and competing sources of authority or to enforce strict discipline in the development and implementation of policy.

Even without the problems created by these constitutional or political limitations on his authority, however, the President faces a multitude of constraints in attempting to make his writ run through the bureaucracy. These constraints derive from the nature of bureaucratic organization itself, the limitations of the political executive system as it currently exists, and the peculiar requirements and limitations of the President and his immediate office.

DYNAMICS OF BUREAUCRACY

Perhaps the most powerful factor determining bureaucratic behavior is the instinct of organizational self-preservation. Like other forms of life, bureaucracies tend to pursue survival before all other goals. Also like other forms of life, they tend to be resourceful in adapting to their environment. Because organizational survival depends on changing political circumstances, bureaucracies rarely hesitate to create various forms of political insurance against the possibility of eventual extinction. Bureaucratic entities are, as a result, notoriously difficult to kill off, even after their original reason for being has disappeared.

Organizational survival is inseparably bound up with organizational identity. Every bureaucracy has an "organizational essence," a set of functions or activities that most clearly define it and justify its existence. Left to themselves, bureaucracies tend to undertake projects and pursue goals that reinforce this organizational essence.

Often, though not always, such goals are at odds with the larger goals that bureaucracies are expected to pursue on behalf of the President and the nation. To take an overworked yet inevitable example, the State Department's organizational essence may be said to be the activity of negotiation and the function of producing agreements (or otherwise promoting harmony in relations with other nations). Yet to seek to compromise differences and conciliate antagonists is not necessarily the best way to safeguard the interests of the United States abroad. There will always be cases where the only attainable agreement is likely to be worse than no agreement at all, or where the defense of a principle is more important than concrete injuries to the United States that result from displeasing a particular country.[4]

The primacy of organizational essence explains an aspect of bureaucratic behavior that is frequently overlooked because it runs counter to a certain popular conception of bureaucracies as ruthlessly expansionist. The fact is that bureaucracies tend to value clarity of mission and autonomy of action more than expansion. Expansion into areas only peripherally related to their organizational essence is often viewed as potentially harmful to bureaucracies by increasing demands for coordination of their operations with other agencies and for oversight from above. In addition, it threatens to dilute or blur the central function which gives the organization its reason for being. The State Department again offers a case in point. Those who have argued over the years that the Secretary of State needs greater authority to coordinate the policies of other international agencies have generally failed to understand the strength of internal resistance to a major enhancement of State Department responsibilities in areas seen as peripheral to its main activity.[5]

To the extent that bureaucracies tend to grow, it is for different reasons. Frequently, an agency will develop new types of expertise for reasons of bureaucratic self-defense, without being strongly motivated to play an independent role in policy development. This leads to a multiplication of bureaucratic entities with overlapping interests, while creating new requirements for coordination and weakening the agency with primary responsibility in the area. In the second place, a trend toward even greater specialization and professionalization seems endemic to bureaucratic organizations. Subdivisions of agencies tend to expand and improve their own capabilities in order to validate their particular missions.

The essentially professional, specialized, or technical character of modern bureaucracies is particularly important for understanding their relationship to political authority. All large organizations develop particular vocabularies and standard operating procedures to cope with their particular functions. This rationalizing or routinizing of administrative activity is of the essence of bureaucracy. Over time, however, bureaucratic procedures and techniques tend to ossify, or to develop in ways that are less than fully rational. Technical language becomes increasingly esoteric and jargonized. Standard operating procedures take on a logic of their own. An organizational tradition and a professional guild spirit come into being.

All this is inevitable and to some degree even salutary. Yet it also accounts for much of what is wrong with bureaucracy, and what lies behind the resistance of career bureaucrats to political control. Specialization and routine lead to narrowness and rigidity of outlook. The tendency to view the functions of bureaucracy in technical terms—a tendency that is especially strong in the American context—usually involves insensitivity to strategic considerations as well as to political requirements. Professional *esprit* tends to encourage dislike and distrust of generalists in general and politicians in particular. Moreover, even with the best will on both sides, it can prove extremely difficult to translate bureaucratic terminology and operating routines into forms that are suitable for political decision. The military establishment provides the most obvious illustration of many of these tendencies; but it is by no means alone.[6]

A widely acknowledged feature of bureaucracy is its resistance to major change or to change altogether. Some argue that the immobilism of bureaucracy has been exaggerated; but there is little doubt that bureaucracies have an instinctive aversion to the disruption of accepted routines. Particularly in the American setting, where change usually requires the involvement and consensus of many actors, the tendency to seek change in small increments (if at all) is a powerful one. But this creates a built-in potential for conflict with decision makers who are attempting to implement political agendas.[7]

The relationship between career bureaucrats and political executives will be discussed more fully in a moment, but one point is worth making here. Because of the increasing interpenetration of career and political functions in the American bureaucracy and erosion of the ideal of a professional civil service, career officials are under increasing pressure to make a choice between overt collaboration with political appointees and a stance of detachment from them. To the extent that enthusiastic compliance with policy guidance

can be considered a liability from a career viewpoint, career bureaucrats are apt to withhold it.[8]

Complex and elusive in its effects, yet of fundamental importance
for understanding the pathologies of bureaucratic culture, is the
entire area of personnel policy and practices. The factors that tend
to be determining here are, first, organizational essence, and second,
the requirements for attracting and retaining competent personnel,
or what can be called organizational morale.[9] Chief among such
requirements are those relating to career development and promotion. Maximization of opportunities for promotion generally explains
a great deal about agency personnel systems. Indeed, the motive is
such a powerful one that it not infrequently interferes in serious
ways with the accomplishment of central organizational missions.
Probably the most damaging personnel-related dysfunction in both
the military and the foreign service bureaucracies is the shortness
of duty tours, especially for those on fast career tracks.[10]

POLITICAL EXECUTIVES

The "illusion of presidential government"—to borrow the title of
an influential recent book on this subject—is nowhere more evident
than in popular conceptions of the role of political appointees in
the federal government. Even if it could be assumed that the seven
hundred or so persons who obtain senior appointments throughout
the executive agencies are wholly the President's men (in fact, as
will be seen shortly, this cannot be assumed at all), the ability of
these political executives to carry out the President's policies is in
general severely limited. There is a tendency to see such people as
the equivalent of corporate troubleshooters who are given authority
to shake up a failing company and restore its profitability. An apter
comparison would be Swift's Gulliver. The typical political executive
is on his own in a strange land, and highly vulnerable to capture
and immobilization by a thousand tiny constraints.[11]

The first problem of the political executive is the tenuousness of
his claim to rule and the thinness of his political base. Political
executives are not elected; and only exceptionally do they have a
direct or close relationship with the President himself. Unless they
happen to have served previously in Congress, they are unlikely to
enjoy a strong base of political support elsewhere. If they have a
base of some sort in the public policy world, they may be tempted

to seek legitimacy through identification with the policies of that constituency rather than the policies of the President.

Second, political executives tend to lack a knowledge of the working environment of their agencies. In recent years, with the increasing specialization and professionalization of bureaucratic existence, there has been a tendency (particularly at subcabinet level) to seek political executives with solid substantive grounding in the relevant policy area. Yet it remains difficult to find candidates who combine such expertise with relevant bureaucratic experience. Lack of personal contacts, unfamiliarity with operational procedures, failure to master the intricacies of civil service regulations, and similar problems can be disabling for an executive who desires to have an immediate impact. The most readily available reservoir of relevant expertise tends to be congressional staffs. But the free-wheeling political environment of Capitol Hill is not necessarily the best preparation for managers of the highly routinized federal bureaucracy.

Third, political executives are transients. A tenure of well under two years is to be expected for them on the average. The reasons for this are entirely understandable—there is often considerable delay in recruiting and clearing prospective appointees at the beginning of an administration, and departure well before a presidential election is a common practice which, if not exactly noble, is not always easy to criticize and would be difficult to correct. On the (probably generous) assumption that a year is required to learn the job, no more than a year of fully effective performance can be expected from any one political appointee in a presidential term. In addition, of course, the expectations career bureaucrats have concerning the tenure of their political bosses can make a great deal of difference in their behavior. Political executives whose departure is anticipated in the near future become lame ducks in the same way presidents do toward the end of their final term.

Fourth, political executives do not really form a cohesive team. They tend to be drawn from all parts of the country and many different professions, with little prior contact and personal knowledge of one another—a "government of strangers," as Hugh Heclo has aptly characterized them. There are no mechanisms that bring them together, other than interagency committee meetings where they are often compelled to defend formal agency positions. Rather than providing each other mutual support, then, they tend to be highly vulnerable to defeat in detail by the bureaucracies over which they preside.

Fifth, the commitment of political executives to the President and his policies can by no means be taken for granted. Recruiting procedures for appointees tend to be haphazard and subject to a variety of political pressures. Party factions generally have to be satisfied, personal favors discharged. Public interest lobbying groups will ask the President to rise above politics and appoint the best man for the job; but the appointment of individuals with strong substantive qualifications carries potential liabilities. They may bring unwanted policy baggage, and their loyalty may be highly conditional. Many if not most political appointees are likely to owe their appointment to personal and professional connections at considerable remove from the President himself. Their future career prospects are likely to depend more on satisfying these private constituencies than on the quality of their service to the President.

Finally, political executives almost inevitably make compromises with the bureaucracy. Political executives cannot do everything themselves, and reliance on punitive methods to discipline bureaucratic subordinates may ensure control but frequently precludes cooperation. Moreover, no matter how fervent their loyalty to the President and how total their embrace of the substance of presidential policies, political executives develop a different perspective. They are necessarily more sensitive to the operational limitations on implementation of the President's policy agenda than is the President himself. They cannot afford to be completely unsympathetic to parochial agency concerns if they intend to operate effectively. In some cases, political executives will strongly embrace agency positions in order to purchase the active support of their subordinates for their own policy agendas. At the extreme, political executives become intellectually convinced or otherwise enamored of agency perspectives and culture, and "go native."

The President's relationship to his cabinet deserves particular attention in this regard. Here again, the analogy with the corporate world is entirely misleading. For an executive to demand a free hand in managing his own department makes perfect sense if he can readily be held accountable for his department's performance. Cabinet appointees regularly make such demands, yet for a number of reasons the President has great difficulty in holding them accountable for their actions and enforcing discipline. To begin with, cabinet officials generally see themselves as answerable to Congress as well as the President, and tend to develop close working relationships and political constituencies on Capitol Hill. Some are prominent figures who come to the job with powerful political connections. In many cases, then, the President must pay a political price for quarreling with a cabinet secretary. Second, as mentioned earlier, the lack of clear standards of performance (such as profit) in the bureaucracy makes accountability elusive. Frequently, presidents find they must tolerate a high level not merely of incompetent performance by cabinet officials but even of obstruction and sabotage of their policies, owing to the difficulty of constructing a case against a particular cabinet member that is actionable in political terms. Finally, presidents tend to be highly sensitive to the political liabilities—international as well as domestic—associated with visible personnel turmoil within their administrations. A few cabinet firings are sufficient to give rise to talk of "massacres" and "crisis of leadership." Expulsion of a cabinet secretary from an important department virtually guarantees the immunity of his successor to similar action.[12]

To say that cabinet secretaries are, in the notorious phrase of Charles Dawes, "the President's natural enemies" is perhaps over-drawn, but reflects an important truth.[13] The fortunes of a cabinet member are inextricably tied to the fortunes of his agency; the incentives for special pleading are powerful. And it is the Secretary, not the President, who controls the levers of power within his agency, and effectively commands the loyalty not merely of the career bureaucracy but of political executives at subordinate levels. Given the practical autonomy enjoyed by cabinet secretaries (especially those of the most important departments), it is entirely understandable that presidents should wish to retain some control over appointments to subcabinet positions. In practice, however, this often proves difficult. A White House Office of Personnel headed by an Assistant to the President is ostensibly responsible for recruiting and obtaining political clearance for candidates for presidential appointments in the agencies. But this office can only do so much in the face of pressure and opposition from an agency head, and the President is rarely able or willing to engage his own prestige in an unseemly struggle with his own appointees over such issues.

As remarked earlier, the Reagan administration has distinguished itself by its systematic effort to place political and ideological support-ers of the President in executive positions throughout the bureaucracy. This effort was less sustained and effective, however, in the case of the national security bureaucracy. The intelligence community has no political positions in the strict sense of the term, though there has been a tendency in recent years for the Director of Central

Intelligence to be seen as a political appointment.[14] In the case of the State Department, both Alexander Haig and George Shultz relied heavily on the Foreign Service, looking to its ranks to fill key positions and successfully resisting White House efforts to increase the number and influence of political appointees within the department itself. Only in the Office of the Secretary of Defense did strong political appointees give their department the unmistakable imprint of the President's policies and ideological outlook.[15]

THE PRESIDENT AND HIS OFFICE

The President differs fundamentally from the chief executive officer of a corporation. It is more tempting in some ways to see him (as many have tended to see Ronald Reagan) as a kind of chairman of the board, concerned to safeguard the interests of the stockholders by monitoring the corporation's activities and on occasion intervening in a critical decision, but content to leave day-to-day management to others. The problem with the analogy, however, is that the President cannot escape managerial responsibility on a day-to-day basis. Yet it is very difficult if not impossible for him to discharge that responsibility effectively.

The overriding difficulty is simply that the President has too many roles, and a span of control that is impossibly broad yet extremely hard to reduce to reasonable proportions. The President is not only chief administrator of the government, but head of state, chief diplomat, commander-in-chief of the armed forces, and titular leader of a political party. Direct access to the President is virtually obligatory for the members of his cabinet, senior military leaders, and senior politicians in the Congress and throughout the country, not to mention foreign leaders and diplomats.

In order to function effectively or indeed at all in these various roles, the President needs the support of a staff that is exclusively his. This requirement was recognized at a relatively early stage in the growth of bureaucratic government in America. In 1939, the Executive Office of the President (EOP) was created to serve as the central administrative office of the presidency, and quartered in close proximity to the White House. Though initially consisting mostly of the Bureau of the Budget (since 1970 the Office of Management and Budget), then a wholly technical organization staffed by career civil servants, the EOP has predictably evolved to encompass a range of political, policy, and operational functions. In the early 1950s, a staff was created to facilitate the work of the National Security Council, which was established by statute in 1947 to provide a mechanism for high-level coordination of foreign and defense policy. In spite of some initial uncertainty, the staff was brought within the EOP and made answerable directly to the President rather than to the Council collectively. Since that time, domestic and economic policy staffs in various configurations have become a permanent EOP feature, as have staff assistant positions for a variety of special functions, especially domestic political ones.[16]

In theory, an extensive presidential staff provides the solution to the multiple problems of presidential governance of the bureaucracy—translating presidential authority into operational policy guidelines, coordinating agency activities from a presidential perspective, and monitoring implementation of the President's policy agenda. In practice, however, presidential staffs have revealed characteristic weaknesses and limitations. Moreover, the nature of the presidency itself imposes certain constraints on presidential management and control of the executive branch agencies.

Perhaps the most fundamental if insufficiently remarked limitation on presidential control of the bureaucracy is the difficulty the President faces in bridging the gap between broad policy goals and operational reality. A President is lucky if he comes to office with a coherent and well thought out set of policies. Rarely is he able to devote much attention beforehand to strategies of policy implementation and the operational implications of the policies he has embraced. This places a burden on White House staffs, whose authority to elaborate operational policy guidelines is likely to be in doubt, while it offers irresistible opportunities for the bureaucracy to redefine presidential policy to suit its own preferences.

Another critical limitation is the necessity presidents are generally under to husband their political resources and make strategic choices between policies to be pursued. Because of the institutional weakness of the executive branch within the wider political system, presidents find that effective implementation of their policies often requires their direct and sustained personal involvement—a scarce commodity. A President who comes to power with a tenuous or mixed mandate is likely to find the problem particularly severe. Failure to appreciate this fundamental reality probably accounts for much of the ineffectiveness of the Carter presidency.[17] In the case of Ronald Reagan, on the other hand, it can be argued that the strategic decision taken at the beginning of the first term to concentrate the political resources of the President on the economic front was a miscalculation based on a failure to appreciate the need for the President to place a firm imprint on national security policy at the outset of his administration—or the relatively modest level of effort that would have been required to do so.

A strong presidential staff seems a logical antidote to the autonomy of cabinet officials as well as the other limitations on presidential power just discussed. Yet it is important to appreciate the weaknesses that have historically hampered the ability of these staffs to protect the President's interests and advance his programs.[18]

Presidential staffs are notoriously the creations of individual presidents, and reflect individual presidential needs and operating styles. This points to what is perhaps the chief weakness of such staffs—the permanent tension between their twin functions. Presidential staffs are inevitably called upon to serve both the personal needs of the President and the administrative needs of a large, complex, and impersonal bureaucracy. They represent the meeting ground of charismatic and rational governance (to appropriate Max Weber's well-known distinction), of the President as monarch and the President as republican manager.

The most serious limitations deriving from this fusion of personal and institutional perspectives have to do with the short time horizons and domestic political focus that are characteristic of presidents in their role as political leaders. The combined weight of American political culture and the short-term orientation of presidential politics works against long-term planning as a White House function. The primacy of domestic politics in presidential perspective works against a sustained and coherent White House staff effort in the field of foreign policy.

In the second place, because of the personalized nature of the operating environment, EOP staffs tend to be extraordinarily unstable in terms both of organization and personnel. The organization of the economic and domestic policy operations has changed kaleidoscopically over the years. Offices rise and fall rapidly in importance as their bosses gain or lose in presidential favor. Changes in administrations lead to virtually total turnover in political-level personnel, with a corresponding loss of institutional memory.

At the same time, bureaucratic elephantiasis is a disease from which presidential staffs are no more immune than any other form of organization. The EOP currently employs over 1,600 persons, and constitutes a bureaucracy probably as compartmentalized in structure and Byzantine in its workings as any in the federal government. The sheer size of the federal bureaucracy requires substantial presidential staffs even for minimum levels of oversight. Yet beyond a certain point, the size of presidential staffs becomes a positive liability, as parochial specializations develop, requirements for coordination multiply, and authority dissipates.

Moreover, there is a very real problem of presidential control over the EOP bureaucracy itself. It is easier for the President to control the loyalties of EOP staffs than those of political executives in the agencies; yet, increasingly, political pressures and party factionalism have been brought to bear on EOP appointments as well. Appointments to the NSC staff are now watched carefully as bellwethers of an administration's foreign policy inclinations. A problem of particular delicacy is the potential of the Vice President to act as an alternate pole of loyalty and source of patronage within the EOP (as happened particularly during the Carter administration).

More generally, however, given the limitations on presidential attention, the temptation must remain strong for senior EOP officials to exploit the authority of the President in ways not intended by him and of which he may remain unaware. Because presidents are often uncertain as to exactly how they should use their personal advisers and staffs, they are apt to be reluctant to spell out their prerogatives in detail, and hence may appear to license policy entrepreneurship.

Under the Reagan administration, the domestic side of the EOP has been used to a much greater extent than previously to translate the presidential outlook into agency policies. In the early years of the administration, the Office of Management and Budget (OMB) played a central role in enforcing presidential priorities. A series of "cabinet councils" was created in economic and domestic policy areas in order to enhance orderly and centralized management of policy development. In a significant departure from previous practice, an Office of Planning and Evaluation (OPE) was established under White House Counsellor Edwin Meese in order to bring an avowedly "strategic" perspective to bear on the President's policy agenda as a whole. In spite of all this, however, the institutional structures of the White House staff remain weak and its jurisdiction and role uncertain.[19]

If anything, there appears to have been a shifting of power away from the White House over the last several years. The departure of

OMB Director David Stockman marked the end of the administration's aggressive employment of that office for enforcement of its policy agenda. The cabinet council system proved cumbersome and was replaced in the second term by cabinet-level committees on economic and domestic policy, chaired respectively by Secretary of the Treasury James Baker and Attorney General Edwin Meese; this move signaled a further decline in the influence of the White House Office of Policy Development, which had staffed the cabinet councils. And the experiment with strategic planning soon ended with the departure of the first director of OPE, Richard Beal, in 1982. As will be seen, the pattern on the national security side of the White House has been essentially the same.

THE PROBLEM OF PRESIDENTIAL GOVERNANCE

Over the last several decades, academic theories of presidential power have had a significant effect on the expectations and attitudes of the American political class with respect to the presidency, if not on the self-understanding of presidents themselves. These theories have in general heavily emphasized the central personal role of the President as national leader and policy advocate, at the expense of the role of the presidency as a political institution. Arguably, such theories contributed to an investment of unrealistic hopes in the presidency during the Kennedy and Johnson years, as well as to exaggerated fears of presidential power in the wake of Richard Nixon. More recently, there has been a tendency in the academic literature to approach the presidency in its institutional and political context. The relevance of the Constitution for understanding the powers and limitations of the presidency has been newly reaffirmed, and the importance of American political culture in general as a determinant of presidential behavior has been emphasized.[20] All this is welcome. Yet it is not clear that adequate attention has yet been given to understanding the implications of modern bureaucracy for presidential governance.

It has been persuasively argued that the presidency was intended by the drafters of the Constitution as neither a strong nor a weak institution, but a mixture of strong and weak elements reflecting the fundamental but conflicting requirements of a political order based on popular consent. In a democratic polity, the executive tends to appear and to be seen as a purely instrumental extension of the will of the people; at the same time, the people also require, in some areas or under certain circumstances, an executive who visibly and forcefully "rules."[21] The President's ruling or commanding function is evident—at least in wartime—with respect to the armed forces. But his relationship to the federal bureaucracy as a whole is ambiguous. The interesting question is whether the need for presidential rule over the bureaucracy as a whole has not been seriously underestimated when not simply lost from sight.

If one looks back over the history of the modern presidency, it is immediately evident that different presidents had very different approaches to the problem of managing the bureaucracy. At first sight, these approaches seem to derive entirely from individual presidential styles. Yet there is also a certain logic to their development over time.

Franklin Delano Roosevelt employed a highly personalized approach which sought to maximize presidential control through fragmentation of bureaucratic authority and active encouragement of conflict between individuals and agencies with unclear or overlapping mandates. Dwight Eisenhower sought to create a system of presidential management modeled to some extent on military staff procedures, but the formal centralization of the interagency structure he effected did not and was not intended to limit in significant ways the prerogatives of individual agencies. John F. Kennedy dismantled the Eisenhower-era interagency machinery, and returned to an informal and personalized approach relying on presidential advisors, ad hoc task forces and a greater degree of operational involvement by the President himself; Lyndon Johnson's approach was similar. Richard Nixon sought to reestablish an orderly and centrally managed interagency process, but with stronger policy leadership from the White House (thus synthesizing the best aspects of the Eisenhower and Kennedy-Johnson systems). For a variety of reasons, including Nixon's personal style and congressional resistance, the attempt to assert control over the bureaucracy was soon abandoned in favor of a unique White House-centered system operating largely independently of the agencies. The fiasco of Watergate served to discredit such an approach, which came to be identified with the "imperial presidency"; and there was a substantial devolution of authority to the bureaucracy under the Ford and Carter administrations. In the Carter period, the pendulum swung back in the direction of increased White House control, under the impact of a strong National Security Adviser and a President committed to rational management and interested in the details of administration; but the institutional mechanisms to support such control were never developed or effectively operated. With the election of Ronald Reagan, an effort was made to reestablish more formal interagency structures for policy development. But it was decided at the same time to rely on political appointees in the agencies rather than a strong White House staff to ensure both the congruence of policy with the President's program and its loyal implementation by the bureaucracy. The role initially played by the Office of Management and Budget in disciplining the domestic agencies owed more to the personal qualities of David Stockman (and to the vacuum resulting from delays in the recruitment of political executives) than to an overarching strategy of centralized White House management.

This very rapid and schematic survey of the presidential-bureaucratic relationship should suffice to make the fundamental point that, with the partial exception of a brief period under Richard Nixon, no modern President has even attempted to assume direct control over the bureaucracy through institutional means. The presidents most interested in exercising policy leadership have used their power in highly personal ways, and have sought to control the bureaucracy by essentially negative methods—by some combination of bureaucratic fragmentation and alliances with or penetrations of subordinate bureaucratic levels. By contrast, except for Nixon, the presidents most interested in institutional management have not cared to assert themselves strongly in a policy-making role.

It is not overly misleading to say that the Reagan approach represented fundamentally a return to the Eisenhower system of presidential governance. The principal difference is that the presidency of Ronald Reagan had a much more coherent ideological basis, and strategic objectives that required more radical change in existing political attitudes and institutions. Accordingly, it was recognized from the beginning that presidential control of the bureaucracy would require special efforts. But it was thought to be sufficient to use the presidential appointment power for this purpose rather than a White House staff system. Recent studies have shown that the Reagan White House has indeed made broader and more systematic use of political appointments throughout the bureaucracy than any other modern administration.[22]

There can be little doubt that the decision to forego a powerful White House staff and thus—or so it was assumed—avoid serious bureaucratic infighting between the President's men and the agencies reflected in considerable measure the personal style of Ronald Reagan. A strong preference for consensus as distinct from sharply defined options and personal confrontation was plainly a Reagan characteristic. Yet a preference for consensus is a trait of most recent American presidents, and appears to go beyond personal predilection. It would rather seem an authentic American cultural trait—a reflection of American management style and personal behavior generally.

But is management by consensus truly possible in the federal government—particularly in the case of national security agencies with long traditions of independence and mutual hostility? This question is closely akin to the classic question Henry Kissinger has posed concerning the efficacy of a foreign policy based on negotiation alone.[23] Just as the use or threat of force may give nations incentives to negotiate while its renunciation may encourage intransigence and make agreement impossible, management by consensus creates strong incentives for bureaucratic recalcitrance. It makes it more difficult to resolve issues at appropriate levels and encourages obstruction and delay. Where powerful agencies have conflicting positions, disputes may fester for extended periods of time before the President is able to take action to resolve them. Furthermore, such an approach tends to give great leeway to agencies in interpreting the meaning of decisions taken and the manner of implementing them. All of these factors work, paradoxically, to exacerbate bureaucratic conflict rather than to minimize it.[24]

Whether management by consensus is desirable is a question with many ramifications. It is usually posed in terms of the relative advantages of an interagency system that produces agreed-upon recommendations and one that produces options for presidential deliberation. Yet what is involved here is much more than technical formats and procedures. It is the fundamental question of whether there is a presidential perspective that is truly distinct from that of the agencies and their executives. The common objection to a system of agreed recommendations is that such recommendations tend to reflect a lowest common denominator of agency positions, or an incoherent compromise of partly or wholly inconsistent views. But this objection assumes that one or another agency position is likely to be fully adequate from the President's point of view. It thus overlooks the possibility that the option that is most likely to satisfy the President may well not be put forward by any agency.

Is there, then, a distinctive presidential perspective? This is surely the case. As indicated earlier, the President combines in his person the functions of national political leader, chief administrator of the national government, chief diplomat, and commander-in-chief of the armed forces. No lower level of government is empowered or able to discharge more than one of these functions; and the function of political leadership is exercised by the President alone. Only the President is in a position to develop an integrated, synoptic understanding of the entire range of issues of national concern, and only the President is capable of forging a strategy to deal with these issues. The perspective of the President is a unique one because the President alone is in a position to exercise strategic leadership of the nation.

That the notion of a uniquely presidential perspective has not been more widely recognized has much to do with the absence in American political culture of the idea of strategy as such.[25] Unappealing as the idea of an integrated national strategy is apt to be for many Americans, it is difficult to dispute in theory the reasonableness of an approach to American national interests that integrates domestic and international perspectives and views the various instruments of national power in their interrelationship. Such at any rate—regardless of the desires or preconceptions of presidents themselves—is the basic logic of the presidency. It goes without saying that the requirements of strategic leadership vary according to circumstances and the purposes of individual presidents. These requirements are most exigent in time of war. Yet their character, deriving as it does from the constitutional and customary functions of the presidency itself, remains fundamentally constant over time.

Recognizing the indispensable role of the President in the development and implementation of national strategy has critically important consequences for the theory and practice of presidential governance. Because the sphere of national strategy belongs to the President alone, and at the same time affects in fundamental ways the business of every agency of the federal government, the President inevitably stands in a relationship of potential conflict with the bureaucracy as a whole. At the same time, if he does the job that is properly his, the President cannot dispense with the bureaucracy. The short-lived experiment of the Nixon presidency with the White House as an operational alternative to the bureaucracy failed deservedly. The President must be able to rely on the bureaucracy to translate into operational terms and into reality the strategic guidance it is his business to provide. This is not to say that the President should not under any circumstances involve his office directly in foreign operations. But, as is apparent from the recent history of NSC-managed dealings with Iran, such operations are always hazardous and liable to run athwart the routine implementation of administration policy by the bureaucracy. It is far preferable for a President to have at his disposal a bureaucracy with the will and ability to carry out sensitive and routine operations alike. But all this means that the President must be prepared to assert his authority over the national security bureaucracy to a greater degree—and in a qualitatively different fashion—than has yet been attempted by any American President.

This is not to suggest that it can be realistically expected—or indeed would be desirable—for the President to exercise command of the bureaucracy in the sense in which he exercises command of the armed forces in wartime. It is merely to argue that the President is in need of greater resources to counterbalance the power of the bureaucracy, and a different approach to managing it.

The President's primary resource for controlling the national security agencies has been, since 1947, the National Security Council and its staff, headed by the Assistant to the President for National Security Affairs. Before turning to an examination of the NSC role, however, some account is needed of the nature of national security and the national security bureaucracy as it currently exists. The strength of the argument for a more active and central presidential role in the management of national security only fully emerges from a consideration of the sources of bureaucratic irrationality or recalcitrance to strategic requirements, as well as of the specific policy failures of recent American administrations in this area.

Chapter 2

National Security and the National Security Agencies

ALTHOUGH THE TERM "national security" has been in relatively general use in the United States at least since the enactment of the National Security Act of 1947, it cannot be said to have won clear acceptance in popular or academic speech, and its meaning remains equivocal for many. "Foreign policy" continues to offer competition as an umbrella term designating the complex of policies that serve to safeguard the position of the United States in the world, and "national security" is often used in a restricted sense to apply only or primarily to military and intelligence matters. This situation is not entirely an accident of language. As has been very clearly apparent in recent debates over U.S. policy toward Nicaragua, Americans remain profoundly resistant to the notion that diplomacy and force are two sides of the same coin. They tend to see military power as an instrument that comes into play only after diplomacy has failed, not one that, in use as well as nonuse, serves the overall political interests of the nation and supports the achievement of negotiated solutions to international disputes.

It is hardly surprising, therefore, that "national security" has traditionally been seen by some in the United States as an ideologically laden concept, one that implies the primacy of the national interest over international cooperation and of military power over diplomacy as a guardian of the national interest. In reality, the term need not and should not carry such ideological overtones. It is employed here in its comprehensive sense, simply because no other term can as adequately capture the domestic as well as the international dimension of national power or the diversity of the instruments comprising it.

What is national security? An exhaustive and precise definition is less necessary for our purposes than a general delimiting of its scope and identification of the agencies involved in it. The core areas of national security are foreign affairs, defense, and intelligence, and the most important agencies are those laying claim to primary responsibility for each of them—the State Department, the Defense Department, and the Central Intelligence Agency. In the area of foreign affairs, the Secretary of State shares cabinet rank with the U.S. Ambassador to the United Nations, although the latter's staff is for most practical purposes a part of the State Department. Two specialized agencies concerned with economic assistance and arms control—the Agency for International Development (AID) and the Arms Control and Disarmament Agency (ACDA) respectively—generally work closely with State, while enjoying a more or less formal autonomy. In addition, several organizations are responsible for disseminating information about the United States and shaping international opinion in a manner that supports American foreign policy—the United States Information Agency (USIA), and the semiofficial Radio Free Europe/Radio Liberty (RFE-RL). These organizations (especially the latter) operate with a considerable measure of day-to-day independence.

In the defense area, the Defense Department is similarly the dominant but not the only bureaucratic player: important responsibilities relating to the development of nuclear weapons are handled by the Department of Energy. In the area of intelligence, the Defense Department has a role at least as vital as that of the CIA. In addition, the Federal Bureau of Investigation (FBI) has very important functions in the area of domestic security and counterintelligence.

Beyond these core areas of national security, there is a more or less well-defined periphery which includes international economic policy, certain scientific and technical issues, mobilization and emergency planning, and space policy. The Treasury, Commerce, Energy, and Agriculture departments (and the cabinet-level Special Trade Representative) all have major international interests that directly involve the nation's foreign relations and overall security. The Federal Emergency Management Agency (FEMA) has an important role in civil defense activities and other aspects of wartime or emergency planning. Finally, the Defense Department and the National Aeronautics and Space Administration (NASA) share primary responsibility for the development of national space policy and for space operations.

THE POLITICAL-MILITARY FAULTLINE

One unfortunate consequence of the American tendency to compartmentalize war and peace is a general failure to approach the national security bureaucracy within a single framework of analysis. As noted earlier, various aspects of bureaucratic organization relating to national security have become politically controversial at different times: State Department and Pentagon reform movements have arisen periodically, yet never coincided. Yet the most critical organizational problems within the national security bureaucracy center precisely on the handling of political-military questions. Remarkably, virtually all of the studies of national security decision making that have been carried out over the years have failed to identify or to highlight sufficiently the weaknesses in political-military planning and operations that are endemic to the national security bureaucracy as a whole.[1] Other bureaucratic faultlines—areas, that is, where major agencies have overlapping responsibilities and fundamental differences of outlook—have also rarely received the attention they deserve in analyses of the national security policy process.

The political-military faultline runs through many of the most sensitive and politically controversial activities of the United States government. Strategic planning, wartime continuity of government and command and control, crisis management and limited military contingencies, low intensity conflict (that is, insurgency and counterinsurgency warfare and counterterrorism), security assistance, overseas basing and alliance relationships, and arms control are the most important such activities. In at least the more conspicuous of these areas, open bureaucratic conflict and confused or inappropriate policies have too often been the rule, in the recent as well as not so recent past.

The nation's difficulties in managing low intensity conflict have been massively apparent at least since the time of the Vietnam War, and recent experience in Central America suggests that there has been little if any fundamental improvement over the years. To begin with more recent history, U.S. political and military support for the government of El Salvador has paid solid dividends, but it is far from clear that the U.S. military has taken advantage of the lessons of Vietnam to develop an effective doctrine and capabilities for counterinsurgency warfare. In Nicaragua, the long-standing CIA involvement in support of the Nicaraguan Contras has only recently begun to produce significant results. For many years, U.S. assistance to the

Contras seems to have been weighted heavily in the direction of providing them with conventional military capabilities and training rather than the ability to conduct a revolutionary insurgency.[2] At the political level, U.S. policy toward Central America has been on the whole vacillating and ineffective. While Congress has certainly made its contribution to this state of affairs, it can be argued that the real damage was originally done by a State Department obstinately wedded to the idea of a negotiated settlement in Nicaragua in defiance of overall administration policy, as well as by severe problems in operational coordination among State, CIA, and military personnel in the theater.[3] In the case of Afghanistan, at any rate, strong support from both Congress and the White House proved unable until quite recently to overcome resistance from State and the CIA to supplying significant quantities of anti-air missiles and other munitions to the Mujahideen.[4]

A study conducted recently under U.S. Army auspices of U.S. strategy and capabilities for low intensity conflict came to the pessimistic conclusion that the United States as a nation lacks an understanding of this form of warfare. "We respond without unity of effort, we execute our activities poorly, and we lack the ability to sustain operations," the study argued, and it called for a "comprehensive civil-military strategy" that would integrate the resources available to the various departments of the government in support of national policy in this area.[5] The recently issued report of the Commission on Integrated Long-Term Strategy has underscored the importance of Third World conflicts in future U.S. strategy and called for a broad rethinking of the U.S. approach to security assistance and related issues.[6] In part responding to similar concerns, and in part in reaction to the widely perceived neglect and misuse of special operations forces by the U.S. military itself, Congress in 1986 passed legislation that strengthens and centralizes both civilian and military control over these forces, which have traditionally played a critical role in low intensity and limited conflict environments.[7] The most dramatic change was the establishment of a new unified Special Operations Command that would have operational control of special operations forces from all the services. But the legislation also creates the new position of Assistant Secretary of Defense for Special Operations and Low Intensity Conflict to exercise oversight of the military in this area, and recommends that the President assign coordinating responsibilities for low intensity conflict for the government as a whole to a new deputy to his National Security Adviser.[8] By all accounts, however, there is much resistance to these changes within the Pentagon, and it is far from clear how meaningful they are likely to prove, especially in the apparent absence of firm direction from political levels of the administration.[9]

Such problems are hardly new. Although the causes of U.S. failure in Vietnam are still the subject of much controversy, it seems relatively clear that the U.S. effort there was plagued from the beginning by fundamental defects in political-military decision making as well as by a flawed approach to military operations in a revolutionary war context. In spite of the strenuous personal attempts of President Kennedy to reorient the armed forces toward counterinsurgency and unconventional warfare, the U.S. military effort in Vietnam never fully adjusted to the requirements of such warfare. At the same time, political and diplomatic considerations caused the White House consistently to deny to the military the forces and the strategic options necessary to win a conventional conflict in Southeast Asia. And the decision-making process, marked as it was by informal and ad hoc arrangements at the highest level, diffusion of responsibility, and overlapping and unclear command relationships, badly exacerbated these problems rather than providing the means to resolve them.[10]

Some progress has plainly been made under the Reagan administration in improving the government's strategic and operational competence in the management of crises involving limited applications of force. Especially by contrast with the inglorious record of the 1970s (the *Mayaguez* and Desert One fiascos), the Grenada operation, flawed as it may have been in a number of respects, nevertheless represented a respectable achievement given the severe constraints imposed by time and secrecy.[11] Interception of the *Achille Lauro* hijackers and the airstrike and related naval activities undertaken against Qaddafi's Libya were well planned and executed operations, and effectively complemented American diplomatic efforts to combat international terrorism. On the other hand, the American intervention in Beirut in 1983 proved a military and diplomatic disaster of the first order, revealing not only serious deficiencies in military command and control but an incoherent approach to the wider political-military situation in the area. Among other things, the episode witnessed a semipublic argument between the secretaries of State and Defense over the propriety of involving U.S. military forces in such situations; and the aftermath of the bombing of the Marine barracks revealed much confusion on the ground as to the exact relationship of American political and military objectives and requirements.[12] Similar confusion about U.S. objectives in the Persian Gulf has accompanied the administration's recent decision to reflag Kuwaiti oil tankers and offer them protection by U.S. naval forces.

Some brief remarks may be added about problems relating to security assistance and alliance management. It is difficult to overestimate the importance of security assistance as a tool of American foreign and defense policy. Unfortunately, powerful bureaucratic incentives have consistently worked to defeat an effective strategic use of this tool. The defense bureaucracy tends to view security assistance through the prism of U.S. military needs rather than those of the recipient country; the State Department tends to view it as a source of diplomatic leverage, and is more interested in gratifying the wants of potential recipients than in serving their genuine military requirements. The problem is particularly acute in the area of support for Third World allies or insurgent movements, which can rarely make proper use of the high technology equipment used by the American military. Insufficient attention continues to be given to developing suitable technologies and associated doctrines and operational concepts for low intensity and limited warfare environments in the Third World.[13]

Fundamental differences in outlook between the foreign service and defense establishments also tend to complicate the effective management of America's alliances generally. The Pentagon is not always sufficiently sensitive to the political and societal impact of a substantial U.S. military presence or a heavily Americanized military in a foreign country (Iran under the Shah is perhaps the classic case). The State Department, on the other hand, is too disposed to sacrifice American military requirements to the maintenance of smooth relations with allied nations. This is arguably a problem above all in the U.S. relationship with its most important allies, the West Europeans. The traditionally Eurocentric State Department tends to be unfriendly to any changes in U.S. military doctrine or practices or new demands on alliance resources that might create political controversy within NATO. By echoing the highly politicized approach most West European governments take to security issues, State has undoubtedly played a key role in the acquiescence of recent American administrations in the erosion of NATO's "flexible response" posture that has been brought about by the massive Soviet military buildup of the last two decades.

Arms control is an area that has increased dramatically in political importance—domestic as well as international—since the early 1970s. As mentioned earlier, the weaknesses of national security decision making in the Reagan years have nowhere been more evident than in arms control policy, where more or less open feuding between the State and Defense departments has gone on almost uninterruptedly since 1981. This history is especially remarkable given the downgrading of arms control as a component of national security policy that was favored by many of the President's political advisers and endorsed by Ronald Reagan himself prior to the 1980 election. In fact, however, the President proved unable to devise an overall framework for arms control policy that could resolve the fundamental differences in perspective between a State Department committed to progress in arms control as an imperative of U.S.–NATO (if not U.S.–Soviet) relations and a Defense Department inclined to emphasize their political and military liabilities. The result has been grinding bureaucratic conflict and, not infrequently, paralysis at the working level, combined with ad hoc presidential interventions to resolve pressing issues. Even then, presidential decisions have often represented only a splitting of agency differences rather than a coherent strategic approach, something that only encourages perseverance in the bureaucratic battle.[14] Examples of the administration's arms control schizophrenia include its prolonged refusal to end U.S. adherence to the SALT treaty regime in spite of its vigorous denunciation of Soviet violations of that regime, and its acceptance of a less restrictive interpretation of the Anti-Ballistic Missile (ABM) Treaty coupled with assurances that the traditional interpretation would continue to be respected as a matter of policy.[15]

The Reykjavik summit meeting between President Reagan and Soviet General Secretary Mikhail Gorbachev in the fall of 1986 startled the world by very nearly producing agreement in principle on a comprehensive arms control regime involving deep reductions in nuclear weapons and the eventual abolition of ballistic missiles. It soon became clear not only that the U.S. position presented at Reykjavik did not reflect an agreed strategy within the NATO alliance, but that it was developed without benefit of detailed analysis by U.S. defense planners or approval by the Joint Chiefs of Staff (JCS). The decoupling of arms control policy from military planning is a gradual development whose beginnings are to be sought in the internal debate over the U.S. approach to strategic arms control in the late 1960s.[16] In spite of the declared intention of the Reagan administration to reverse this trend, it has if anything only worsened in recent years, as the influence of the State Department in arms control matters has grown and the JCS has become increasingly disinclined to buy political trouble for itself by going on record in opposition to prospective treaties.[17] Whatever one's view of the merits or dangers of a Reykjavik-style accord, it has to be acknowledged that there was something flawed in a process which so limited military participation in decisions that could radically reshape the defense posture of the United States and its NATO allies for the rest of this century.[18]

THE DEFENSE ESTABLISHMENT

If the nonparticipation of the Joint Chiefs in critically important administration deliberations on arms control has not aroused more criticism, at least part of the reason lies in the widely perceived ineffectiveness of the JCS as an organization and as a source of advice on matters of strategy and policy. The Joint Chiefs of Staff, the nation's supreme military authority, is essentially a committee made up of the chiefs of staff of the uniformed military services (Army, Air Force, Navy, and Marine Corps), presided over by a separate chairman selected on a rotating basis from one of the services and supported by a staff of officers detailed from their services for relatively brief tours of duty. Like a number of other Western democracies, the United States has recently moved toward a more "joint" or centralized military staff structure. The proximate author of this change has been the U.S. Congress, through informal pressure as well as formal legislation (the Goldwater-Nichols Department of Defense Reorganization Act of 1986). But attitudes on Capitol Hill have reflected a widely shared feeling within senior military ranks as well as among civilian defense experts that the relative autonomy of the individual military services has limited the operational effectiveness of U.S. forces in the field and prevented the JCS from playing a more central role in national-level decisions on military strategy and resource allocation. A presidentially appointed blue-ribbon panel chaired by former Deputy Secretary of Defense David Packard reached very similar conclusions and anticipated the key elements of the congressional reorganization plan.[19]

While spirited resistance to centralization has been offered by the Navy and Marine Corps (which have traditionally feared encroachment on their independence by the other services), there seems little question but that the recently enacted reforms are a reasonable response to very real problems. Particularly over the last decade or so, critics of greatly varying political orientations have joined in making the case that the performance of American military forces over the years has left a great deal to be desired, and that these inadequacies can be traced to systemic flaws in the structure and culture of the U.S. military establishment. The chief counts of the indictment are that the U.S. military is divided against itself by crippling rivalries between (and within) the services, that it is preoccupied with budgetary questions and with the protection of its existing programs, that it produces an officer class of managers and technicians rather than "warriors," that it is overly reliant on high technology as a solution to military problems, that it has failed to appreciate the operational or campaign level of warfare and to exploit such classic elements of operational art as maneuver, deception, and surprise, and that it has wholly neglected the art of strategy.[20]

This is not the place to adjudicate the various claims of the advocates of military reform. It will suffice for present purposes to discuss briefly the most salient issues bearing on the organization and bureaucratic behavior of the defense establishment: reform of the JCS, the relationship of the JCS and the Office of the Secretary of Defense (OSD), and the relationship of the uniformed military to the policy agencies and to civilian authority generally.

The Goldwater-Nichols bill addressed a number of key problems hampering the effective functioning of the joint military structure. These included the insufficient authority allowed the commanders-in-chief (CINCs) of the unified and specified commands[21] and their lack of weight in Washington-level decision making, the inadequate preparation of military officers for joint staff work and the lack of career incentives supporting it, and the weakness of the joint perspective at the level of the JCS itself, given the committee-like nature of the organization and the Chairman's lack of independent authority. The most important single reform instituted under the bill is the designation of the Chairman of the JCS as the President's principal military advisor, with full authority over the Joint Staff and the right to provide advice independently of the services. Apart from creating a powerful counterweight to service parochialism, this step was believed to be essential in any effort to improve the quality of military planning at the national level and increase the focus on strategic issues that cut across service responsibilities.

Some have questioned whether it makes sense to enhance the ability of the JCS to conduct strategic planning without more radical changes both in the organization of the defense establishment as a whole and in military education, training, and personnel practices. The single most important issue in this connection remains the relationship between JCS and the civilian side of the Pentagon.

What gives the Defense Department much of its unique complexity is its very extensive civilian component. Each of the services reports to its military chief of staff, but also to the civilian secretary of the corresponding military department (though the staffs of these officials have now been partially amalgamated as a result of the recent legislation). A variety of civilian defense agencies deal with common functions such as logistics and communications. Within OSD itself, there is another civilian bureaucracy which for some twenty-five years has been centrally involved in the formulation of national-level policy and strategy affecting U.S. military forces as well as in decisions on particular defense programs and on defense resource issues generally.

Participants in the recent defense reform debate have reemphasized the extent to which the civilian defense bureaucracy has burdened the uniformed military by micromanaging or duplicating functions that can be performed equally by the military itself. What is at issue here, however, is not merely managerial efficiency, but also—and more importantly—the proper conception of civilian and military expertise and responsibility. OSD's peak of influence occurred in the 1960s during the tenure of Robert McNamara as Secretary of Defense; it was at this time that the essentially civilian "systems analysis" approach to defense program issues gained ascendency in the Pentagon. Although the limitations of this variant of corporate cost-benefit analysis in dealing with military problems are by now widely recognized, OSD has never fully succeeded in redefining its role in a way that would complement rather than compete with essentially military functions, or help correct the lack of strategic focus created by the traditional decentralization of U.S. military planning and the demands of the budget process. As its critics in Congress and elsewhere like to point out, OSD is organized by functions that tend to duplicate those performed by various military organizations, instead of by missions (such as strategic nuclear deterrence, power projection, or defense of NATO Europe) that cut across organizational lines. It thus only exacerbates the key weakness of the defense decision-making structure as a whole—its tendency to focus on "inputs" rather than "outputs," programs and resources rather than the strategic purposes and national policies these should be serving.[22]

The relationship of OSD to the uniformed military tends to mirror the relationship of civilian to military authority in the United States generally. That relationship is a complex and in many ways paradoxical one, at once overly intrusive and overly remote, and marked by much uncertainty as to the proper spheres of civilian and military responsibility. The model of civil-military relations that seems to be generally accepted today as both the fact and the norm for the United States is what Samuel Huntington has called "objective control"—undiluted civilian control of a military enjoying virtually complete internal autonomy and devoted solely to professional military tasks. The reality, however, more closely approximates Huntington's model of "subjective control," which involves both greater civilian penetration of the professional military sphere and a greater involvement of the uniformed military in the determination of national policy.[23]

One indication of this state of affairs is the substantial presence of active duty or retired military officers in key positions throughout the civilian defense bureaucracy as well as in the State Department and the staff of the National Security Council.[24] Another is the relatively independent role that the JCS organization frequently plays in interagency committees dealing with questions of fundamental political-military policy. The presence of JCS representatives at such meetings would be unproblematic were they there simply to offer professional military judgments. Yet in practice there is often little discernible difference between the basis or scope of JCS positions and those of the civilian agencies; and the relationship of JCS to OSD in such forums tends to be one of equality rather than subordination.

At work here are factors that go beyond organization in any narrow sense. Military officers whose education extends beyond essentially technical or managerial subjects tend to develop expertise in international relations as currently taught in American universities, and it is this expertise they bring into play (rather than any specific military knowledge) when serving in political-military assignments throughout the national security bureaucracy. This has several consequences. In the first place, it blurs the difference between the uniformed military and civilian policy makers. But perhaps more insidiously, it can lead to a certain loss of focus on (or even distortion of) the operational military realities that need to be taken into account if policy is to have a sound basis.

Another aspect of the problem is visible in the critical area of war planning. Strategic and operational planning for war in the United States is wholly the responsibility of the unified and specified commands and of the JCS. Even at the most strategic level, there is no civilian involvement of any kind in the development or review of such plans, even though they unavoidably rest on a host of assumptions about the strength of U.S. alliance relationships and the crisis or wartime role of American diplomacy that plainly exceed the competence of the military by itself or indeed of the defense establishment as a whole.[25] In truth, this situation is an atavism, reflecting the World War II era arrangement under which the JCS assumed responsibility for the formulation of national strategy in its most comprehensive sense, subject only to the authority of the President as commander-in-chief of the armed forces.[26] Its effect in practice is to make impossible any coherent peacetime planning for the coordinated use of military, diplomatic, and other elements of U.S. power in crises and war.

This is by no means to suggest that the blame for current deficiencies in the area of strategy and planning lies with the military alone. All too often, guidance provided to the military by OSD, the White House, or the State Department is nonexistent or so general as to be virtually worthless, and military planners are forced to reconstruct a hypothetical national-level policy or strategy on the basis of public speeches and news reports. And the military's desire to protect its traditional prerogatives in war planning is understandable in view of the endemic leakiness of the bureaucracy and the lack of interest or competence in such matters in the civilian agencies. Nevertheless, it has to be recognized that the current situation is an unsatisfactory one from the point of view of presidential management of the national security policy process as a whole.

THE FOREIGN POLICY ESTABLISHMENT

As indicated earlier, Americans are not wholly accustomed to considering diplomacy as an integral aspect of national security, or the State Department as a component part of a larger community of national security agencies. At the same time, State has long enjoyed a dominant position in the formulation not merely of foreign policy but also of national security policy in the larger sense. State's role in such critical areas as arms control, intelligence and counterintelligence, security assistance, international economic and scientific affairs, and the management of the nation's military alliances continues to be very important if not decisive. There has been a surprising degree of consensus over the years by observers of very different professional and political orientations (including many veterans of the Foreign Service) that the performance of the State Department has been far from satisfactory, especially in those areas not central to its overriding institutional mission. Like the defense establishment, State and the foreign policy establishment generally have been the subject of numerous studies and reports diagnosing the relevant pathologies and prescribing reforms of various kinds.[27]

Perhaps the most common complaint about State is that it is wedded to a tradition of genteel diplomacy that is of decreasing relevance in the contemporary world. By the early 1960s, it had become the fashion to speak of a "new diplomacy" extending beyond the traditional methods of state-to-state diplomacy to incorporate a panoply of unconventional instruments such as propaganda, economic and security assistance, paramilitary operations, and covert action.[28] Although the attractions of such an activist approach to diplomacy have since faded markedly for the American political class, and in spite of formal recognition and accommodation of some of these functions within the foreign policy establishment as a whole, State remains vulnerable to similar charges today. It is now more usual to hear the Foreign Service criticized for its lack of specialized knowledge of economics and of global issues such as energy and the environment. Yet few would deny that State remains seriously deficient in expertise in the other nondiplomatic instruments of national power. In spite of State's critical role in the formulation of arms control policy, for example, its expertise in military affairs has generally been extremely thin. Foreign Service Officers tend to disdain the information or public diplomacy function, and are happy to see it performed by a separate agency. They tend to disparage intelligence reporting and to be sceptical of the utility of covert action. Generally speaking, they are more apt to regard U.S. military, informational, and intelligence activities abroad as alien and unwelcome intrusions than as a valuable adjunct to American diplomacy.

The organization of the State Department reflects its underlying institutional culture. A variety of functionally oriented offices exist within the department, but they tend to be small, bureaucratically weak, and unattractive to the most talented and ambitious officers. Institutional power and professional prestige reside almost entirely in five regional bureaus, among which the European bureau (EUR) has traditionally been preeminent. Within the bureaus, the basic unit of organization is the Country Desk. While regional and subregional integration is performed within the bureau at the level of Deputy Assistant and Assistant Secretary, there remains a persistent bias in the department as a whole toward bilateral political issues as the core concern of diplomacy. Some functional integration occurs at the level of Under Secretary, but the Under Secretary positions (of which there are currently four—Political Affairs; Economic Affairs; Security Assistance, Science, and Technology; and Management) have historically been understaffed and lacking in true line authority. Longer-range policy integration and strategic planning are formally the responsibility of a Policy Planning Staff. In spite of its prestige and proximity to the Secretary, however, this office has rarely been able to hold its own against the regional bureaus, and at present is regarded as almost wholly ineffective in the bureaucratic competition for influence within the department.

The dominance of regional and bilateral issues and of a short-term perspective in State's approach to foreign policy follows logically from the department's basic mission, which is to carry on diplomatic relations with other countries and conduct negotiations. Necessary as this mission is, there can be little question but that it tends to create in its practitioners—in combination with other factors more specific to the American context—an unusually powerful and pernicious *déformation professionelle.* "Clientitis" is a term frequently given to the tendency of State Department personnel to adopt the outlook of foreigners and become advocates for their interests.[29] This tendency is a function partly of the general effect of spending time in another country and gaining firsthand appreciation of its problems, partly of the liberal-internationalist assumptions that continue to influence the way educated Americans view the world, and partly of the pragmatic or problem-oriented outlook characteristic of Americans generally. Efforts have been made over the years to combat the effects of clientitis by a variety of administrative means, particularly the frequent rotation of Foreign Service personnel through a variety of countries and regions. Unfortunately, such methods often have adverse side effects, particularly by devaluing regional and language expertise and disrupting policy continuity and institutional memory.[30]

It would be wrong to hold the State Department responsible for all the mistakes that have been made in the management of U.S. relations with the Soviet Union in recent years, and State's approach to dealing with the Soviets cannot be characterized as a case of clientitis in any simple sense. Nevertheless, the pathologies of the department are nowhere more apparent or more damaging than in this critical area. Faced with an adversary that has traditionally viewed the United States as "the main enemy" and employed a range of unconventional instruments in a coordinated and long-term effort to undermine the American position in the world, State persists in believing that the threat is one that can be deflected or contained by essentially diplomatic methods, and hence that the maintenance of good relations with the Soviets is a prime objective of U.S. national policy. State appears constitutionally incapable of understanding the extent to which Soviet purposes are governed by a revolutionary ideology and shaped by an operational tradition in which diplomacy is seen primarily as a form of psychological or political warfare.[31] That the reforms recently instituted in the Soviet Union by General Secretary Gorbachev will fundamentally alter Soviet behavior in these respects seems highly unlikely. While the Soviets have certainly shown an increased willingness to consider negotiated solutions to outstanding problems (notably, the war in Afghanistan), the new adroitness of Soviet diplomacy under the Gorbachev regime is surely not an unambiguous benefit for the West. It is far from clear that State has adjusted itself to the new Soviet style in diplomacy, especially its much more sophisticated approach to public and media relations.

This failing is perhaps most worrisome in the area of arms control. As indicated earlier, State has always played a significant role in the formulation of U.S. arms control positions as well as in actual talks with the Soviets, and its domination of the Reykjavik summit and of subsequent negotiations on an intermediate-range nuclear forces (INF) treaty has been virtually complete. Yet State has shown little sensitivity to the record of negotiating deception and violation or near-violation of existing agreements that the Soviets have established since at least the early 1970s;[32] and it has generally failed to compete effectively with the Soviets in turning arms control developments to public relations advantage. Other areas in which State has played a questionable role over the years include technology transfer, academic exchange programs, and counterintelligence. In all of them, State has tended to ignore or downplay concrete damage to clear national interests in the name of undemonstrable and frequently implausible improvements in relations with the Soviets.[33]

It is not customary to think of the State Department as posing the same kind of implicit challenge to the nation's political leadership as the uniformed military. Yet the Foreign Service is a corporate body with a degree of cohesiveness, independence, and uniqueness of outlook that invites comparison with the military in every respect. Particularly since the passage of the Foreign Service Act of 1980, the authority of presidential appointees over career personnel at

State is very limited, and Foreign Service officers are uniquely able to serve in political slots without being considered part of agency management. Moreover, a very large number of slots which could be filled by noncareer appointments are currently and have regularly been held by Foreign Service Officers (FSOs), including many that are of critical importance for maintaining control of the department (such as the Under Secretary for Management) as well as key ambassadorships. The Foreign Service has consistently resisted efforts to bring its personnel system under the kind of oversight exercised over the Civil Service by the Office of Personnel Management.[34]

The question of presidential appointment of noncareer ambassadors is a perennial topic of dispute in Washington. While there is no denying that marginally qualified persons continue to be appointed to ambassadorships with some regularity (or that deserving FSOs are often forced to retire before obtaining one), the issue cannot be settled by a simple appeal to foreign policy professionalism. The idea that there is a body of knowledge of foreign affairs comparable to operational military expertise and available only to career professionals is, at bottom, a fallacy. A good knowledge of history and languages and common sense are probably the most important requirements in an ambassador. Unfortunately, as indicated earlier, they are no more likely to be found in today's Foreign Service than among persons in other walks of life.[35]

An important and long neglected aspect of American foreign and national security policy is the complex of activities that are frequently grouped together under the term "public diplomacy."[36] As it has evolved in recent American practice, public diplomacy includes three distinct though related functions: international information, international political affairs, and what might be called strategic public affairs. It will be well to discuss each of these areas briefly.

International information refers to the activities principally of the United States Information Agency (USIA), the Voice of America (VOA) (a semiautonomous division of USIA), and Radio Free Europe/Radio Liberty (RFE-RL), although the State and Defense departments have also come to play a significant role in recent years in disseminating information relating to national security both abroad and at home. In addition, a radio station was established in 1985 within the Voice of America specifically for broadcasting to Cuba. The establishment of this station—"Radio Marti"—signaled a renewed appreciation within the U.S. government of the value of so-called surrogate broadcasting operations to the Communist world. Like RFE-RL, which continues to broadcast to Eastern Europe and the Soviet Union from sites in Western Europe, Radio Marti provides to its target audiences information not otherwise available to them about their own countries. These radios serve the specific strategic purpose of creating an informed public opinion that acts as a constraining influence on the international behavior of Communist regimes.[37]

International political affairs, the second component of public diplomacy, refers to a range of activities including certain kinds of multilateral diplomacy, support for foreign political parties and organizations, and support for a variety of private organizations abroad that serve to promote democratic institutions and values. In June 1982, the President delivered a speech to the British parliament outlining a new U.S. strategy to promote the growth of democracy and democratic institutions throughout the world. One result of this initiative was the creation of a quasi-governmental entity called the National Endowment for Democracy to serve as a mechanism for disbursing U.S. funds abroad in support of such activities.[38]

Strategic public affairs is to be distinguished from the public affairs activities normally discharged by various government agencies. It attempts to develop strategic approaches to shaping the domestic political agenda and to engaging the public more actively in serious consideration of fundamental security issues. The most ambitious effort to date in this area has involved the establishment of State Department and White House offices to promote administration policies in Central America.

The United States Information Agency (USIA) was created in 1953 in recognition both of the importance of the international information function and the problems that had been experienced in the State Department's handling of it. In a reorganization in the 1970s, USIA acquired additional functions formerly belonging to State in the area of education and cultural affairs. Both of these areas tend to be regarded not only as marginal to the central concerns of the State Department, but also as a source of potential complication and difficulty for the conduct of traditional diplomacy. Accordingly, State's attitude toward them has been a compound of neglect and intervention in the name of tactical diplomatic requirements.

From this perspective, the assignment of public diplomacy functions to autonomous agencies makes sense insofar as it represents an acknowledgment of the strategic character of these functions. The shaping of fundamental political attitudes in foreign populations and support for the development of democratic institutions are long-term or strategic objectives which are not necessarily in harmony with the day-to-day management of bilateral relations with foreign governments. On the other hand, it has to be acknowledged that there are dangers in too sharp a divorce of the international information function (if not of education and cultural affairs) from current policy. Some would argue that the U.S. information agencies have tended in recent years to lose any sense of strategic purpose and to model their activities to an unwarranted extent on those of the commercial media, and a good case can be made for a closer integration of the public diplomacy activities performed by State and by USIA.[39] At all events, the inherent differences in perspective between the information agencies on the one hand and the State and Defense departments on the other make public diplomacy another critical faultline within the national security bureaucracy.

THE INTELLIGENCE COMMUNITY

It has long been the practice in the United States to treat intelligence as a problem virtually *sui generis*, rather than as an instrument of U.S. national security policy in the broad sense. There are a number of reasons for this. In the first place, what may be called the traditional view of the relationship between the American intelligence community and the policy agencies has stressed the importance of segregating the intelligence analysis function as much as possible from the making of policy, so as to avoid contamination of the intelligence product with the views and concerns of policy officials. In the second place, the prominent role of covert action in the history and institutional ethos of the Central Intelligence Agency (CIA) has fostered the widespread impression that this organization tends to operate semiautonomously, directed but not truly controlled by the President and with a relationship to other governmental departments or to the nation's broader foreign policy interests that is tenuous at best. To the extent that the CIA's role has been regarded as problematic, however, the problem has been seen primarily as one of insufficient negative control of the agency by the President and the Congress. Less attention has been given to the need for positive guidance of its activities by senior policy officials, or of closer integration with the work of the other national security agencies.

At its origins, the CIA was very much a part of the overarching national security apparatus created by Congress after World War II to bring greater coherence and central coordination to the management of national security affairs by the executive branch. Contrary to a widespread assumption, the chief motivation behind its creation was not the desire for a peacetime covert action arm, but rather the desire for a central coordinating agency for intelligence analysis, and one that would serve national needs rather than the parochial needs and interests of the military services in particular.[40]

Whatever expectations may originally have been entertained about the CIA's bureaucratic role in the production of national intelligence, it has not displaced the various military intelligence organizations, or the intelligence arms of civilian agencies such as the State Department. The CIA enjoys a hegemonic but not wholly dominant role within what has come to be called the intelligence community. This is a loose federation of intelligence agencies or components, headed by the Director of Central Intelligence (DCI), who also serves concurrently as director of the CIA. The most important members of the intelligence community apart from the CIA are the National Security Agency (responsible for communications security as well as communications intelligence), the Defense Intelligence Agency, the intelligence components of the individual military services, and the Federal Bureau of Investigation. The State Department's Bureau of Intelligence and Research has had a significant role in the preparation of key national intelligence estimates; the intelligence components of other civilian agencies (such as Treasury or Agriculture) have more specialized responsibilities for the collection and analysis of intelligence in areas relevant to their concerns.[41]

An important part of the reason for the CIA's imperfect dominance of the intelligence community is simply that it is not necessary—and would be difficult or impossible—for it to duplicate the specialized operational intelligence activities of the military or the civilian policy agencies. Traditionally, the CIA role has been considered to be distinct from that of the other agencies because its focus is principally at the strategic or national level. At the same time, however, an excellent case can be made that strategic or national-level intelligence should not be left to the CIA alone.

The primary institutional vehicle for the analysis and dissemination of strategic intelligence is the National Intelligence Estimate (NIE). NIEs are formal reports on key issues produced periodically by the National Intelligence Council, a high-level group working directly under the DCI. The development of NIEs is a cooperative activity of the intelligence community as a whole, but one that in the past has been essentially controlled by the CIA. During the 1970s, the CIA's record in estimating the growth of Soviet strategic forces and Soviet defense spending, among other matters, came under scrutiny from independent analysts, and it is now very generally accepted that the CIA approach in these areas suffered from fundamental defects in methodology and in basic assumptions about the Soviet Union.[42] Largely as a result of this, a relatively wide consensus has developed over the last decade or so in support of competitive intelligence analysis by different agencies of the U.S. government. In practice, this means in the first instance strengthening the analytic capabilities of the Defense Intelligence Agency (DIA) and enhancing its role in the development of NIEs on the Soviet Union and other key strategic issues.

That a central intelligence organization reporting directly to the nation's political leadership will automatically be free of bureaucratic bias is a notion that runs counter both to theory and to experience. In the case of the CIA, the very claim to institutional objectivity has been transformed over the years into a kind of bias. This is evident in the first place in the agency's disposition to discount analyses by military intelligence organizations that support so-called "worst case" assumptions about the capabilities or intentions of adversaries, on the grounds that these are motivated solely by a desire to defend or promote U.S. military programs.[43] It is further evident in what an informed observer has called the "idealism" of CIA analysts—a disposition to demonstrate the independence and integrity of the CIA's analytic mission by challenging the policy preferences not only of the military but of the administration as a whole.[44]

All this suggests that there is as much a problem of political control in the case of the CIA as there is with the defense and foreign policy establishments. As indicated a moment ago, the traditional view of intelligence in the United States has stressed the importance of protecting the intelligence analyst from the interference or influence of the policy maker. In recent years, however, there has been a growing recognition of the inadequacy of such a view, and of the need for closer integration between intelligence collection and analysis and national security policy making generally. While there are undoubtedly hazards in too close a relationship between intelligence analysts and policy makers, the temptation to slant intelligence reports to conform to the expectations of policy makers is one that is present to some degree in any event; and the penalties associated with poor communication between the two can be substantial. In addition, there has been greater recognition of the difficulty of separating intelligence analysis from policy development. Especially in the American setting, where policy makers often lack elementary information about national security affairs or a theoretical framework for understanding current events, it is almost certainly unrealistic to require intelligence analysts to limit themselves to the presentation of bare "facts" devoid of a policy context. This is especially the case in areas of high uncertainty where there is much room for interpretation of the data available. In such areas (which include many that are of the greatest importance from a policy point of view), the "facts" presented to policy makers are in actuality judgments arrived at through a process of bureaucratic negotiation and compromise, and are not essentially different from the judgments or interpretations that are regularly made by policy makers themselves. All too often, however, the intelligence community has refused to acknowledge the policy assumptions or biases present in intelligence analyses, particularly those of a more strategic or political nature, and has resisted efforts by the policy agencies to clarify or adjudicate intracommunity disagreements.[45]

That important bureaucratic dysfunctions exist in other areas of the intelligence business as well has been argued by a number of practitioners and observers. In the area of collection, the U.S. has invested enormous sums over the years in highly sophisticated technical collection systems such as photographic reconnaissance satellites. As with many expensive defense programs, however, technology tends to determine policy and requirements rather than the other way around, and resource allocations tend to occur with insufficient attention to the "outputs" of interest to intelligence consumers.[46] In another critical area, counterintelligence, the performance of the CIA and the intelligence community as a whole is widely agreed to be very inadequate. This has to do partly with the institutional conflicts within the community (especially between the CIA and the FBI), and partly with the generic institutional disinclination of all intelligence organizations to submit their information, personnel, and procedures to the rigorous scrutiny that an effective counterintelligence effort requires.[47] A closely related disability is the lack of interest or even hostility most intelligence organizations tend to show toward evidence of deception directed at them by an adversary. There is good reason to believe that the CIA in particular has seriously underestimated the scope and sophistication of Soviet strategic deception efforts in recent years.[48]

As remarked earlier, the CIA is virtually identified in the popular mind with covert action, although this side of the agency's activities in fact involves a relatively small fraction of its resources and personnel. That the CIA has frequently acted as a "rogue elephant" in the covert action area is a notion that gained currency in the wake of the congressional investigations of the agency during the 1970s, but one that has little relationship to the historical record. The fact of the matter is that the CIA has always been responsive to presidential direction. The problem is a subtler one. It is not the failure of the CIA to conform to political guidance in conducting its operations, but rather the lack of well-developed mechanisms for ensuring the coordination of those operations with other activities of the U.S. government. The nature of the agency's mission and its operational code have consistently worked against close collaboration with other agencies; yet—for reasons that are easy to understand in the light of recent revelations in the Iran-Contra matter—the White House has rarely been eager to involve itself actively in the implementation of covert action projects. The relationship between the CIA and the State Department—and between CIA personnel overseas and the local American ambassador—is a perennial source of difficulty. But the key problem lies in the CIA's relationship to the military in supporting paramilitary activities in the Third World. As indicated earlier, lack of strategic and operational coordination of U.S. military and intelligence personnel in Central America has probably had much to do with the modesty of the accomplishments of American policy in the region to date—and helps to explain the growing White House involvement in the conflict there during the Reagan administration.

The military-intelligence faultline is perhaps the least explored aspect of bureaucratic contention in the national security arena. In the paramilitary area, the military as an institution tends to be sceptical and unsupportive of a CIA role for essentially the same reasons it is sceptical and unsupportive of military special operations forces; the CIA, on the other hand, tends to regard the military as too unimaginative and bureaucratically rigid to carry out such activities effectively. In the area of collection, the military is generally unhappy about the level of CIA support for operational military intelligence requirements. The creation several years ago of a clandestine human intelligence collection unit within the Army reflected the general military dissatisfaction with the CIA on this score. In the area of analysis, mention has already been made of the perennial tensions between the military and the CIA in interpreting the Soviet threat.

Related problems are apparent in the area of "net assessment"—that is, the analysis of U.S. forces and capabilities in relationship to the forces and capabilities of adversaries. Because it is centrally dependent on strategic intelligence and yet forms an integral part of military planning, net assessment has always been a difficult function to handle in bureaucratic terms. Improved net assessment is one of the reforms of the defense establishment recently recommended by the Packard Commission.[49]

PERIPHERAL AREAS

Something should be said briefly about what was characterized earlier as the peripheral aspects of national security. At issue here are a variety of security-related issues in diverse areas such as economics, science and technology, mobilization and emergency planning, and space. These areas are united by the fact that they are not generally thought of in a national security context, and are handled within the U.S. government by agencies that are not primarily concerned with national security affairs. For this very reason, however, they pose unique bureaucratic problems, situated as they are on the fault-line that divides national security policy from domestic policy generally.

Economic issues loom large as an aspect of U.S. foreign policy, and many of these issues are of truly strategic significance for the countries involved if not for the United States itself. Traditionally prominent among these are trade and monetary issues, and the Treasury and Commerce departments have long played a key role in the formulation and implementation of U.S. policy in these areas. More recently, a Special Trade Representative has been created within the White House with cabinet rank, and this office too has come to play a significant role in the development of international trade policy. The Department of Agriculture has also had a long-standing interest in agricultural developments abroad, and a special Foreign Agricultural Service forms part of the foreign policy establishment. On the foreign policy side, an Under Secretary for Economic Affairs is the senior economic official in the State Department, supported by a bureau of Economic and Business Affairs (EB). The Agency for International Development (AID) is an operating arm of the State Department in the area of economic assistance, though one that has gained considerable autonomy in practice.[50]

The growing importance of scientific and technological issues for U.S. foreign policy was signaled by the creation in the 1970s of an Under Secretary of State for Security Assistance, Science, and Technology, as well as of a new bureau of Oceans, Environment, and Scientific Affairs (OES). The oil crisis of the early 1970s underlined the vital importance of natural resources such as oil and nuclear power for the security of the United States and the Western alliance. Both the Department of State and the Department of Energy have been prominent bureaucratic players in this arena. In addition, the Defense Department has important institutional interests and responsibilities relating not only to energy (the Strategic Petroleum Reserve) but to strategic minerals that are essential in the construction of modern military hardware. Another area of central concern for all of the national security agencies as well as many domestic ones is telecommunications and data processing. Recently, the State Department created a new assistant secretary position and an expanded staff to handle the international dimension of these matters, but the close interlocking of commercial, foreign policy, and security aspects of telecommunications and data processing issues makes them uniquely difficult to handle within the government.

Less familiar areas of international economic and technology policy, but ones whose importance for national security is being increasingly recognized, are financial security and technology transfer. Very recently, some attention has begun to be given to Soviet penetration and manipulation of the international banking system and measures to counter it.[51] The fundamental importance of export controls on sensitive technologies has been demonstrated yet again by the revelation of illegal transfers to the Soviet Union by Japanese and Norwegian firms of equipment that has allowed the Soviets to make dramatic advances in submarine quieting. It has become clear that illegal acquisition of Western technology by the Soviet bloc has cost the United States tens of billions of dollars and years of competitive advantage in key areas of military technology.[52]

Mobilization and emergency planning is an area that continues to suffer from severe neglect for a mixture of political and bureaucratic reasons. Industrial mobilization for crisis and wartime, continuity of government, and civil defense are the key activities involved here. Although a serious effort has been made under the Reagan administration to overcome past neglect and mismanagement of all of them, much still remains to be done.[53]

In the area of space policy, the loss of the *Challenger* shuttle has brought the U.S. space program under close scrutiny over the last year or so, and there is wide agreement that management of this program both within NASA and at the national level has left much to be desired. Fundamental divergences between scientific, commercial, diplomatic, military, and intelligence perspectives on the U.S. role in space, not to speak of the high public visibility and political salience of certain aspects of U.S. space operations, make this an extraordinarily contentious policy area. The central problem lies in the roughly coequal status enjoyed by NASA and the Defense Department (with the Air Force as principal player) in the development of space policy, and the absence of a strong and consistent hand in the White House to set fundamental strategy and adjudicate disputes. Although some critics complain about a growing military influence on space policy, it can also be argued that NASA's civilian perspective remains the dominant factor, and has led the nation into gross errors (notably, overreliance on the shuttle at the expense of the development of a new generation of expendable, heavy-lift launch vehicles). At all events, the inexorable growth in the importance of space not only for national security but for U.S. national strategy in the most expansive sense of the term suggests that special efforts will need to be made in the years ahead in order to overcome the bureaucratic pathologies that have stood in the way of a coherent and effective U.S. policy in this area.[54] The new national space policy approved by the President in early 1988 is a hopeful sign that this is now occurring.[55]

Chapter 3

The NSC and the NSC System

THE NATIONAL SECURITY COUNCIL (NSC) came into being shortly after World War II, in the wake of an extended debate over the peacetime organizational requirements of the U.S. national security establishment generally. The NSC was created by the National Security Act of 1947, which also mandated the establishment of a unified Department of Defense and a Central Intelligence Agency. The National Security Council, currently consisting of the President, the Vice President, the Secretary of State, the Secretary of Defense, and other cabinet and subcabinet officials in an advisory capacity as required, is empowered to "advise the President with respect to the integration of domestic, foreign, and military policies relating to the national security" so as to enable the departments of government to "cooperate more effectively in matters involving the national security." The act specifically assigned to the NSC the responsibility to "assess and appraise the objectives, commitments, and risks of the United States in relation to our actual and potential military power, in the interest of national security, for the purpose of making recommendations to the President in connection therewith."[1]

It is one of the abiding ironies of this sweeping reform of U.S. national security policy making that the NSC came to function in a way that was diametrically opposed to the intention of many of its original proponents. Many in the military and in Congress at the time believed that an institution such as the NSC would act as a constraint on the President by tying him more closely and formally to his cabinet advisers. In fact, the result has been to lessen the President's dependence on his advisers by giving him greater control of the policy process and a staff that can effectively represent the presidential perspective in national security matters. From the beginning, presidents have been highly sensitive to any encroachment on the authority of their office potentially arising from the NSC, and have carefully maintained the council's status as a purely advisory body.

The National Security Act authorized an NSC staff headed by an Executive Secretary. In 1953, the position of Special Assistant to the President for National Security Affairs was created to serve as head of a senior-level Policy Planning Board that was created within the NSC staff. This position has since become a permanent one (its formal title is now Assistant to the President for National Security Affairs), and the individual occupying it serves by custom as director of the NSC staff in addition to acting as personal adviser to the President. The existence of an NSC adviser and staff separate from the National Security Council itself has been a fertile source of confusion. In the early days, NSC staff members were career bureaucrats on temporary duty from their agencies, and the function of the staff was seen as a purely technical or professional one. Though the question of whether the staff owed formal allegiance to the NSC as such or to the President was soon resolved in the latter's favor, in practice the staff operated very much as a secretariat rather than as a personal or political staff to the President. With the administration of John F. Kennedy, the NSC staff acquired the semipolitical character and identification with the presidential perspective which it has retained to a greater or lesser degree ever since. With the administration of Richard Nixon, the NSC adviser and his staff (this institutional collectivity will be referred to henceforth simply as "NSC," while the parent committee will be identified as "the council" or "the NSC principals") became for the first time a powerful and independent bureaucratic actor.

Before reviewing the history of the NSC, an analysis of the functions the organization can or should perform is essential. Many treatments of this subject are vitiated by simplistic assumptions as to the alternative NSC arrangements that are available to presidents. Too often, the alternatives are seen in starkly polarized terms—as if an NSC that does not compete with the State Department over the day-to-day running of foreign policy must be reduced to insignificant paper shuffling. Other observers too frequently dismiss the question of the organization and functions of the NSC on the grounds that it is merely an extension of individual presidential styles or preferences—as if presidential preferences cannot or should not be shaped by an understanding of what is intrinsically desirable. In fact, the NSC is a highly flexible instrument. It can serve a variety of functions, and offers a range of possible modes or degrees of control which can be tailored to a President's personal requirements, while at the same time fulfilling certain basic and recurring needs of the presidency as an institution.

NSC FUNCTIONS

The functions or categories of functions performed by the Assistant to the President for National Security Affairs (or the National Security Adviser, the informal if more convenient term) have been characterized in a variety of ways, all too often with little effort at analytic precision or completeness.[2] At a later point, these functions will be discussed systematically and prescriptively; here, it will suffice to identify them in general terms in order to facilitate discussion of the NSC's history. The functions that are currently or have at some time been carried out by the NSC may be grouped under the following headings: (1) routine staff support and information, (2) crisis management, (3) policy development, (4) policy implementation, (5) policy advice, and (6) operations.

Routine Staff Support and Information

Though seldom given much attention in discussions of the NSC role, this is an important and frequently burdensome staff function. Routine staff support includes the preparation of routine presidential speeches and messages, the handling of state visits, and the handling of presidential trips abroad. In theory, it should be possible to hand off many of these chores to other agencies, particularly the State Department; yet the time pressures involved often make this difficult or impossible, and presidents tend in any case to prefer that such matters be handled primarily or exclusively within the White House.

Equally little-noted but much more important is the information function. In the world of bureaucracy, knowledge is power; and the extent and type of information available to presidents is critical to their ability to arrive at sound independent judgments concerning external events or developments within the bureaucracy. Presidents will always have their own information channels, but the severe demands on their time and the restricted circle of persons with whom they are in daily contact can dangerously divorce them from the larger world. The National Security Adviser is in the best position to ensure that information available in the bureaucracy is brought to the attention of the President in a timely manner, and in a form and level of detail appropriate to his understanding and the demands of his schedule. This includes intelligence information of all types, information memoranda forwarded by the cabinet secretaries, administrative or personnel developments, and the like. He can also help ensure that alternate channels to the President remain open.

Crisis Management

That crisis management is preeminently a White House or NSC function has been generally recognized at least since the Cuban missile crisis of 1962. The rapidity of modern communications and their effect on the pace of world events, the domestic political pressures on the White House to react immediately to developing international crises, and the ineffectiveness of normal bureaucratic routines under such circumstances have together made sustained presidential involvement in crises virtually unavoidable. Where decisions must be made quickly and where disciplined coordination of the activities of several departments is needed, only the President or a proximate representative can ensure that this will occur. Moreover, where the use of military force by the United States is imminent or possible, the President is directly involved in his capacity as commander-in-chief, and his relationship to the bureaucracy in general shifts perceptibly toward a stance of command.

Policy Development

That the NSC has some role in policy development is generally acknowledged, but the exact nature of this role has been controversial. At one extreme, the NSC has been viewed (ideally or in fact) as performing a purely technical staff function in managing the decision process for the National Security Council principals and the President. At the other extreme, it is seen as having an independent role in identifying policy issues and formulating presidential initiatives.

The NSC policy development role is perhaps best analyzed in terms of three distinct subfunctions: strategic planning, the catalyzing of decision, and the management of decision.

Strategic planning can encompass a variety of short- to long-term, formal or informal types of planning exercises. It may be undertaken wholly within the NSC staff, in conjunction with other elements within the Executive Office of the President, or in conjunction with elements within the bureaucracy.

Catalyzing decision can involve a range of more or less intrusive interventions in agency and interagency policy deliberations. The most frequently used of these techniques is the tasking or assigning of studies. By focusing the energies of the bureaucracy on specific topics and forcing agencies to provide information and take positions on them, the NSC can have a very important effect on the structure and content of the agenda before high-level policy makers. More intrusive techniques—formal identification of issues for decision and initiation of the decision process—require NSC control of interagency committee machinery, which has frequently been partial or uncertain. Regular chairing of interagency meetings by NSC staff allows a much more thorough shaping of the bureaucratic agenda than is otherwise possible.

Management of the decision process is an indispensable NSC function, and one that may also be exercised in more or less interventionist fashion. It involves actions such as choosing the forum for deliberation and appropriate participants, settling questions of schedule and timing, ensuring the consideration of all relevant options, exercising quality control over agency analyses and argumentation, and ensuring full integration of agency contributions and their presentation in a form suitable for consideration by the council and presidential decision. While the casual observer may imagine that such chores are purely clerical, the fact of the matter is that, given the nature of committees and committee products, and given the compressed timeframe for high-level decision and the value of the stakes, they can be of surpassing importance for ensuring decision outcomes that meet even minimum standards of rationality, not to mention conserving the very valuable time of high officials.

Policy Implementation

Policy implementation is a function that has been performed less frequently and less systematically than policy development, though it is arguably of similar importance. Policy implementation may involve the recording and promulgation of decisions, liaison with operational planning, monitoring of operations, and assessment of results.

The promulgation of decisions is an important function, and one that can involve considerable complexity and delicacy where sensitive matters are at issue. Tradeoffs must always be faced between the advantages of transmitting formal and explicit orders to all concerned organizational elements and the risks of premature public disclosure of information. Because of such complications, record keeping and the management of information relating to presidential decisions becomes a function of some importance in its own right. That considerable policy slippage can occur in the process of converting decisions into bureaucratic actions is a frequent experience of presidents, not to speak of cases where presidential directives are consciously circumvented or simply ignored. It is thus altogether understandable that the NSC tends to assume some responsibility for oversight and monitoring of policy implementation. Here as elsewhere, the extent of NSC intervention can vary considerably, from mere observer status to active participation in operational planning to the exercise of formal or informal vetoes over operational decision making. Assessment of the results of existing policy as carried out by the relevant agencies is a function logically associated with those just discussed, but there is little evidence that the NSC has ever attempted it.

Policy Advice

There would seem to be no particular inevitability in the National Security Adviser assuming the role of substantive policy adviser to the President, especially where the Adviser is appointed with the clear understanding that this would not be the case. On the other hand, it is necessary to understand the various pressures and incentives that can lead presidents in this direction. Simple proximity and personal contact with the President, to begin with, are an immeasurable advantage enjoyed by the National Security Adviser in contrast to cabinet secretaries or other agency heads. The fact that the Adviser, alone of the President's senior counsellors, is answerable to no institution or authority other than the President himself helps further to cement a relationship of loyalty, familiarity, and trust. When two cabinet secretaries clash on important issues, the President is apt to want to know where his Adviser stands; and he is particularly likely to rely on the Adviser's substantive judgment in cases where time pressures or sensitivities of various kinds preclude formal adjudication of agency differences. Even when his other advisers are not split, however, the President may seek out the views of the National Security Adviser. If a particular cabinet secretary proves insufficiently competent or responsive to his requirements, the President may prefer to use his National Security Adviser as principal policy adviser in that area rather than pay the political costs associated with removal of a member of his cabinet. Finally, the President may come to value the Adviser as a source of strategic advice that is unavailable from other sources.

Operations

At times, and particularly during the tenure of Henry Kissinger as National Security Adviser, the NSC has been directly involved in the execution of operational tasks normally performed by other agencies. Operational activities (other than those relating to crisis situations) have mainly involved the preparation of secret diplomatic initiatives (Kissinger's opening to China is the classic case), the conduct of sensitive negotiations, private consultations with U.S. ambassadors and high-level foreign visitors, private press contacts and briefings, and public appearances by the Adviser. The propriety of NSC involvement in some or all of these activities has since been sharply challenged (most recently following revelation of the Reagan NSC's covert dealings with the Khomeini regime in Iran); and there is very general agreement that they are at best a serious distraction that can interfere with the performance of more central NSC functions. At the same time, however, it is well to recognize that circumstances of various kinds will most likely continue to make certain types of operational involvement by the NSC an attractive option for the President.

The foregoing analysis is meant to be descriptive rather than prescriptive. It recognizes that there is a wide range of possible NSC functions that have been given legitimacy by the history of the institution or its internal logic, and that differing circumstances may lead presidents to use the NSC in differing though equally legitimate ways. At the same time, the point cannot be made too strongly that it is impossible to leave the matter at saying that any NSC arrangement is as good as any other if it reflects the personality and operating style of a particular President. This assumes that presidential personalities or styles are simply immutable, or that organizational arrangements have no reality or utility except as extensions of the chief executive himself. These propositions are demonstrably incorrect. Some presidents have made great efforts of will to overcome aspects of their personalities they considered ill-suited to the office (Nixon is perhaps the classic case). Those presidents (FDR, Kennedy, and Johnson) who tolerated or actively cultivated bureaucratic chaos cannot be said to have developed an alternative method of governance, and some of the key policy failures of their administrations (particularly in the national security area) can be traced to their disregard for organizational realities.

A closer look at the recent history of presidential management of national security policy should illuminate the problems individual presidents have faced and the merits and limitations of the solutions they have chosen.

MANAGING NATIONAL SECURITY:
From Roosevelt to Carter

The history of the NSC system cannot be properly understood without some appreciation of the circumstances that gave rise to it and the problems it was designed to address. The United States had just emerged victorious from a world war, but with a greater consciousness of the need for coherence and continuity in its peacetime national security posture. The Joint Chiefs of Staff had only been created under the pressure of war so that the American military establishment could present a unified front to its British counterpart. Yet wartime cooperation between the Navy and the Army (and the Air Force, then an autonomous organization subordinated to the Army) was imperfect at best, and coordination between the military services and civilian defense agencies had left much to be desired. A State-War-Navy coordinating committee had come into existence during the war, anticipating the NSC structure and intended to serve similar purposes. But this committee never functioned effectively, and did not even attempt to deal with the fundamental issues of national strategy. National strategy was uniquely the province of the military establishment and its commander-in-chief, Franklin Delano Roosevelt.[3]

Like most of his successors, FDR did not have a high opinion of the State Department. He attempted to exercise personal control over foreign policy by deliberately undercutting the authority of his Secretary of State, Cordell Hull. When war came, Roosevelt had no intention of permitting State to play a significant role; and, in any event, the characteristically American tendency to think of war and diplomacy as unrelated spheres greatly favored military ascendency in the formulation of overall national strategy. The dominance of a purely military perspective, together with the often amateurish and erratic strategic leadership of FDR, can be credited with producing a number of fundamental strategic errors that seriously weakened the international position of the United States in the postwar world.

The consequences of the strategic errors committed by the allied powers in the course of World War II were not widely understood in the years immediately following 1945, but there was strong support in Congress as well as in the Army for unification of the American military establishment under a single Secretary of Defense. Unification was strongly opposed, however, by the Navy, and the struggles between the services over the unification issue were the key factor in the evolution of the National Security Act of 1947. The idea of a National Security Council including the Secretary of State and a civilian responsible for defense resource and mobilization issues was first broached in the Eberstadt Report, a study of postwar defense organization commissioned in 1945 by Secretary of the Navy James V. Forrestal. As the unification debate developed, a National Security Council was accepted not so much as something desirable in its own right but rather as necessary to securing Navy acquiescence in a unified Department of Defense. However, the NSC was viewed by its proponents in both services (and by some in Congress) as a useful mechanism for harnessing the President to the advice of the uniformed military, thus precluding a repetition of the undisciplined strategic leadership of FDR. As indicated earlier, such expectations revealed a fundamental misunderstanding of the role of the presidency in the American political system, and would prove wholly wide of the mark.

Largely for the reasons just sketched, Harry Truman was unenthusiastic about the NSC, and in its first years (until the outbreak of the Korean War) rarely attended its meetings. Meetings of NSC principals were chaired during this period by the Secretary of State, and the State Department tended to dominate the Council's proceedings. This was owing in part to continuing turmoil in the defense establishment, in part to the existence of a competent planning group in State, the Policy Planning Staff, and in part to the presence of a Secretary of State (Gen. George C. Marshall) with a strong strategic orientation. Many NSC papers were prepared by the Policy Planning Staff, most notably NSC-68, which laid the groundwork for the reconstitution of American military forces during the Korean War in response to a newly perceived Soviet global threat. With the advent of that war in June 1950, Truman came to recognize the value of the NSC as a forum for debate and a mechanism for policy development. After this time, the influence of State was considerably reduced, and an NSC staff—made up largely of career officials temporarily assigned by their parent agencies—firmly established as the immediate staff element for the council.[4]

Dwight Eisenhower undertook major changes in the NSC system after commissioning a report on it from Robert Cutler, whom he then appointed to the new position of Special Assistant to the President for National Security Affairs. Cutler had recommended that the NSC staff be made more clearly answerable to the President as distinct from NSC principals. A major step in this direction was the creation of an interdepartmental Planning Board under Cutler's chairmanship; in addition, he was given responsibility for overall management of the NSC staff, the Council, and its operations. The Planning Board was made up of high-ranking (Assistant Secretary level) departmental representatives, while support and continuity were provided by the NSC staff proper, which became a relatively permanent professional cadre. The Planning Board appears to have played a relatively active and independent role in catalyzing policy decisions as well as in strategic planning, while the staff occupied itself principally with management of the decision process. Some months later, a new interagency committee, the Operations Coordinating Board (OCB), was formed to improve policy implementation. Chaired by the Under Secretary of State, the OCB was intended both to coordinate operational planning and to monitor implementation of national-level policy. This NSC machinery seems to have worked well on the whole. During the eight years of the Eisenhower presidency, the NSC itself met 366 times, almost always with the President himself in the chair; such activity has not been equaled since.[5]

The Eisenhower NSC system was much criticized in its last years on the grounds of formalism, overconcern with agency consensus, and unwarranted demands on senior officials.[6] It is far from clear to what extent such criticisms are justified.[7] Eisenhower expressed bafflement at the charge that he or his advisers encouraged interagency consensus, and on a number of occasions he went outside the bureaucracy altogether in an effort to stimulate fresh thinking and new initiatives in controversial areas of national security.[8] Nevertheless, as Nelson Rockefeller argued forcefully at the time, the NSC planning system as a whole remained dominated by the perspectives of the individual agencies, and hence denied the President a full airing of policy options. There is evidence that Eisenhower had some sympathy for Rockefeller's radical proposal of a "first secretary" for foreign policy and national security who would have cabinet rank and directive authority over his colleagues.[9] In any event, Eisenhower became increasingly dissatisfied with interagency performance of the policy implementation function. In 1957, the National Security Adviser was given formal membership on the Operations Coordinating Board, and the OCB was integrated into the NSC staff; in 1960, the National Security Adviser was made chairman of the OCB, in recognition of the need for a presiding official who would be seen to be impartial in adjudicating agency disagreements.

John F. Kennedy assumed the presidency in 1961 determined to dismantle the elaborate NSC apparatus of the Eisenhower years and replace it with a more open and fluid system. JFK's assault on the interagency national security machinery meant in the first instance a devolution of authority to the State Department, and the President repeatedly exhorted State to take the leading role in foreign policy formulation. At the same time, however, Kennedy assumed an activist stance relative to the bureaucracy, and immersed himself in the details of policy. As his National Security Adviser McGeorge Bundy was to put it, the Kennedy administration "deliberately rubbed out the distinction between planning and operation" that governed the NSC structure during the Eisenhower period,[10] apparently in the belief that policy is much more affected by the rush of day-to-day events than by any systematic or long-term planning effort. Kennedy himself made a point of dealing directly with officials in the agencies at the level of assistant secretary or even below. Perhaps more significantly, JFK established (during the Berlin crisis of 1961) the dubious precedent of disrupting the military chain of command in order to exercise operational control over military units in the field.

The NSC under Bundy was considerably reduced in size from what it had been previously, and staffed primarily with persons from outside of government. However, its influence was considerably enhanced, owing both to the President's general encouragement of an activist White House role and the direct personal access he allowed not only to Bundy but to a number of his subordinates. Partly because of the presence of a very strong Secretary of Defense in the person of Robert S. McNamara, partly because of the inclinations of Kennedy and Bundy, the NSC staff involved itself almost exclusively in foreign policy matters. Because of the predictable failure of State to occupy the organizational vacuum the President had created for it, the NSC acted increasingly as an alternate source of policy development and policy advice.

Lyndon B. Johnson shared Kennedy's penchant for an informal

approach to the management of national security policy, and there was broad continuity between the two administrations in terms of personnel and structure alike. However, Johnson was less personally interested in foreign policy issues than his predecessor and more inclined to delegate to the departments. Accordingly, the NSC staff declined in importance, reverting to its role as manager of the policy process rather than catalyzer of decision or source of policy advice (although Bundy's successor Walt Rostow personally assumed a vigorous advocacy role with respect to Vietnam). The Council itself was moribund. In its place, LBJ instituted informal weekly meetings (the "Tuesday Lunch") with his secretaries of State and Defense and his National Security Adviser. These provided a confidential forum for high-level discussion of issues relating to the increasingly controversial war in Vietnam. But they caused severe problems for the bureaucracy. They were not adequately prepared, there was no clear record of decisions reached, and the results were rarely promulgated widely enough to provide adequate guidance to the agencies; at the same time, the arrangement tended to paralyze lower-level efforts at interagency coordination. In 1966, Johnson made a gesture in the direction of more systematic interagency procedures when he assigned to the State Department responsibility for managing a Senior Interdepartmental Group (SIG) and a variety of Interdepartmental Regional Groups (IRGs), to be chaired by State officials at the Under Secretary and Assistant Secretary level respectively. But this new system was never effectively supported by the President or by Secretary of State Dean Rusk.[11]

There can be little question but that the principal national security disasters of the Kennedy and Johnson administrations—the abortive Bay of Pigs invasion and U.S. strategic and operational ineptitude in Vietnam—owe much to these presidents' organizational choices and individual operating styles. Richard Nixon, at any rate, was inclined to trace "most of our serious reverses abroad since 1960" to the abandonment of the old NSC system in favor of "catch-as-catch-can talkfests" among the President and his advisors.[12] In private conversation with Henry Kissinger, his National Security Adviser-to-be, Nixon made clear his distrust of the State Department and CIA and his desire for a White House-centered mechanism for the formulation of foreign and national security policy. Nixon wanted, as he put it, the Eisenhower system "without the concurrences"— that is, a system that would provide the President with a full range of options for decision rather than a single agreed interagency view.[13]

The system that resulted resembled the Eisenhower NSC in many respects, yet also took over features from the Kennedy-Johnson era. Most importantly, the NSC staff was based more on the Kennedy than the Eisenhower model, utilizing young, capable foreign affairs professionals largely recruited from outside the government. Kissinger retained the State-chaired IRGs (renamed Interdepartmental Groups, or IGs) and SIG (replaced by the Under Secretaries Committee), but had them report to an NSC Review Group chaired by himself. The regionally oriented IGs had responsibilities in the area of contingency planning as well as policy development, while the Under Secretaries Committee (of which Kissinger was also a member) was intended to take on some of the operational coordination functions of the old OCB. In addition, Kissinger chaired new senior-level committees dealing with crisis management (the Washington Special Actions Group), covert action (the Forty Committee), and arms control (the Verification Panel), as well as an ad hoc committee on Vietnam (the Vietnam Special Studies Group). In the defense area, a Defense Program Review Committee (DPRC) was established with high-level representation from State and the NSC as well as the OMB and the Defense Department to review major defense fiscal policy and program issues in a broad strategic context.

The first six months of the Nixon administration's new national security apparatus were largely taken up with a series of studies of U.S. policy conducted at the request of Kissinger and within the framework of the interagency IGs and NSC Review Group. During this period, the system as a whole functioned for the most part in accordance with these formal arrangements. Soon, however, a combination of personalities and circumstances worked to concentrate effective power in the hands of Kissinger, largely at the expense of the State Department headed by William P. Rogers. The Defense Department, under the resourceful leadership of Melvin Laird, kept its distance from Kissinger and the White House (the DPRC in particular quickly turned into a dead letter). At all events, Kissinger soon came to dominate both the formulation and the execution of administration foreign policy in the most critical areas, particularly the Vietnam peace negotiations, policy toward the People's Republic of China, and the negotiations with the Soviet Union over strategic arms control. In addition, and equally unprecedented, Kissinger stepped forward as the architect and principal spokesman of a national security policy which laid claim to conceptual cohesion and strategic scope. As the rivalry between NSC and State sharpened, the original NSC system broke down, and the Adviser and his staff increasingly assumed operational responsibilities to the complete exclusion of State.

When Kissinger assumed the position of Secretary of State in September 1973, he retained his White House job as well, thus consolidating his control over the forms of interagency coordination as well as the substance of policy. Gen. Brent Scowcroft replaced Kissinger as National Security Adviser after Gerald Ford's accession to the presidency, but this produced little real change. Scowcroft's NSC can be understood as a kind of throwback to the Eisenhower (if not the Truman) era, with the staff acting more nearly as a secretariat for the Council and its principals than as a personal staff for the President.[14]

Jimmy Carter's choice of Zbigniew Brzezinski as his National Security Adviser seemed at first to mark a return to the Nixon-Kissinger era. Like Kissinger, Brzezinski was an academic authority on international affairs with well-developed policy views of his own. Brzezinski himself conceived the NSC role in the broadest terms, as a source of strategic planning and advice that was unavailable within the bureaucracy as well as a mechanism for interagency coordination; and his initial plan for the NSC system envisaged a structure of seven committees much like that established by Kissinger. However, Carter refused to go this far, and the system that emerged was a compromise between a White House- and a cabinet-centered arrangement.[15] The NSC structure itself was greatly simplified: a Policy Review Committee (PRC) would handle foreign policy, defense, and international economic issues, and was to be chaired by the appropriate cabinet secretary, while a Special Coordinating Committee (SCC) chaired by the National Security Adviser would handle sensitive functions such as arms control, crisis management, and covert action.

At the same time, Carter signaled his support for a stronger NSC role by giving his National Security Adviser cabinet status. The SCC chaired by Brzezinski, unlike its Kissinger-era equivalents, was actually a cabinet-level committee, including all NSC principals except the President himself; and Brzezinski sat as a full member of the PRC as well as serving as manager of the policy development process. This enhancement of the Adviser's formal status was itself an important development, but the President strongly reinforced it by his apparent inclination to look to Brzezinski as an alternate source of foreign policy advice of coequal standing with Secretary of State Cyrus Vance. The ideological differences between Brzezinski and

Vance predictably led to a revival of State-NSC animosity, a situation the President was unable or unwilling to resolve in spite of the generous airing the dispute received in the national press. One consequence of all this was increasing discussion of the question whether the National Security Adviser position should be given statutory cabinet rank and made subject to confirmation by the Senate. Brzezinski himself is on record as favoring such a step.[16]

THE NSC UNDER THE REAGAN ADMINISTRATION

The controversial nature of the Kissinger and Brzezinski experiments and their adverse political fallout were very much on the minds of Ronald Reagan and his advisers when they turned to the task of reorganizing the White House in 1981. The President's original National Security Adviser, Richard V. Allen, was himself convinced of the need for a reduction in the NSC role, and supported the appointment of a strong Secretary of State in the person of Gen. Alexander Haig. The President himself made clear to Haig his own commitment to cabinet government and to restoration of the primacy of the State Department in foreign policy.[17] However, Haig's asserted claim to function as the President's "vicar" for the full range of U.S. policy concerns abroad triggered alarm and resistance within the White House staff, and derailed Haig's effort to put in place a new NSC structure that would formally authorize a central role for State. The problem had become visible as early as March 1981, when the chairmanship of a new interagency crisis management committee was given to Vice President Bush rather than to the Secretary of State.[18]

The administration's concentration during its first year on domestic and budgetary questions contributed to the drift in national security policy resulting from White House uneasiness over what was perceived to be bureaucratic self-aggrandizement on the part of the Secretary of State. Haig's marked reliance on the Foreign Service rather than political appointees, and incipient differences between State and the Defense Department over arms control and other issues, further exacerbated the problem. Nevertheless, elements of a new NSC system were put in place during 1981. Interdepartmental Groups and Senior Interdepartmental Groups were established in a number of regional and functional areas, almost all of them under the chairmanship of State Department officials; a Special Situation Group for crisis management was created under the Vice President; and a National Security Planning Group was set up as a less formal alternative to the National Security Council itself. At the same time, Allen's NSC staff had difficulty establishing its authority and defining its role either within the White House or relative to the bureaucracy, and was widely viewed as ineffective.[19]

In January, 1982, after the replacement of Allen by William P. Clark as National Security Adviser, the White House finally issued a presidential directive formally establishing the new NSC system. According to National Security Decision Directive (NSDD) 2, the National Security Council would remain the principal forum for consideration of national security policy issues, while the National Security Adviser would be responsible for "developing, coordinating and implementing" national security policy in consultation with NSC principals. At the same time, this document described the Secretary of State as the President's "principal foreign policy advisor," with responsibility for "the formulation of foreign policy and for the execution of approved policy" as well as for "the overall direction, coordination, and supervision of the interdepartmental activities incident to foreign policy formulation, and the activities of Executive Departments and Agencies of the United States overseas" (excluding military forces). The Secretary is specifically charged with "preparation of those papers addressing matters affecting the foreign policy and foreign relations of the United States for consideration by the NSC." The directive similarly describes the Secretary of Defense and the Director of Central Intelligence as the President's "principal advisors" in their respective areas, and with similar responsibilities for interdepartmental coordination and the preparation of papers for NSC consideration.

NSDD 2 also established a framework of interagency committees to support NSC decision making. Separate SIGs were created for foreign policy, defense, and intelligence, chaired respectively by the deputy secretaries of State and Defense and the Director of Central Intelligence, and with the National Security Adviser as a member. These groups were assigned responsibilities in the area of policy implementation as well as policy development, and were supposed to have permanent secretariats drawn from personnel of the lead agency. In support of the SIGs, the establishment of a number of IGs was mandated or permitted under the chairmanship of the appropriate agency under secretaries or assistant secretaries. State was required to establish five regional IGs and two functional ones in the areas of political-military affairs and international economic affairs. The regional IGs were specifically empowered to prepare contingency plans and create working groups to support NSC crisis management operations. The Director of Central Intelligence was required to establish an IG for counterintelligence, while the Secretary of Defense was authorized to create IGs "corresponding to the functional areas within the Department of Defense."[20]

Other important structural innovations were undertaken early in Reagan's administration in the traditional NSC areas of crisis management and covert action. As mentioned earlier, the Carter-era SCC was replaced by a Special Situation Group (SSG), chaired by the Vice President, for crisis management, while covert action responsibilities were taken over by the National Security Planning Group. In May 1982, a Crisis Pre-Planning Group (CPPG) was established under the chairmanship of the Deputy National Security Adviser to support the higher-level SSG. At around this same time, a permanent crisis planning element was created within the NSC staff, with advanced data processing capabilities and a mandate to develop a government-wide communications system and set of agreed procedures for prior planning and operations relative to international crisis situations. By the end of 1983, a Crisis Management Center, including a conference room equipped with sophisticated audiovisual equipment and a powerful computer, had become operational adjacent to NSC offices in the Old Executive Office Building.[21]

The National Security Planning Group (NSPG) is a significant innovation of the Reagan administration, if one that has received relatively little attention. The membership of this group and its precise charter have not been publicly revealed, but it has evidently included NSC principals as well as the President's senior White House advisers, with meetings structured so as to allow maximum opportunity for a free exchange of views. The existence of this forum facilitated the handling of covert action questions, but its confidentiality also proved conducive to discussion of other sensitive matters in a less structured setting, thus serving a function akin to the Tuesday Lunches of the Johnson administration.[22]

In view of the history of dissension over NSDD 2 and the ambiguities of the document itself, particularly as regards the ultimate locus of authority for management of the NSC process, it is not altogether surprising that reality did not conform very closely with the procedures it laid out. On the one hand, the three agencies involved were slow to take on responsibility for establishing and managing the interagency groups assigned to them. The SIGs for defense and intelligence have met only rarely, and only then in response to White

House pressure. The SIG for foreign policy never developed a recognizable identity (none of the SIGs ever established the permanent secretariat required by NSDD 2), and the regional IGs have met irregularly at best. For the most part, State tended to use the SIG-IG framework as a convenient method for handling ad hoc problems as they arise, rather than as a mechanism for the systematic development of policy. Partly as a result, these groups tended to decline in importance and level of representation and to assume a more operational role.

On the other hand, a number of expedients were devised to strengthen centralized control and coordination of the interagency process in key areas. In June 1982, a new SIG was created for international economic policy, with the Secretary of the Treasury as chairman and the Secretary of State as vice chairman. This tendency to split agency differences through co-chairing arrangements was also evident in the arms control area, where State and Defense were given joint responsibilities for chairing a number of committees on issues on which disagreement between them was often profound; predictably, paralysis or bad feeling were frequently the result.[23]

At the same time, however, the National Security Adviser and his staff began to play a larger role, particularly during the tenure of Clark, a close personal friend of the President who had initially joined the administration as Deputy Secretary of State under Haig. Clark's arrival put the Adviser for the first time on an equal footing with the White House "troika" of James Baker, Michael Deaver, and Edwin Meese, and his access to and influence with the President soon made him a conduit for growing conservative dissatisfaction with the Secretary of State as well as some of his White House critics.[24] But Clark was also convinced that firm White House management of the NSC system was essential for its proper functioning. Accordingly, he attempted to bring greater discipline to the mechanics of interagency policy development. Most significantly, he did not hesitate to take on responsibility for the chairing of interagency committees in areas of particular sensitivity or bureaucratic contention.

Clark thus created and assumed the chairmanship of a SIG on space policy and a SIG-level committee on emergency preparedness (the Emergency Management Preparedness Board). In early 1983, the President established a cabinet-level committee (the Special Planning Group) under Clark's leadership—the level of the group was itself a significant departure—to improve the planning and coordination of administration activities in the public diplomacy area.[25] Under this umbrella authority, a committee was established under the chairmanship of the NSC deputy to plan and coordinate technical, diplomatic, and budgetary aspects of U.S. international broadcasting, and another under the co-chairmanship of the NSC deputy and the White House Director of Communications dealing with public affairs issues relating to national security. In another area, Clark assumed the chairmanship of a SIG-level Verification Committee that was intended to impose discipline and a greater national perspective on the bureaucratically contentious and politically charged process of assessing verification and compliance with arms control agreements. By mid-1983, disputes between State and Defense over arms control issues had become so intense that Clark stepped in to assert NSC control of the arms control policy process as a whole through the establishment of a Senior Arms Control Policy Group under his chairmanship. Finally, Clark took a strong interest in the systematic development of broad policy or strategy across the spectrum of national security issues. In the spring of 1982, he initiated a major study of U.S. military strategy within the context of national strategy as a whole. A follow-on study in 1983 reviewed U.S. international information policy.[26]

Clark's personal role as policy adviser and catalyst of presidential decisions on policy and personnel questions must also be emphasized. Clark evidently had a key part in forcing the resignation of Haig as Secretary of State in July 1982 in connection with a dispute over Middle East policy.[27] By the end of his first year in office, Clark seems to have come to the conclusion that he could not adequately discharge his responsibilities merely by acting as an "honest broker" of agency differences. In what was almost certainly his most forceful policy intervention, Clark moved to toughen U.S. policy toward Nicaragua, blocking State Department efforts at accommodation with the Sandinistas and engineering the departure of the champion of this approach, Assistant Secretary of State Thomas Enders.[28] Mention should also be made of Clark's active intervention in international economic policy matters (particularly technology transfer and energy security), where the NSC at times played a pivotal role in fierce disputes between the Defense Department on the one hand and State and a variety of domestic agencies on the other.[29]

In addition to assuming a higher personal profile, Clark came to see the need to strengthen the bureaucratic position of the NSC staff. A reorganization, announced in July 1983, brought an upgrading in status for senior staff, eight of whom were formally designated

Special Assistant to the President. It was also at this time that the position of Executive Secretary was resurrected in order to improve communications between the NSC and the secretariats of the agencies as well as within the White House complex itself. The increasing publicity Clark sought during 1983 also seems to have been calculated to enhance the standing of the NSC in the internal bureaucratic struggle.[30]

Clark's sudden departure in October 1983 to become Secretary of the Interior highlighted what has proven to be perhaps the most characteristic and enduring problem in the management of national security affairs under the Reagan administration: tension between the National Security Adviser and the White House staff. Originally, in line with the intention to downgrade the importance of the position, the Adviser reported formally to the President through White House policy chief Edwin Meese, and his clout within the White House was extremely limited. Though Meese was sympathetic to national security concerns, the initial White House preoccupation with domestic policy turned the reporting arrangement into a roadblock. By the time Clark arrived on the scene, the situation had become confused by Meese's relative loss of influence and the rise of James Baker and Michael Deaver, who tended to view national security issues from a domestic political perspective and were more inclined to seek accommodation with Congress, the bureaucracy, and the media. Because of his personal relationship with the President, Clark was able to regain direct access to the Oval Office and to raise the salience of national security issues in the White House generally. In so doing, however, he was perceived as posing a fundamental threat to the existing balance of power among White House factions. The resulting feud, which was increasingly seen as a contest between "conservatives" and "pragmatists" throughout the administration, seems to have been the critical factor in Clark's eventual departure. Reportedly, Baker himself sought to replace Clark at the NSC, while the conservative wing promoted Jeane Kirkpatrick for the position. A compromise candidate was eventually settled on in the person of Clark's then deputy, Robert C. (Bud) McFarlane.[31]

The weakness of McFarlane's position within the White House became clear when a reorganization in April 1985 abolished the NSC international economic policy SIG and established a new Economic Policy Council chaired by Jim Baker, who had taken over the Treasury portfolio from Donald Regan early in 1984. This move marked the end of NSC efforts to play an independent role in the international economics area. Evidently, McFarlane was unable to work out a modus vivendi with new White House chief of staff Don Regan, and growing tensions between the two men seem to have been the main cause of McFarlane's abrupt resignation in December 1985.[32] According to one analysis, McFarlane had attempted to shore up his position within the White House through an alliance with the State Department, but in so doing had antagonized other NSC principals, who increasingly took their case directly to Regan.[33] If this is correct, it indicates that NSC–White House problems under the Reagan administration have been systemic rather than simply ideological in character—although this need mean no more than that they are rooted in a particular presidential management style.

That McFarlane was succeeded by Rear (later Vice) Adm. John M. Poindexter rather than by a figure of independent political standing suggests continuing resistance within the White House to a strong NSC role. As NSC deputy under McFarlane, Poindexter acquired a reputation as an effective and cool-headed crisis manager, and is reported to have played a key role in planning the U.S. military operation against Grenada as well as the interception of the Egyptian jet carrying the *Achille Lauro* hijackers. Poindexter's evident dislike of the media and concern over the leaking of national security information resulted in an NSC operation even less visible than that of his predecessors. Accordingly, it is difficult to assess the role played by the NSC and by Poindexter himself in perennially contentious areas such as arms control. Press attacks on his handling of the decision to cease compliance with the SALT II agreement were predictable, and in any case appear to have been abetted by the office of Don Regan.[34] Other credible press accounts, however, suggest that the NSC staff declined further in influence under Poindexter in areas other than those relating to crisis management and covert operations.[35] All of this stands in striking contrast to the image of an overreaching and omnipresent NSC operation that emerged from the "Irangate" drama.

The controversy set off in the fall of 1986 by the exposure of ex-NSC Adviser McFarlane's secret trip to Teheran on behalf of the President, together with questions regarding NSC staff involvement in facilitating the transfer of profits from clandestine arms sales to Iran to the Nicaraguan Contras (as well as in other activities in support of the Contras), suddenly gave renewed prominence to the issue of the role of the NSC. The abrupt departure of Poindexter and of Lt. Col. Oliver North, the appointment of Frank Carlucci as the new National Security Adviser, and the creation of a bipartisan presidential commission with a broad mandate to investigate NSC operations seemed to set the stage for a fundamental reappraisal of the NSC role and for sweeping changes in administration practice if not in existing legislation.

In fact, however, this did not occur. While it criticized the President's "management style" as overly lax, the Tower Commission accepted the existing NSC system as essentially sound, and gave no encouragement to those attracted to further legislative constraints on presidential power. At the same time, the new Carlucci regime, in spite of its rough handling of the NSC staff inherited from Poindexter and other early indications of radical change, does not appear to have operated in ways markedly different from its predecessors.[36] Carlucci reemphasized the importance of the Adviser's direct access to the President, and received assurances on this score. Predictably, both Carlucci and the Tower Commission agreed on the need for a tightening of procedures dealing with covert action, as well as enhanced status for the NSC legal adviser. In addition, both recognized that the Iran-Contra episode was at bottom, in the words of Senator Tower, an "aberration," and that the NSC's fundamental problem in the Reagan years had been insufficient authority rather than too much of it.[37] The Tower Commission recommended that the NSC return to the practice of chairing key interagency committees. Carlucci, evidently recognizing the atrophy of the agency-chaired SIGs created by NSDD 2, quietly moved to supersede this system by the creation of a new high-level committee, the Policy Review Group (PRG), chaired by the Deputy National Security Adviser. The function of this group was to review unresolved issues arising in IG-level committees in all regional and functional areas and to improve the process of readying such issues for presidential decision. Whether it has made a significant difference in the operation of the NSC system as a whole is as yet unclear.

In spite of the impressive span of his experience, Frank Carlucci is by all accounts a skilled bureaucratic manager rather than someone possessed of a distinctive strategic outlook and agenda. Given Ronald Reagan's evident reluctance—in spite of appearances created by the Poindexter-North operation—to use the NSC as an active instrument of his presidency, the political inhibitions created by the Iran-Contra affair, and the inevitable waning of White House influence in the final years of the administration, there was little reason to expect any significant departure from established patterns in national security policy making during Carlucci's tenure. Nonetheless, Carlucci was evidently not prepared to play a wholly subordinate role in administration policy making. By mid-1987, reports had begun to surface of fresh tensions between NSC and State. Well-advertised trips by the new National Security Adviser to Central America and Europe, and other direct diplomatic contacts by NSC staff members, gave rise to complaints in Foggy Bottom, while George Shultz's emphatic testimony before congressional investigators concerning the need for a reduction in the NSC's size and role apparently irritated Carlucci.[38]

In November 1987, Carlucci moved from the NSC to the Department of Defense following the departure of Caspar Weinberger, and was succeeded—in a by now familiar pattern—by his deputy, Lt. Gen. Colin L. Powell. An infantry officer with extensive command experience (as well as several staff tours in the Pentagon, the last as Weinberger's military assistant), Powell reportedly resisted his original NSC assignment with some vigor. In an interview in October, Powell had defended a military presence on the NSC staff, but expressed the view that the Adviser position is a political one and should be held by a civilian.[39] Powell's elevation thus appeared to signal a White House preference for a caretaker NSC regime in the final days of the administration, and acquiescence in the reemergence of Shultz's State Department as the primary engine of national security policy-making.

Chapter 4

Rethinking the NSC Role

How SHOULD the President employ the NSC and the NSC system? This fundamental question transcends the sphere of management in any conventional sense, and bears directly on the issue of the nature and role of the presidency in the American political system. At the same time, the question is of considerable practical importance, with large implications for the day-to-day functioning of the national security bureaucracy.

That systemic disorders of a serious character exist within the national security bureaucracy, and that the NSC system is not now (if it ever has been) capable of dealing with them effectively, has been the burden of the argument thus far. It will undoubtedly be said that something that is not manifestly broken should not be fixed, that differences in presidential style are too great to permit drawing up a meaningful general blueprint for NSC reform, or that fundamental change is impossible in any case. In response to the first (and probably most common) objection, two points can be made. First, organizational disorders in the national security arena are rarely visible—even to those in a position to know something about them—until they turn into disasters. Second, perhaps even more important than the potential for disaster is the reality of lost opportunity. Bureaucratic pathologies may or may not have visible symptoms, but they act as a constant drain on the system of government by absorbing energies that might otherwise have been turned outward and making certain kinds of activity difficult or impossible.

That these afflictions are chronic and incurable is a view many hold, but one that is overly pessimistic. Presidential styles and organizational arrangements really do make a difference. And it is wrong to suppose that any strengthening of the White House role in national security decision making is sure to be resisted *à outrance* by the agencies involved. The logic of the policy process itself demands a measure of central direction. Agencies have many good reasons for supporting a strong NSC—it ensures a modicum of orderliness and predictability in the process, offers protection or leverage with respect to bureaucratic competitors, and provides political cover for controversial decisions, to name a few. The NSC can expect to find natural allies particularly in smaller or less powerful agencies. But even major departments such as State or Defense recognize that there are critical functions of coordination and direction that can only be performed or performed effectively from the White House.

There can be little question but that the NSC role very much depends on the requirements of individual presidents. These requirements are in turn a function of presidential personality, operating style, and—perhaps most importantly—political agenda. Presidents who seek to achieve an ambitious political agenda must overcome endemic bureaucratic resistance to change. A President who prefers to remain relatively aloof from day-to-day decision making will have greater need of a strong staff if he wishes to maintain control of the bureaucracy; the same is true of a President who has no taste for direct argument with members of his cabinet.

At the same time, there would seem to be rather clearly definable limits within which such factors can or should affect the basic institutional structure of the federal government. As suggested earlier, presidents should expect to pay severe penalties for indulging quirks of their personalities or fantasies of charismatic leadership at the expense of institutional arrangements that reflect the basic logic of the presidential office.

The basic logic of the presidency, to repeat the point stated earlier, is strategic leadership of the nation. Understanding the NSC in terms of the central task of strategic leadership offers an unaccustomed angle of attack on the much-discussed problem of NSC-State rivalry. But it also brings into relief the equally important yet generally neglected question of the relationship between the NSC and the defense and intelligence establishments. In this perspective, it is evident that the conventional opposition between the NSC as policy coordinator and the NSC as source of policy advice or direction is profoundly misleading. While the existence of separate agencies with distinct missions certainly makes an NSC coordinating role indispensable, the NSC must also be involved directly in the business of all of the major national security communities—yet in a carefully delimited way.

STRATEGY AND PLANNING

That the NSC's role has become a public issue at all is owing entirely to the open feuding between the NSC adviser and staff and the State Department that took place during the tenures at the NSC of Henry Kissinger and Zbigniew Brzezinski. Strikingly, the NSC role was virtually invisible during the Eisenhower years in spite of the high level of activity associated with the Council itself and the inter-agency structure supporting it. This suggests that the State-NSC conflicts of the past are at least as much a result of the personal styles and strategies of those advisers and (more importantly) inadequate management by the President as they are a reflection of enduring institutional tensions. In fact, only in recent years has it become clear to what extent Eisenhower himself controlled foreign policy formulation through the NSC mechanism. That Secretary of State John Foster Dulles was the dominant figure in this area is a myth that was almost certainly encouraged by Eisenhower himself, so as not to undercut Dulles's effectiveness as foreign policy spokesman for his administration.

Why was the Eisenhower NSC system able to operate so smoothly? The fundamental reason would seem to be that Eisenhower maintained a very clear view of the proper function of the NSC. For him, the proper function was not policy coordination simply, and still less day-to-day decision making, but the development of national strategy. Eisenhower's articulation of the NSC system as a whole followed directly from this approach. Freely adapting the model of military staff procedures, Eisenhower created the NSC Planning Board to carry out the strategic planning function, while the Operations Coordinating Board was to develop coordinated plans for translating approved national strategy into agency operations. The departments were fully involved at every step of this process and their operational responsibilities were respected, thus minimizing the potential for sharp bureaucratic conflict; yet at the same time the White House was able to exercise substantial control over the process as a whole.

The breakdown of the NSC system in the Kennedy administration and subsequently would seem to have had less to do with the politicization of the NSC staff beginning at this time than with a loss of

appreciation on the part of the White House of the distinction between strategy and operations. With the abolition of the Eisenhower-
era OCB, the idea took hold that the only way to ensure the execution
of presidential policy was through direct operational involvement
by the White House. At the same time, a change occurred in the
way in which policy itself was conceived. Kennedy and Johnson
had little patience with what they regarded as paper exercises in
strategic planning. Increasingly, "policy" meant operational decision
making, and policy development became indistinguishable from the
day-to-day management of national security. Under these circumstances, any strong White House role in policy development was
bound to come into direct conflict with the prerogatives of the
agencies, and especially the State Department. The end of this particular road was reached under Kissinger. In spite of Nixon's professed
desire to recreate the Eisenhower NSC system, Kissinger's strong
operational orientation (not to speak of his personal ambitions) im-
parted an entirely different spirit and meaning to what looked like
very similar institutional arrangements.

It would be a mistake, however, to idealize the Eisenhower system.
The insistence of Kennedy and Bundy on the importance of the
operational dimension of policy, and their dislike of government
by committee, obviously reflected a dissatisfaction with the Eisenhower approach that extended across the political spectrum. As
indicated earlier, Eisenhower himself came to recognize the need
for a closer integration of the OCB with the policy side of the NSC
and a stronger White House role in managing it. By the same token,
as was argued at the time by Nelson Rockefeller in particular, the
Policy Board itself remained overly dependent on the agencies that
staffed it, and thus produced options that reflected agency positions
rather than genuine strategic choices.

Contrary to the view that gained currency under Kennedy (and
remains strong today), strategic planning is not inherently a futile
exercise. That such planning often occurs at a level of generality
so high as to be relatively meaningless in practical terms is true,
but this reflects planning exercises by committees dominated by
agency perspectives. Agencies see it as in their interest to drive
interagency planning to abstract levels, since this preserves their
own freedom of action. Contrary to the popular notion that "keeping
options open" is peculiarly in the interest of the President,[1]
avoiding genuine strategic choice is in the interest of the bureaucracy, since
policy then devolves to the operational level, where it is more difficult

for the White House or other agencies to make their influence felt. The issuance of general yet carefully defined strategic policies by the President helps to constrain and shape the operations of the agencies in a variety of ways. Even when operations are not directly or immediately affected, clarification of the assumptions and aims of policy can serve useful educational and morale-building purposes. This is a function much underrated by pragmatically minded Americans, for whom the word "doctrine" tends to conjure up alien and unsavory images; yet an excellent case can be made that rigorously formulated doctrinal concepts are as essential for the effective functioning of the national security establishment as a whole as they have proved to be for the uniformed military. For the development of the national security strategies and doctrines, the President requires a planning staff that has competence in policy analysis at the strategic level, and at the same time is not constrained by any concern to protect the operational flexibility of the agencies.

Strategic planning conducted by dedicated staff elements is usually discounted on the grounds that any distinction between planners and operators tends to transform planning into a mere paper exercise. The disjunction of planning and operations is obviously a valid concern. Yet the almost axiomatic dismissal of the very possibility of autonomous planning staffs that regularly recurs in the literature on the NSC system is really a reflection of the historical weakness of planning within the State Department rather than of the working of any universal law. In fact, of course, military planners function as self-contained units, yet they are closely coupled into operations by virtue of the basic organizational structure of military staffs. There is no reason in principle why procedures cannot be devised that would maintain national-level planners in appropriate operational loops.

To speak of a strategic planning function for the NSC, then, is most emphatically not to envision an NSC planning staff that is hermetically sealed off from the rest of the bureaucracy. Strategic planning cannot meaningfully be conducted in the absence of full and reliable information concerning the operational implications of strategy, and this obviously requires some form of participation by the agencies responsible for operations. By the same token, operational planners themselves benefit from direct access to those responsible for the formulation of strategy.

A further source of misunderstanding of the relationship of the NSC to the bureaucracy arises from the common confusion of planning with strategy in the largest sense of the term. Here too, the history of State's Policy Planning Staff has helped to muddy the waters. Contrary to the usual view, there need be no conflict whatever between planning elements at State and at NSC, since the planning in each case can and should occur at quite a different level. NSC planning should be at the level of national strategy (or grand strategy, as it is sometimes called); planning at State and throughout the agencies should be at the level of agency-specific strategy and of agency-specific or interagency operations. While it is obviously not possible to make completely clean distinctions in such matters, the analogy with military planning can again prove helpful. Very different yet equally necessary sorts of planning occur at the levels of the service staffs and Joint Staff, the staffs of the unified and specified commands, and the staffs of major military formations (fleet or naval task force, field army or corps), corresponding to the requirements of military strategy generally, theater strategy, and operations or operational art. Precisely because of the overlap between these requirements, planners at the different levels routinely interact and reciprocally affect one another's outlook; but they retain specific and well-defined responsibilities.[2]

The notion that State can or should do planning at the level of national strategy is a legacy of the brief and in many ways atypical period during which State's Policy Planning Staff dominated the fledgling NSC process under the Truman administration. That Policy Planning has subsequently failed to repeat this experience or anything remotely like it is hardly surprising, especially given the enduring bureaucratic culture of the department. Yet even the much-acclaimed NSC-68, a planning document which called for dramatic increases in U.S. defense spending to meet the global Soviet threat, would almost certainly have remained a dead letter had it not been for the outbreak of the Korean War. The fact is that the relationship of Policy Planning not only to the military establishment but even to the rest of State has always been tenuous, and for reasons that are systemic rather than personality-related. There is a strong likelihood that any Policy Planning study with a strong military component will remain a paper exercise given the organizational and cultural barriers to direct State-Defense cooperation. In addition, Policy Planning has always been in a weak position within State itself because the organization of the department, built as it is around powerful regional bureaus, is inherently hostile to any central or functionally oriented staff element. Career incentives, training, and a host of other cultural factors stack the deck further against Policy Planning. These factors can be countered to some degree by leavening Policy Planning's staff with outside experts, as has been done increasingly in recent years; but this only exacerbates its bureaucratic isolation and ineffectiveness.

The implications of this analysis for the organization of the State Department itself will be pursued at a later point. It must be emphasized that none of this is intended to deny the need for a planning function at State; indeed, the State planning mechanism should be greatly strengthened. The point is that State can in no way substitute for the NSC as a locus for the planning of national strategy. Perhaps the clearest evidence of the current incompetence of State in this area, as discussed earlier, is the department's approach to dealing with the Soviet imperium. But this is only the most obvious and persistent example of State's constitutional inability to look at the problems of U.S. foreign policy in strategic perspective.

A serious strategic planning effort at the national level cannot in any case limit itself to foreign policy narrowly understood. It must encompass elements of military strategy as well as strategic intelligence, and integrate them with the diplomatic and political dimension of national security. In addition, it cannot avoid at least some consideration of economic as well as domestic policy (and political) factors. As indicated above, what is needed here goes well beyond mere coordination of the work of the separate agencies involved. Serious strategic planning must rest on an analysis of the international situation and of U.S. national objectives and strategy which exceeds the mandate of any single agency, and at the same time has direct implications for agency roles and missions and for resource allocation within as well as across agencies. Particularly where resource allocation questions are involved, differing agency approaches to such matters cannot be "coordinated" but must be actively adjudicated within the White House.

While it is of fundamental importance that NSC prerogatives in strategic planning and policy development be recognized in principle, in practice the NSC role can and should vary considerably depending on personalities, events, and the extent of controversy—bureaucratic, political, or substantive—surrounding a particular policy area. The point is a critical one, since most discussions of the NSC role simply assume that the relationship of the NSC to the agencies (or to the foreign policy agencies) must be essentially uniform across all areas of policy. Yet there is no reason at all why this should be the case.

In fact, of course, some differentiation in the NSC role is tacitly admitted by most analysts, since the NSC is generally seen as having a much more central role in foreign policy than in other areas of national security. The very common view that the NSC shares essentially the same policy arena as the State Department is, however, an erroneous one, although it contains an element of truth. As discussed earlier, State resembles the NSC and differs from other agencies by the fact that it is concerned with the coordinated exploitation of the various instrumentalities of national power. It is not surprising, then, that the NSC has historically been much more involved in the foreign policy arena than, for example, in defense policy. At the same time, however, it has to be recognized that the relative lack of NSC involvement in defense matters also reflects fundamental differences in the organization of the foreign policy and defense bureaucracies. The State Department has no equivalent to the Office of the Secretary of Defense, with its far-reaching responsibilities for the development of defense policy and oversight of its implementation by the military services. In many respects, OSD has served as a counterpart or extension of the NSC in the defense area; that the two organizations have frequently been bureaucratic allies is not accidental.

The fact of the matter is, however, that OSD has not been able to substitute satisfactorily for the NSC in the defense area. This is partly due to its inability to exercise clear authority over the uniformed military, and partly to its difficulties in representing effectively the defense point of view in interagency political-military policy deliberations. The chronic weakness of interagency political-military planning and operations discussed earlier is a strong argument for a vigorous NSC role in this general area, and points up one of the basic flaws in the common view of the scope and functions of the NSC. A similar argument holds relative to other critical faultlines in national security policy such as public diplomacy, strategic economics and technology, space policy, emergency planning, and counterintelligence.

In the light of recent experience, there are a number of political-military policy areas that stand out as candidates for a particularly vigorous NSC role. Foremost among these is arms control. While something can perhaps be accomplished in this area by restricting or reassigning agency responsibilities (as will be discussed at a later point), the salience of arms control issues in political and bureaucratic struggles in Washington as well as in relations with Western Europe and the Soviet Union have made this an area of prime strategic concern, and one requiring meticulous and rapid coordination among interested elements of the executive branch as well as between the executive branch and Congress. Only an NSC visibly in control of the arms control policy process as a whole (including the chairing of all key interagency committees) can hope to accomplish this very difficult feat. The other major area that needs to be mentioned in this connection is low intensity conflict. Experience has also shown (and the Congress itself has recognized) the vital importance of strong White House leadership in the setting of policy and in planning relative to insurgency and counterinsurgency operations and counter-terrorism.

However, as remarked above, it is not sufficient to define the NSC role with reference to those areas which currently suffer from divided bureaucratic responsibilities. To argue that the NSC should be the principal locus within the government for strategic planning is to argue that it should become more involved than is currently the case in operational planning and decision making now carried on largely or exclusively within the departments of State and Defense. In the case of the State Department, the change would not be a drastic one, except insofar as it involved a much greater degree of formal planning (operational or otherwise) than now occurs within that department. In the case of the Pentagon, however, it would involve an NSC role in the area of wartime and contingency planning, which has traditionally been the private preserve of the uniformed military. As suggested earlier, an excellent case can be made that the time has come to move away from this tradition; but doing so would almost certainly involve a major struggle, and could give unwanted political visibility to sensitive issues of civil-military relations. It may be added that a stronger NSC role in national security resource planning would undoubtedly raise difficult questions about the relative responsibilities of the NSC, OSD, and JCS (not to speak of the Office of Management and Budget) in shaping the defense budget.

Does a strong strategic planning role for NSC necessarily mean that the National Security Adviser will act as an independent policy adviser to the President? That the President will always have incentives to turn to the Adviser for substantive advice was noted earlier. The real question is rather to what extent the strategic planning function of the NSC will be supported by strategically competent and bureaucratically cooperative agencies. Presidential recognition of the National Security Adviser as his chief strategic planner is an important precondition, but much will also depend on the commitment of the cabinet secretaries and on the quality of the working-level personnel assigned to this task, as well as on unpredictable factors such as personality and the pressures of the political environment. Yet even assuming a smooth collaboration between the National Security Adviser and the agency heads, it is to be anticipated and accepted that the Adviser will on occasion offer independent advice, for there can be no guarantee that agency heads will in all cases subordinate their own interests and perspectives to the strategic perspective represented by the Adviser. The Adviser should be considered to have the right to provide advice *in his capacity as strategic planner,* and this advice should be seen by the President as having equal standing with the advice provided by his cabinet. This is not to say that the Adviser's advice should for that reason always prevail. The President is perfectly entitled to put greater weight on tactical, political, or personal factors than on the strategic factors laid out for him by the National Security Adviser. The point is that only the Adviser can be relied on to keep the strategic perspective within presidential view.

ELEMENTS OF STRATEGIC PLANNING

Strategic planning properly understood cuts across the missions of all the agencies involved in national security. But strategic planning itself is a multifaceted activity, and involves distinct types of functions and personnel. Six types or elements of strategic planning may be identified for purposes of this analysis: (1) strategic intelligence; (2) net assessment; (3) long-term planning; (4) short-term planning; (5) resource allocation; and (6) crisis planning.

Strategic Intelligence

To assert that strategic intelligence is an integral aspect of strategic planning is to argue that intelligence should not be seen merely as a given to be presupposed by the President, but rather as something to be actively selected and structured to serve his unique needs.[3] The disinclination of the CIA in particular to collect and process intelligence in a way that is responsive to the requirements of the presidential office and of the policy agencies generally points to the need for an independent capability for strategic intelligence evaluation in the NSC. This capability need not and should not duplicate functions that are performed by the intelligence community. Rather, it should in the first place perform a liaison function with the intelligence community by formulating strategic intelligence requirements and reviewing intelligence community operational planning based on those requirements. Secondly, it should have an important role in reviewing intelligence community strategic analyses and estimates at various stages in their production, and should be responsible for the dissemination of this information within the White House. NSC intelligence personnel should (in collaboration where appropriate with the members and staff of the President's Foreign Intelligence Advisory Board [PFIAB]) provide the President with independent analyses concerning such matters as the nature and extent of disagreement on particular issues within the intelligence community, the possible role of institutional bias, implicit policy assumptions, and the susceptibility of the analysis to external challenge.

Of particular importance in this connection is the question of an NSC role in intracommunity analytic disputes. As matters currently stand, the importance of competitive intelligence analysis is recognized in principle, yet in practice the CIA regards itself as the arbiter of intracommunity disagreements and resists efforts by the White House or the policy agencies generally to probe their sources. To assign the NSC an independent role in the assessment and adjudication of such disagreements is, given the current organization of the community, to create a valuable check on the institutionally preponderant CIA. It may be added that there are significant advantages in assigning this and other oversight functions to an organic element of the bureaucracy rather than to the PFIAB. An oversight board consisting of distinguished private citizens can be very useful by bringing high-level attention to bear on a limited number of major issues, but may not be as effective where more sustained and systematic analysis and follow-through is needed across a spectrum of issues.

Net Assessment

Closely related to strategic intelligence is "net assessment"—analysis of U.S. military forces or other capabilities in relationship to the threat posed by adversaries. As indicated earlier, net assessment has always been a bureaucratically problematic function, given traditional CIA-military rivalries as well as sensitivities within the military itself. Net assessment at the strategic level is currently the responsibility of an Office of Net Assessment within OSD. In the past, however, a

*

net assessment function has sometimes been housed in the NSC, and the case is strong for a return to some such arrangement. An NSC umbrella would make it easier to extract strategic-level intelligence at all classification levels from the intelligence community, lend greater credibility to evaluations of U.S. military capabilities by removing them from the Pentagon's jurisdiction, make them more responsive to national requirements, and greatly facilitate their use by national-level planners and decision makers.[4]

Net assessment is usually thought of in narrowly military terms. Yet strategic net assessments worthy of the name must take account of nonmilitary factors, and it can be argued that such factors are most likely to receive adequate emphasis when the net assessment function is located in the White House. National-level net assessment could prove particularly useful in bureaucratically contentious areas such as arms control. Net assessments of the impact of prospective arms control agreements on U.S. and Soviet security have been notable for their absence within the U.S. government, for reasons that are not difficult to understand. It can be argued that the only hope for comprehensive and honest assessments of the verifiability of agreements, their long-term impact on force planning, and similar questions lies in the establishment of a net assessment element at the NSC.

None of this is meant to suggest that the NSC can or should go it alone in this area, merely that it should have recognized authority to provide overall guidance and coordination for major net assessment efforts throughout the national security bureaucracy. The inevitable objection to a leading NSC role in both net assessment and strategic intelligence is that, far from guaranteeing impartiality, NSC involvement will threaten the integrity of otherwise professional analysis out of a concern to protect the personal and political standing of the President. There are surely legitimate grounds for such concern. Yet the corruption of analysis by policy can equally occur within the bureaucracy itself, and it can be argued that a stronger NSC role would considerably increase the probability of the President accepting and acting on unwelcome analysis. By providing increased control of the process and thus confidentiality, it would increase the credibility of the analysis while at the same time shielding the President from bureaucratic pressures that might otherwise be generated by it. There are also procedural measures that could be taken within the NSC staff to minimize the potential for a direct contamination of policy and analysis.

Long-term Planning

That long-term, national-level planning by the U.S. government is useless or impossible (or both) is virtually an axiom for those experienced in the workings of the American political system.[5] One does not have to be wholly optimistic about the likely impact of such planning to wonder whether it should be dismissed as unthinkingly as is usually done. Certainly, the frequency of presidential elections, the independent role of the Congress in national security policy, and the permeability of the federal bureaucracy pose special problems for long-term planning in the United States, by contrast not only with Communist systems but also with parliamentary democracies such as those of Western Europe. There may well be particular areas—for example, procurement of major strategic weapon systems—where such planning is bound to be defeated by the raw facts of domestic politics. Still, it is not at all evident that certain kinds of planning could not be sufficiently insulated from the political process to serve a useful purpose. Even in cases where drastic changes in agreed-upon plans subsequently prove necessary, the planning process itself may be of considerable value as a way of encouraging disciplined strategic thinking about long-term goals.

That long-term, national-level planning is not simply impossible is demonstrated by the example of contemporary Communist states. The Soviet Union and its allies plan comprehensively not only in the economic sector but across the entire spectrum of foreign and national security affairs, and they do so not merely in five year cycles, but in cycles of fifteen to twenty years as well. It is a misunderstanding of the Soviet approach to see it as intended to impose a system of rigid constraints on strategic and operational planning. Rather, Soviet planning has considerable room for operational flexibility as well as for alteration or amendment to take account of new strategic realities. The purpose is to provide a basic direction and broad guidelines for government action.[6]

That much state planning in domestic economic matters (even by states with nonmarket economies) is futile when not actively counterproductive may be readily granted. It is less clear that this must be the case in foreign and national security affairs (at least for great powers that retain a significant degree of initiative in the international arena), where government is able to exercise more effective control. In the United States, defense planning at the strategic level is largely preoccupied with resource allocation issues, thanks in no small measure to the inefficiencies and micromanagement of Congress in this area. There is no reason in principle, however, why military planning could not be conducted within more of a strategic framework, and broadened or supplemented by some consideration of national strategy as a whole. Indeed, Congress itself has recently recognized the need for better planning of this sort by requiring the President to submit an annual report on national strategy at the beginning of the budget cycle.[7]

Obviously, any national-level strategic planning effort by the United States would have to take due account of the congressional role and the cycles of the American political process. To discuss in detail the structure of such a planning effort would take us too far afield. The key requirement is executive-congressional agreement on a procedure that will uphold executive primacy in the planning process while improving communication between the two branches and integrating national-level planning with the congressional budget cycle. The recent history of executive-congressional deliberation over modernization of the U.S. intercontinental ballistic missile (ICBM) program offers a cautionary case in point. The creation of a special presidential advisory group (the so-called Scowcroft Commission) to wrestle with this contentious issue effectively demonstrated the need for more coherent and integrated planning within the executive branch in the area of strategic forces and arms control; but the solution arguably represented more nearly an abdication than a sharing of executive branch responsibility for policy development in this critical area.

Short-term Planning

That strategic planning is synonymous with long-term planning is a common misconception. Actually, important strategic decisions are not infrequently forced by events over a very brief period of time. Crisis events are often of this nature; but not all crises involve matters of strategic moment (terrorist incidents, for example), while a variety of noncrisis events may well do so. A good example of the latter is congressional budget action, which often requires rapid reassessment of fundamental aspects of the nation's military strategy. Another example is Soviet arms control proposals. Here, the intense political pressure to develop immediate responses to major Soviet initiatives can stampede the process of decision on important strategic issues. The cumbersome nature of executive branch decision processes, particularly on questions of defense resources and arms control policy (but also on many other matters), constitutes a strong argument for giving the NSC a particular and recognized responsibility in this area. To some extent this is already the case. Yet the NSC could undoubtedly act with greater effectiveness to catalyze and manage the short-term planning process. In matters involving the Congress, there is an inevitable tension between the NSC perspective and the tactical and political orientation of White House congressional liaison personnel. Unfortunately, in recent years the NSC has too often taken a distant second place in this contest. As far as public diplomacy is concerned, there is little need to belabor the difficulties the U.S. government continues to have in putting together coordinated and effective short-term responses to events with major policy implications, such as Soviet arms control proposals or unanticipated incidents like the Daniloff case.

Resource Allocation

The importance of resource questions for policy planning in all areas of government is generally recognized. In the national security area, the defense budget is of course a topic of perennial political controversy which tends to overshadow other national security resource issues. There are, however, substantial funding requirements for other instruments of national security policy—most notably, intelligence, but also foreign economic and security assistance and public diplomacy.

Few would dispute that the allocation of resources in the national security area is guided only very imperfectly if at all by a coherent national strategy. To the extent that the White House exercises discipline over the budgets of the national security agencies, it does so principally through the Office of Management and Budget (OMB) rather than through the National Security Adviser and his staff. In recent years, it has been increasingly recognized that the OMB performs functions that are inescapably political or policy-relevant, and the agency has been staffed by growing numbers of political appointees at senior levels. At the same time, the mechanisms for ensuring that OMB decision making is informed by substantive policy considerations remain underdeveloped. The problem is particularly acute in the national security area, owing to the inevitable tendency of OMB management to focus on domestic economic questions and reflect a congressional perspective. Under the Reagan administration, ultimate responsibility for adjudicating budget questions was originally given to a Budget Review Board, consisting of the Director of OMB and the White House Counsellor and Chief of Staff; subsequently, this was dropped in favor of a less formal arrangement. In any event, White House senior staff have dealt directly with agency heads, thus circumventing the NSC entirely. At earlier stages of the budget process, the NSC may have opportunities for formal or informal comment on agency resource planning. But there is no mechanism for formal review of agency budget submissions from the perspective of overall administration national security policy and strategy.

The result of all this is a persisting disjunction between resource allocation for national security and actual national security policy. There is no satisfactory arrangement for injecting fundamental policy considerations in decision making concerning the general magnitude of spending for national security, tradeoffs between national security and domestic funding priorities, or tradeoffs between various national security agencies and programs. This works strongly against national security agencies and programs that lack significant political support in the Congress. Congress has been and remains notoriously reluctant to provide even minimally adequate funding for agencies such as the State Department or vitally important programs such as security assistance.

It has to be recognized that national security resource planning will always remain hostage in some measure to the actions of a sceptical and unpredictable Congress. At the same time, a more disciplined executive branch approach could increase pressure on Congress to address national security issues in a more integrated and strategic perspective, and it could help correct some of the more extreme institutional biases that Congress brings to the consideration of these issues. Essentially, what is needed at the national level is something analogous to what the Packard Commission has recommended for the Defense Department, a closer integration of budgetary and policy responsibilities. In addition, however, a significant readjustment is needed in responsibilities within the White House itself, with a much strengthened role for the NSC relative to the OMB and the President's domestic advisers. Institutionalizing a significant role for the NSC in this area is essential in order to compensate for the informal political pressures that inevitably work against a strategic approach to resource questions within the White House itself.

Crisis Planning

As pointed out earlier, crisis management is generally thought of as an essentially operational activity, and presidential involvement in crises as an exceptional excursion of the White House into the operational realm. Yet crises can have the potential for forcing fundamental strategic decisions (the Cuban missile crisis, for example, set the subsequent course of U.S. policy toward Castro's Cuba). Further, crisis management can involve not merely crisis operations but more or less elaborate crisis pre-planning.

Under the Reagan administration, a crisis planning function was firmly established for the first time within the NSC. In 1983, a Crisis Management Center (CMC) became operational in the Old Executive Office Building, reporting to the National Security Adviser though with a staff separate from that of the NSC. The CMC is equipped with powerful computing capability and sophisticated audiovisual technology for the integration and display of data from a variety of sources, and has developed procedures for the management of crisis-related information and decision making. According to an authoritative description, the CMC not only serves as the focal point for actual crisis management operations, but "conducts pre-crisis collection and analysis of information about likely crisis areas in an effort to anticipate events and to provide extensive background information to decision makers as a crisis preventive," and generally serves as "an institutional memory for the policy makers so that past decisions and events can be more comprehensively integrated into consideration of a current crisis."[8] The crisis planning role of the CMC is supplemented by the interagency Crisis Pre-Planning Group (CPPG), chaired by the Deputy National Security Adviser, which provides policy and planning guidance from the earliest stages of an incipient crisis.

These arrangements represent a dramatic improvement in the national-level approach to crisis management. To what degree the systems and procedures currently in place have actually succeeded in revolutionizing crisis operations in the White House remains to be seen. Also not clear at this time is the exact relationship between the Crisis Management Center and the NSC staff, and the responsibilities of the two staffs in the crisis management area. If the NSC is to restrict itself as much as possible to a strategic as distinct from an operational role, it would make sense to assign operational crisis management responsibilities primarily to the CMC, while mandating close coordination between the NSC and the CMC in crisis planning matters. However, it may be desirable to restrict the CMC staff (as in fact appears to have occurred) to a primarily technical support role rather than interposing an additional staff layer in White House dealings with the bureaucracy.[9]

POLICY DEVELOPMENT AND IMPLEMENTATION

To identify strategic planning as the primary NSC role implies certain consequences for NSC involvement in policy development generally; but it would not appear to require a single approach to policy development, and a strong argument can be made on behalf of utilizing varying approaches for different policy areas. Emphasizing the strategic planning role does seem to require, on the other hand, a deemphasis on NSC involvement in policy implementation. At the same time, however, some involvement in policy implementation remains essential as a check on the tendency toward operational autonomy that is endemic even in well-disciplined bureaucracies.[10]

As discussed earlier, policy development may be conveniently analyzed in terms of the subfunctions of strategic planning, the catalyzing of decision, and the management of decision. The burden of the argument thus far has been that the NSC should exercise both formal and substantive control of strategic planning, though with appropriate involvement by agency representatives. The planning and decision making that should (ideally) flow from approved national strategies should be substantively the responsibility of the involved agencies. Yet there remains a need for some degree of formal NSC control of the overall process of planning and decision making at this secondary level, which may be characterized (in a loose analogy with military affairs) as the "operational" as distinct from the strategic and tactical levels of bureaucratic activity. (The operational level of bureaucratic activity in this sense belongs to the sphere of policy development; policy implementation strictly speaking occurs at the tactical level.)

There are two reasons for an NSC role here: to ensure that agency operations do indeed reflect national strategies, and to effect coordination between different agencies with complementary or overlapping policy responsibilities. In order to avoid the potential danger of paper planning, it is essential that careful attention be given by the NSC and the National Security Adviser to procedures for the translation of basic national strategy into operational plans and concepts. At the same time, a strong NSC role is critical in order to adjudicate among the differing interests and perspectives of the various national security agencies, and to ensure that the requirements of interagency consensus are not permitted to become an excuse for obstruction and stalemate in the decision-making process.

This suggests that the criteria for NSC involvement in policy development are somewhat different and more stringent than what is often understood by the term "coordination." If the primary mission of the NSC is to oversee the development of operationally effective national strategies, NSC responsibilities cannot be limited simply to the refereeing of interagency differences, but should extend to oversight of the activities of an individual agency in policy areas where other agencies do not play a significant role. While care should be taken to reserve the primary operational policy role to the agencies, the NSC should be accorded sufficient formal control of the process to allow it to influence to some degree the substance of policy decision. In particular, the NSC should have wide authority to catalyze operational planning and decision through the assigning of studies and the establishment of priorities, reinforced where necessary or desirable by the prerogative of chairing interagency committees. It should also have clearly defined authority to manage the overall decision process down to the operational level. This authority should be understood to include key questions relating to the interagency committee system as a whole and the venue, participants, classification, timing, and structure of particular meetings, as well as formats of decision documents and procedures for handling them. It should also include, if only on an exceptional basis, the right to exercise quality control of interagency documents, incorporating where necessary neglected options or missing rationales or caveats.

If or to the extent that the NSC is able to shape operational planning and decision making, there would seem to be less need for NSC involvement in the actual implementation of operational plans and decisions than might be the case under current arrangements. However, an argument can be made that the NSC should at least have recognized authority to monitor agency operations on a regular basis, and should be required to do so in especially important or politically sensitive matters or in matters directly involving the President. Outside observers tend to underestimate the extent to which bureaucracies are prepared to ignore, willfully misinterpret, and even sabotage nationally approved policies with which they happen to disagree.

Such behavior—which can involve practices as subtle as altering nuances of phrasing in cables or as gross as advising foreign governments on ways to circumvent or reverse established U.S. policies—is not always easy to detect or prove, short of a detailed investigation requiring intimate familiarity with the recent history of policy in a particular area. Full and systematic monitoring of agency operations by the NSC or anyone else is therefore an impossibly demanding assignment. Yet there would be considerable deterrent value even in a very sporadic monitoring effort. As matters stand, the NSC is not formally empowered to uncover agency abuses, and staff members who have managed to do so have probably been at greater risk than the offending agencies themselves. Only very exceptionally has the NSC Adviser acted in recent years to impose discipline on an agency in the name of the President. The visible failure of the NSC and the White House generally to assert such control over the bureaucracy has seriously vitiated the NSC's authority in every other area of its activity.

In addition, it would be very useful to have some formal mechanism, preferably one activated and directed by the NSC, for assessing the results of operations and their implications for policy ("lessons learned"). This is of particular importance in cases of major failures or disasters—the Iran raid, the bombing of U.S. marines in Beirut, and the like. Bureaucracies are notoriously resistant to exercises in self-criticism; yet it should not be necessary to establish special commissions of inquiry to deal with every apparent inadequacy in the system (as was done in the two cases just cited). The NSC can perform a critical service in this respect as a relatively detached and impartial yet authoritative investigative body. Of course, the NSC itself can be expected to have a vested interest in the success of policies in the planning of which it was a central participant. Nevertheless, there are a number of steps the Adviser could take to minimize potential NSC partiality, such as barring any role for individuals previously involved in the area or employing outside consultants.

OPERATIONS

It has been the fashion for some time to deplore the tendency of recent NSC Advisers to assume operational roles at the expense of cabinet officials with legal responsibilities for the carrying out of national security policy. Criticism of the NSC on this score became intense following exposure of the NSC role in transferring arms to the Khomeini regime in Iran and in support for the Contras. As noted earlier, however, the President may have excellent reasons for turning to his NSC Adviser not only for day-to-day policy advice but for the performance of certain operational tasks. It is easy to say (as Henry Kissinger among others has said[11]) that a President who lacks confidence in a cabinet official should replace that official rather than undercutting his authority through reliance on the Adviser. Yet, to repeat the point made earlier, the firing of a cabinet official is a dramatic step that is likely to prove politically difficult and cannot be often repeated. Nor is it self-evident that a judicious (and inconspicuous) use of the Adviser for such purposes must necessarily result in a diminution of the authority of cabinet officials.

Having said all this, however, it should be added at once that an extensive involvement by the NSC Adviser in operational matters is without doubt undesirable. If the substantive policy responsibilities of the Adviser are limited to strategic planning, the NSC is better positioned to exercise formal authority over the policy process as a whole. By competing with the agencies on their own operational ground, the Adviser only opens to challenge by the agencies his dominance of strategic planning and the policy process. In addition, of course, any attempt by the Adviser to master a significant range of operational issues is apt to overload his span of attention and reduce his effectiveness elsewhere. Further, it can be argued that there are real dangers in NSC involvement in matters such as sensitive negotiations and consultations with foreign leaders. Impatience with diplomatic niceties and a desire for results proportionate to the investment of NSC time and energy can act to undermine the U.S. bargaining position and stampede decision making. The cutting of red tape involved in an NSC operational intervention almost inevitably severs some essential connections with other aspects of overall U.S. policy. And providing an alternate point of contact for foreign ambassadors and leaders creates rich opportunities for them to play off the State Department and the White House against one another.

This problem is even more acute when it comes to relations with the media. To quarantine the NSC completely from the media is difficult and almost certainly undesirable, but an active media presence and role for the Adviser can easily become counterproductive, apart from being an unjustifiable drain on his time. A useful rule of thumb might be that the Adviser and his staff should act as public spokesmen for the administration only in those areas that do not clearly fall within the purview of a single agency or where the NSC has primary responsibility (strategic planning, crisis management, the policy process) or a leading bureaucratic role. Limiting even private contact between the NSC and the media on controversial issues of foreign and defense policy would make sense as a way of discouraging media exploitation of NSC-State differences and minimizing incentives for competitive leaking. Nevertheless, it is unrealistic to expect the NSC Adviser to disarm unilaterally in the face of predictable State Department efforts to interpret policy in its own way and constrain presidential decision. The problem of leaking is a larger one, and susceptible to significant improvement only by fundamental changes in bureaucratic procedures and the political culture of Washington.

At the same time, it has to be recognized that there are a number of operational activities—broadly understood—that are necessary or proper for the NSC because they reflect specific presidential requirements. Remarkably, almost no attention has been paid to many of these activities in recent political commentary or in the literature on the NSC. They may be conveniently characterized in the following terms: (1) routine staff support and information, (2) personnel management, (3) speechwriting, (4) personal representation and negotiation, (5) staff support for diplomatic requirements, (6) staff support for military requirements, and (7) crisis management.

Routine Staff Support and Information

As discussed earlier, routine staff support and the collection and processing of information to fulfill specifically presidential needs are unheralded but vital functions performed by the NSC as well as the White House staff generally. Routine staff support includes the preparation of routine presidential (and vice presidential) speeches and messages, the handling of state visits, the handling of presidential (and vice presidential) trips abroad, and the like. Some of these functions are shared by the NSC and various White House as well as State Department personnel, and the extent of NSC involvement in them has varied over time. While some NSC role in such matters is probably unavoidable, NSC staff generally can and should be spared for other duties.

The most important staff support function performed by the NSC is the information function. This includes many routine activities, but also such complex and highly sensitive functions as the management of the flow of intelligence to the President and the dissemination of sensitive presidential decisions. Recently, as discussed above, the NSC has acquired sophisticated data processing capabilities in connection with the establishment of the Crisis Management Center; these capabilities have greatly increased the scope for centralized information management relating to a range of national security requirements.[12]

Generally speaking, the National Security Adviser has a twofold responsibility in the information area, corresponding to his dual role as personal adviser to the President and institutional manager of the NSC system. On the one hand, he must serve the information needs of the President by ensuring that the President receives, in an appropriate form and level of detail, vital national security information generated within the government, as well as information, opinion, and advice from independent sources. On the other hand, he must serve the needs of the administration as a whole for authoritative record keeping and information management concerning national-level policy and presidential actions. Improved management of such information can make a large contribution to the effectiveness of NSC oversight of policy implementation throughout the bureaucracy.

Personnel Management

In Washington, personnel questions take on an importance that has few parallels elsewhere, given the political complications that inevitably attend hirings and firings at high levels of government as well as the magnitude of the stakes involved. As noted earlier, the President labors under unique pressures and constraints in this regard. The National Security Adviser, because of the extent of his access to highly restricted policy deliberations and day-to-day diplomatic and intelligence reporting, is almost inevitably drawn into controversies over the performance of individual high-ranking officials. His proximity to the President makes him the logical person to referee serious personnel disputes or to bring such disputes to the attention of the President himself, in cases where the overall interests of the President and his administration may be affected. Particularly where the President has troubled relations with members of his cabinet, the Adviser may be called upon to monitor the performance of cabinet and subcabinet officials on a regular basis, and at the extreme, to advise the President concerning possible actions to be taken against an offending agency head or his subordinates. A serious effort to monitor the implementation of presidential policy, as discussed above, will inevitably involve the Adviser more actively in personnel questions.

Speechwriting

Given the cumbersomeness of bureaucratic processes and the factors limiting the President's room for policy maneuver, presidential speeches offer an important vehicle for the launching of presidential initiatives and the articulation of an administration's strategic vision. The link between strategic planning and speechwriting is a natural one. State's Policy Planning Staff has generally had responsibility for preparing major speeches for senior officials of the department, and has often had a large hand in presidential speechwriting as well. In recent years, the tendency has been to move presidential speechwriting more into the White House, with the NSC dividing the labor with the speechwriting staff of the White House Director of Communications. However, the continuing bureaucratic weakness of the NSC in relation to State makes NSC control of the substance of presidential national security speeches uncertain at best. Obviously, the locus of speechwriting activity in any administration is apt to depend heavily on the distribution of speechwriting talent as well as the extent of the President's personal interest in the substance and style of his speeches; and the NSC must accommodate to a greater or lesser degree the political and tactical concerns of other White House offices. Still, the argument for a preeminent NSC role in the composition of major presidential speeches on national security issues seems a compelling one.

By the same token, it may be added, the NSC should have clear authority to review and approve major policy speeches by cabinet officials or their immediate subordinates. Cabinet officials tend to guard jealously their prerogatives in this area, and presidents are generally reluctant to discipline their cabinets (especially the secretaries of State and Defense) for dubious or inappropriate policy pronouncements. The fact of the matter is, however, that speeches by senior administration officials are an integral tool of overall administration strategy. A President who is interested in exercising genuine control of his government cannot afford to permit cabinet officials autonomy either in the substance or in the form and timing of major speeches.

Personal Representation and Negotiation

The National Security Adviser is an ambiguous figure, poised between the roles of bureaucratic functionary and personal adviser and assistant. Whether or to what extent it may be appropriate for the Adviser to act as a personal agent for the President in contacts or negotiations with the Congress or with foreign governments is, therefore, not an easy question, apart from the operational complications it is likely to create. That it is not desirable for the Adviser to serve routinely as an alternate point of contact for foreign government officials was argued earlier. However, this should not be understood to rule out the President's use of the Adviser as his personal emissary on an extraordinary basis. Such a role might be appropriate, for example, in negotiations with allied or neutral governments involving highly sensitive military or intelligence matters where the credibility of the American interlocutor was a key consideration. It can certainly be justified in the case of secret diplomatic ventures such as Henry Kissinger's opening to Communist China. It should be emphasized, however, that a key aspect of the rationale for such operations is the personal prestige of the Adviser himself. It is not clear that it makes particular sense to rely on NSC staff members to substitute for the Adviser rather than, for example, special presidential envoys (to take a recent example, Gen. Vernon Walters, whose unusual linguistic and diplomatic talents have been put to use by a number of presidents in this way).

The Adviser's unique credibility as a spokesman for the President, as well as his extraordinary span of knowledge and authority also point to the potential for a similar role with respect to the Congress— one that has been realized to a growing extent in recent years.[13] This issue will be considered below in connection with the question of the Adviser's relationship to Congress generally.

Staff Support for Diplomatic Requirements

The President is the nation's chief diplomat. As head of the government of the United States, he has ultimate responsibility for managing the nation's foreign policy and for handling relations with heads of government elsewhere in the world. The Secretary of State is, of course, the President's executive agent for most foreign policy operations. Yet there is one class of operations which the President cannot safely or conveniently delegate to the State Department: those involving his personal relations with foreign leaders. Most presidents place considerable value on the cultivation of personal bonds with key foreign leaders, especially the heads of government of major allied nations (and not infrequently the leaders of key neutrals and adversaries). There is no denying the palpable hazards in such relationships. Presidential vanity, the dangers of cultural misperception, and the confusion that frequently results from verbal understandings are factors that argue for minimizing personal contact at the highest levels. At the same time, it has to be recognized not only that presidents have a human side, and hence are unlikely to be easily dissuaded from such contact, but also that the human side of their counterparts may offer possibilities for dramatically advancing the nation's foreign policy interests.

If it is admitted that management of the President's relations with foreign leaders is a function of potentially critical strategic importance, it must also be granted that this function is almost certainly one that should be operationally controlled if not totally managed by the White House. Intelligence relating to the personal and political health and behavior of foreign leaders can be, for obvious reasons, extremely sensitive; records of personal communications between the President and foreign leaders and of meetings with them are often equally sensitive. There is every reason to give the National Security Adviser operational responsibilities for the handling of such information and its utilization in strategic planning and in the actual conduct of presidential diplomacy.

U.S.–Soviet summit diplomacy is the most critical and hazardous form that such presidential contact can take. While difficult to separate from the general state of U.S.–Soviet relations, summit diplomacy has a large personal component which is of undeniable importance in shaping Soviet perceptions of national purpose and will. There is little evidence that recent presidents have attempted to devise careful strategies for the management of their personal relations with Soviet leaders, and much evidence that summit preparations tend to be dominated by a State Department that is preoccupied with seeking improvements in diplomatic relations with the USSR. Another important channel of contact between the U.S. and Soviet leadership that should be mentioned in this connection is the Direct Communications Link ("Hotline"), a teletype circuit which is available for use in crisis situations. It seems doubtful whether the White House or any other agency has developed adequate policy and doctrines governing the use of this sensitive and potentially hazardous communications tool.[14] A greater NSC role in both these areas would almost certainly be beneficial.

Staff Support for Military Requirements

The responsibilities of the President as commander-in-chief of the armed forces are among the most important of his office. Yet there has been remarkably little systematic analysis—or indeed, public discussion of any kind—of the implications of this presidential role for the functioning of the NSC and the White House generally.

Given the character of contemporary warfare, the President himself is a vital operational link in the military chain of command. Without the personal authorization of the President, the military cannot (at least in theory) use nuclear weapons to respond to a Soviet assault on the United States or its allies. Yet the rapidity and shock of a ballistic missile attack would greatly complicate rational decision making. The question of presidential decisions and actions under conditions of nuclear attack may be thought an excessively theoretical issue. In fact, however, the ability of the President (or, more correctly, the National Command Authority, consisting of the President, the Secretary of Defense, and their designated successors) to execute nuclear retaliatory options is an integral and critical element of the nation's deterrent posture.

Nor is this all. Equally important for deterrence—especially in view of Soviet doctrinal assumptions in these matters—is assurance of the continuity of government functions during a protracted nuclear or general war, including central civilian direction of the military effort. Continuity of government requires not only the physical survival of the President and/or his designated successors, but the survival of staff and support capabilities sufficient to allow him to exercise more than nominal command and control of military forces as well as essential diplomatic and domestic functions. A survivable central authority of this kind is indispensable not only for the effective prosecution of a general war but for making and communicating decisions concerning termination of hostilities.

It is not possible to do more than speculate about the operational arrangements currently governing what is obviously a highly sensitive area. However, there is evidence in the public domain that raises serious questions about the way these matters have been handled in the past, and suggests that existing operational arrangements (which have been for the most part the responsibility of the White House Military Office) may be less than perfectly integrated into the larger strategic and political context of the presidency as an institution.[15]

In general, it has to be recognized that there are inherent tensions in the relationship between the military and the commander-in-chief, in war as well as during peacetime, which make it inadvisable for the President to rely entirely on his line authority to maintain effective control of the armed forces and support his unique needs. In matters such as nuclear release procedures and technical support of presidential command, control, and communications (C^3) requirements, the military as an institution tends to be indifferent where not actively hostile to presidential desiderata.[16] More generally, military advice to the President is inevitably shaped by military operational preferences and cannot be counted on to reflect the strategic perspective of the President, even when it is responding to presidential guidance. This is not to argue that the President should be permitted or encouraged to disregard operational military realities. It is rather to suggest that failure to prepare the President adequately to face up to those realities may well result in ill-considered action or in civil-military confrontation under conditions of real crisis or war.

What all this suggests is that there is an important role for the NSC and the National Security Adviser in aiding the President in the exercise of his responsibilities as commander-in-chief. In peacetime, the Adviser should have the authority to review all briefing materials for the President's use in the event of a military emergency to ensure their compatibility with national policy and strategy and their conformity with the needs of the President. This emphatically includes the nuclear retaliatory options of the Single Integrated Operational Plan (SIOP). Furthermore, the NSC should have some responsibility for overseeing White House Military Office activities relating to procedures and equipment for presidential command and control, and it should play a major role in government-wide planning to ensure continuity of federal government operations under emergency conditions.

In periods of severe crisis and war, the NSC (together with key personnel on the White House domestic policy side) should be prepared to function as a wartime staff for the President, with enhanced responsibilities for strategic and operational planning and for coordination of the operations of all federal agencies. While encouraging close collaboration with military planners in the JCS, the President should maintain the organizational integrity of the NSC as a civilian agency reporting directly to himself. The NSC should be authorized and expected to give the President independent advice integrating military considerations in the larger perspective of national strategy. A particular NSC task should be to undertake longer-range planning focusing on war termination and postwar political conditions. A recognized NSC role in this area would help avoid a repetition of the U.S. experience during World War II, when immediate military requirements were allowed to dictate war termination policy and completely overshadowed efforts to plan for the postwar period.

Crisis Management

There is little disagreement on the need for heightened operational involvement of the President and his staff in crisis situations. The need for centralized management of information on a breaking crisis, the need for rapid White House response to building domestic and international pressures, and the need for rapid and carefully coordinated decision making under such circumstances all argue strongly for a special NSC responsibility for crisis management. Granting the NSC a special crisis management role means that it must be granted a degree of authority in crises that it normally lacks. Defining and circumscribing this authority in some *a priori* fashion is, however, extremely difficult.

What is a crisis? A true crisis is one involving an imminent threat to the lives or property of American citizens or the actual or prospective engagement of U.S. military forces. In such circumstances, the President has special responsibilities as commander-in-chief of the armed forces, and severe time pressures make it necessary or advisable to deviate from standard operating procedures. Whether or when the President is justified in violating the military chain of command in crises is a hard question. But there can be little question that, given modern communications technology, the President will have the capability and should therefore have the right to make quick decisions affecting operational military matters that have key strategic or political implications. The NSC should by the same token have commensurate authority concerning decision-making procedures for crisis management as well as the implementation of presidential orders.

Managing crises potentially involves a number of the other operational NSC functions discussed above. The collation, analysis, and formatting of information is a critical aspect of crisis operations, and one that the NSC is currently positioned to do much more effectively than in the past. Presidential communications (both public statements and diplomatic messages) can play a major role in crises. Finally, in a genuinely stressing crisis—one involving a direct U.S.–Soviet confrontation with some potential for escalation to general war—the NSC should be authorized and prepared to supervise a government-wide transition from peacetime to wartime modes of operation.

Chapter 5

The NSC as an Organization

A COMMON FAILING in both the theory and the practice of bureaucracy is to assign roles and missions to an organization that is not optimally staffed, structured, or positioned to execute them. Clarity about its roles and missions is essential if the NSC is to perform effectively. Hardly less important, however, is an adequate understanding of its organizational requirements. This is particularly so because the NSC is in many respects a unique organization within the federal government. Its very broad responsibilities, key position in the bureaucratic chain of command, and small size combine to magnify the importance of administrative details of all kinds. Moreover, the NSC is uniquely dependent for its proper functioning on a series of formal and informal relationships with individuals and organizations in the White House as well as throughout the bureaucracy.

Perhaps the most obvious and important consequence of the NSC's size and position is the enhanced role of particular individuals in its operations. This is true in the first instance of the President himself, whose personality and operating style inevitably affect the NSC in more or less direct ways. It is very obviously true of the National Security Adviser. But it is true to a significant degree as well of virtually the entire senior NSC staff. Individual intellectual abilities, career affiliations, personality, and (not least important) moral character can play a much more decisive role in the NSC's overall organizational performance than is generally possible in larger and more routinized government agencies. As a result, questions relating to staffing take on an importance at the NSC that they rarely have elsewhere.

Another critical factor is the NSC organizational chart. There has been considerable fluidity over the years in the internal organization of the NSC staff. This has reflected in part changing policy priorities, but in part also mere administrative convenience or internal bureaucratic maneuvering. There are good reasons for maintaining a degree of flexibility in any bureaucratic organization. However, the structure of the NSC staff is fraught with policy implications to a much greater degree than is the case in most organizations. The structure of the NSC staff reflects willy-nilly a certain view of the proper architecture of the federal government in the national security area, and sends important messages to the bureaucracy concerning White House priorities. There is little reason to think that past National Security Advisers have been especially sensitive to this aspect of their operation. Casual staff reorganizations have often done little to improve staff performance, while they have wiped out hard-won gains in continuity and institutional memory.

At least as important as formal organization are the internal staff procedures that govern the actual functioning of the NSC. This aspect has received considerable attention in the wake of the Iran-Contra scandal, but its generic significance is still not widely recognized. There are many pressures that work against a centrally controlled and coherent NSC staff operation. Security requirements are of course a powerful incentive for compartmentalization within the NSC staff. These requirements apply not merely to covert or other intelligence-related matters, but to a wide range of issues of political or diplomatic sensitivity that must regularly be handled by the NSC. In addition, however, there are strong incentives for individual staff members to maximize their own autonomy. In some cases, staff members develop de facto alliances with the agencies with which they regularly associate, and attempt to maintain exclusive control of issues of interest to those agencies. In other cases, staff members become absorbed in defending or extending their bureaucratic "turf" out of personal ambition or in order to promote a policy agenda of their own. Finally, the sheer volume and pace of business create many practical difficulties for intrastaff coordination and centralized management. Failure of the National Security Adviser and of NSC administrative officers to cope effectively with these problems is by no means unique to the Reagan administration.

Finally, the NSC is even less a self-contained organization than other agencies of the federal bureaucracy. It is a brain without a body. What is more, it is not the only brain inhabiting the federal organism. The NSC's proper functioning requires a proper relationship not only with the national security bureaucracy, but with other autonomous centers of decision making that potentially affect its operations. These centers are located in the White House itself and on Capitol Hill. The question of the relationship of the NSC and the National Security Adviser to the Congress has recently gained salience, as Congress has become sensitive to an NSC operational role beyond the reach of congressional oversight. Equally important, however, is the question of the relationship of the National Security Adviser and his staff to White House domestic policy and budget officials as well as to the White House Chief of Staff.

STAFFING

By far the most important staffing question with respect to the NSC has to do with the qualifications of the National Security Adviser himself. As indicated earlier, the status and role of the Adviser is an anomalous one in that his relationship to the NSC staff has only a customary rather than a formal basis. Properly speaking, the National Security Adviser is a personal assistant to the President, while the NSC staff works for the National Security Council. In practice, of course, much of the Adviser's power derives from his control of the NSC staff, with its unique access to information from and about the national security bureaucracy and its strategic placement athwart the lines of paper communication between the bureaucracy and the White House. By the same token, the Adviser is in an important sense personally hostage to the NSC staff, and must exercise effective control of it in order to protect his own position, if for no other reason.

The Adviser therefore cannot afford to neglect the administrative or managerial side of his job. Yet it is a fundamental error to conceive of the Adviser as a mere manager or bureaucratic technician whose chief concern is to ensure the smooth operation of the interagency NSC machinery. The Adviser cannot operate effectively even in a technical administrative sense unless he is, and is seen to be, a personal representative of the President. A prime requirement for any Adviser is a relationship to the President that permits him to act credibly in this role. Also vital, because it reflects the central and unique function of the NSC, is the requirement of strategic competence (which may be understood to encompass political ability). Bureaucratic and operational skills, though important and even indispensable in some measure, are a secondary consideration.

How close does the relationship of Adviser and President need to be if the former is to do his job effectively? Personal closeness, while no doubt desirable, is not necessary; prior friendship or association between the two men is likely to remain very much the exception (William Clark is so far the only case). Political or ideological sympathy is more important, and some degree of it is clearly necessary, especially in the case of a President (such as Ronald Reagan) who holds strong or unorthodox views on policy questions. There is an inescapable political dimension to the Adviser's job, and he must be fully prepared to represent the specific policy ideas of the President and his party to the national security bureaucracy and attempt to give them operational reality. At the same time, it has to be recognized that a penalty is paid in the appointment of an Adviser who is widely viewed as having markedly partisan political credentials.

The key consideration, however, is really the nature of the working relationship between the President and the Adviser. The President must develop sufficient personal confidence in the Adviser to give him the authority that is essential if his job is to be performed effectively. This means among other things that the President must view the Adviser as a peer whose advice carries a personal authority comparable to that of major cabinet figures, while at the same time not being unduly concerned that the Adviser's political standing or ambition will pose a challenge to his own authority. It should be added that much depends on the nature of a personal bond that, forged as it is in the heat of battle, will always have an element of the idiosyncratic and unpredictable.

The most fundamental intellectual qualification in a National Security Adviser is strategic expertise. What is at issue here, however, is not so much the Adviser's intellectual ability or accomplishments in a conventional sense as a particular habit of mind. The qualities required include a sense of history and the ability to look beyond the events of the day, the ability to assimilate and integrate large amounts of very diverse information, the mental discipline to identify fundamental objectives and pursue them tenaciously, and the mental flexibility to adjust to foreign ways of thinking and anticipate an adversary's moves. It is probably fair to say that such a combination of qualities is more apt to be found outside government than in it. Yet it has to be recognized that a strategic habit of mind is not common in any walk of American life. A pragmatic or problem-solving approach, orientation to the short term, and cultural insularity are pervasive American traits. It is not accidental that the most strate-

gically minded National Security Advisers—Kissinger and Brzezinski—have been foreign-born.

In practice, most Advisers in recent years have been either academics or military officers. Those with an academic background (with the exception of the economist Walt Rostow) have been specialists in international relations; few of them could claim any expertise in military, intelligence, economic, or technical matters. Of the military officers, two (Scowcroft and McFarlane) held higher degrees in international relations, though only one (Scowcroft) had extensive career experience in political-military affairs within the military. All four officers served as NSC Deputy before succeeding to the Adviser's job itself; two (Scowcroft and Poindexter) originally entered the White House as Military Assistant to the National Security Adviser, an essentially administrative post. William Clark was the first lawyer to serve as National Security Adviser. More significantly, Clark was the first Adviser appointed on the basis of his personal and political relationship with the President rather than any independent substantive expertise (though he had served briefly as Deputy Secretary of State before moving to the White House). At the other extreme is Frank Carlucci. Originally a career Foreign Service Officer, Carlucci had the distinction of being the first person appointed to the Adviser position who had had extensive experience at high levels of all of the major national security agencies, as well as in the domestic bureaucracy and in private industry. Carlucci's demonstrated expertise, however, was bureaucratic and operational rather than strategic, and he lacked an identifiable political orientation.

The NSC has been at its strongest and most independent under Advisers who had an academic base. In all cases, the appointment of military deputies to the Adviser position has reflected an intention to relegate the NSC to a subordinate role relative to the White House and the national security agencies. Two of the military Advisers (Poindexter and Powell) remained on active military duty during their tours in the White House—something that probably would have generated more criticism under an NSC regime that was perceived to have a more independent role. The military Advisers have generally been seen as politically neutral technicians whose chief function is coordination of differing agency positions, rather than as an independent source of strategic advice (although McFarlane, with his greater political background and coloration, should perhaps be placed in a different category). As just indicated, only one of the three military Advisers (Scowcroft) had a military background

of the sort that could be considered proper preparation for service as National Security Adviser.

Academics and military officers tend to bring different strengths and weaknesses to the Adviser position. Although the place accorded security issues in the discipline of international relations is greater today than it was twenty years ago, academic specialists in the discipline still tend to have a traditional foreign policy orientation. The acute State-NSC rivalry of the 1970s (and the relative neglect by the NSC of military issues) almost certainly reflected in important measure the academic backgrounds of Kissinger and Brzezinski. Moreover, the question must at least be raised whether university professors do not tend to be deficient in certain of the intellectual and moral virtues that are necessary to perform effectively in the Adviser's job—a job wholly different in its demands and of immeasurably higher stakes than the one to which they are accustomed. The temptation to pursue grand designs or to validate personal theories, and the desire to remain in good standing with former and future academic colleagues, are subtler but no less dangerous sources of corruption than more venal motives.

Unfortunately, there is little reason to expect that general officers in the U.S. armed forces will have acquired a solid grounding in higher strategic studies or in political-military affairs. Capable military officers who have reached one-star rank are much more likely to have a technical or managerial background and a predominantly single-service orientation. A pervasive weakness in American military officers of all backgrounds is a lack of feel for the political side of national security policy making. On the other hand, military officers tend to bring unique strengths. They are accustomed to a uniquely disciplined organizational structure and procedures, and in the frequently chaotic White House atmosphere generally act as the guardians of orderly process. They also possess a level of operational knowledge of military organizations and capabilities that can be highly useful for the performance of certain NSC functions, especially crisis management. Finally, military officers tend to possess personal qualities that are highly desirable in the NSC environment—coolness under stress, steadiness of purpose, common sense, and dedication to the national interest.

Consideration of the very disparate requirements for NSC leadership almost inevitably suggests the solution of a civilian Adviser and a military Deputy Adviser. Generally speaking, it seems wise to seek an Adviser who is not only not a military officer, but someone

without (at least) recent career service in any other part of the national security bureaucracy. At the same time, there remains a need for military expertise and presence in the NSC front office which is unlikely to be satisfied by a civilian candidate. In fact, the combination of civilian Adviser and military Deputy has been a recurrent pattern in the recent past, under Kissinger (Haig and Scowcroft), Allen (Admiral Nance), Clark (McFarlane), and Carlucci (General Powell). During the Carter years, although the deputy position was formally held by a political civilian (David Aaron), Brzezinski used the strategically minded Col. (now Lt. Gen.) William Odom as a de facto deputy for military affairs.

Several remarks are necessary with respect to the Deputy Adviser and to the role of military officers at NSC generally. Almost inevitably, the NSC Adviser and his Deputy arrive at a division of labor between them, rather than being equally involved in all matters. The Deputy Adviser tends to assume large responsibilities for the more technical, operational, or administrative issues which demand front office attention. This means that the Deputy will frequently be in the position of speaking for the Adviser or indeed the President himself on matters with which these officials cannot be expected to be intimately familiar. Accordingly, the status, rank, and authority of the Deputy are even more critical considerations than might otherwise be the case, particularly as regards his relationships with military organizations.

A good case can be made that insufficient sensitivity has been shown in such matters in the past. For an officer to function effectively in the Deputy slot relative to the uniformed military, three star rank is probably essential, and four star rank would be highly desirable. It is probably also desirable that such rank be earned legitimately within a military career context, rather than being bestowed in consequence of White House service (as was the case with Haig and Scowcroft). Most critical, however, is the question of the propriety of a military Deputy (or any other senior military officer in the NSC) remaining on active duty. Career loyalties and expectations are factors whose importance it is difficult to overestimate. Although many officers assigned NSC duty have served the Adviser and the President unaffected by such factors and in some cases in heroic disregard of them, it would be a healthier practice for at least a military Deputy to resign his commission. As will be argued in a moment, the same is probably true of any other officers of flag rank on the staff, as well as of comparable senior officials from the Foreign Service or the intelligence community.[1]

The ideal military Deputy would be a retired four star officer whose background combined operational command in a key joint assignment, joint or service planning experience, and political-military experience. In terms of substantive knowledge, the most valuable areas of expertise in a military Deputy would probably be nuclear weapons and strategy, high technology (especially relating to space), and low intensity warfare. Of these, low intensity warfare is arguably the prime candidate. As suggested earlier (and as will be further argued below), the recurrent problems the U.S. government has faced in developing and implementing coherent approaches to insurgency and counterinsurgency warfare and counterterrorism point to the need for special attention to these areas at the national level.

There has been considerable public discussion in recent years as to the proper makeup of the NSC staff as a whole. In the first Reagan administration, the NSC staff under both Allen and Clark was frequently attacked on the grounds that it was dominated by conservative "ideologues" who lacked professional expertise and were bureaucratically ineffective. More recently, with the breaking of the Iran-Contra scandal, concerns have been expressed about the growing presence and role of military officers on the staff. What kinds of individuals should the National Security Adviser recruit to work for him?

That the NSC of the 1980s was populated with "ideologues" to a much greater degree than, for example, the Kissinger or Brzezinski NSC is a canard, and reflects a serious misunderstanding of the facts of the matter as well as the working environment at the NSC during the Reagan years. In fact, with only a few exceptions, the most senior and influential NSC staffers in this period were career bureaucrats with no strong conservative political orientation. That the NSC of the Reagan presidency was ineffective, while undoubtedly true at least in some areas, was less a function of the quality of individual staffers than of the constraints under which the organization as a whole labored.

If it is true that the strategic planning function should be central to the NSC's role, and that this function is inseparable from a concern with the President's political agenda, it must be granted that the presence on the NSC staff of politically oriented individuals with suitable professional qualifications is not only not objectionable but much to be desired. Such persons are necessary to counterbalance the inevitable tendency of a purely bureaucratic NSC to reflect the institutional interests and culture of the various agencies from which the staffers come rather than the perspective of the President. At

the same time, for reasons already indicated, it is unnecessary and would be undesirable to staff the NSC entirely with politically oriented persons, on the model of a congressional staff. A strong case can be made for having NSC staffers with operational knowledge of the various national security agencies and sensitivity to their concerns.

This general point is one that would probably be granted by most informed observers. Where the conventional wisdom fails, however, is in not grasping the critical importance of according an appropriate status to the political appointees on the staff. A cardinal error of recent years has been the failure of the NSC leadership to create a cadre of senior political appointees with clearly defined authority both within the staff and relative to the bureaucracy. The NSC as a whole cannot operate effectively unless there are individuals in each of the major areas of its activity who are able to represent the NSC and the President credibly at the level of Under Secretary. These individuals should all be political, in the sense that they should at least not be current employees of any of the national security agencies on temporary assignment to the NSC (though they could certainly be career bureaucrats—including military officers—who have resigned or retired), and should at best have a demonstrable commitment to the President's political outlook and agenda. And they should enjoy a position on the NSC staff that gives them both authority over subordinates who are detailed from the bureaucracy and special access to the NSC front office.

The procedural dimension of all this is important, and will be discussed in greater detail in a moment; but the fundamental point is that the NSC must recruit individuals of visible seniority and stature who are able credibly to represent the presidency as an institution both within and outside the executive branch. As in the case of the National Security Adviser himself, the chief professional qualification for serving in such positions should be strategic expertise and talent. Some mix of academic and bureaucratic (or military) backgrounds would be appropriate, though it is worth stressing once again that career affiliation is not as important for good performance of the job required as less tangible personal qualities and habits of mind.

ORGANIZATION

The NSC staff has gone through frequent reorganizations over the years. Unfortunately, these changes can be tracked only very imperfectly in the public record. Rather than attempting to reconstruct this aspect of the institution's history, I shall simply lay out what I believe to be the optimal organization chart for NSC. Inevitably, such a chart must reflect what are or should be current priorities in U.S. national security policy; but its overall structure derives directly from the basic functional requirements of the NSC as discussed earlier in this study.

Some preliminary remarks are in order. The size of the NSC staff has been intermittently an issue ever since Henry Kissinger turned the organization into a miniature State Department. Under the Reagan administration, the staff remained in the neighborhood of fifty to sixty (substantive) professionals, down somewhat from the Kissinger days (although this does not include the staff of the new Crisis Management Center). In reaction, apparently, to the perceived excesses of the McFarlane-Poindexter NSC, Carlucci announced that significant staff reductions would occur (a measure also supported by Secretary of State Shultz during the Iran-Contra hearings); in fact, however, there was a slight expansion at this time. A good case can be made that the sixty to seventy range is more nearly optimal given the wide span of responsibilities that must be assumed in some fashion by the NSC. Particularly with a staff of this size, however, it is essential to establish clear hierarchies in order to provide the NSC front office with a manageable span of control. Both for this reason and because of the need for more senior individuals for external representation of the organization, there needs to be a clearly demarcated senior staff element in charge of staff groups or subunits.[2]

It will be well to begin by simply enumerating these major subunits. They are: (1) Planning, (2) Political Affairs, (3) Defense Policy, (4) Political-Military Affairs, (5) Arms Control Policy, (6) Economic, Scientific, and Technological Affairs, and (7) Intelligence.

Planning

Discrete planning groups have existed on the staff from time to time in the past, but their mandate and influence have generally been modest.[3] Establishment of a well-staffed planning operation with the proper authority both within and outside the NSC is the single most important innovation that will be suggested here. More than any other institutional mechanism, such a group would contribute to ensuring that the Adviser and the staff as a whole perform adequately the central NSC function of strategic planning.

In addition to a senior Special Assistant[4] for Planning who would have overall direction of the group, it should include staff members responsible for the following functions: (1) strategic intelligence, (2) net assessment, (3) long-range planning, (4) short-range and crisis planning, (5) economic and resource planning, and (6) speechwriting.

There is no need to reiterate here the arguments made earlier for a special NSC role in all of these areas. Several points should, however, be strongly underlined. First, all planning functions should ideally cut across all areas of national security affairs, emphatically including military affairs. Long-range planning should thus encompass planning for general war as carried out at the level of the unified and specified commands and the joint staff, while short-range and crisis planning should extend to the military aspects of planning for crises and limited military contingencies. For this reason, it would be highly desirable to staff one or both of these positions with a general officer with experience as a military planner. The Director of Short-range and Crisis Planning should probably serve simultaneously as Director or Deputy Director of the Crisis Management Center. Second, special attention should be given to devising procedures that ensure the thorough coordination of the Planning Group's work with that of the staff's other subunits.

Political Affairs

It is almost certainly necessary for the NSC to have a separate staff element organized around the major regions of the world, mirroring the regionally focused organization of the State Department. Most planning at State and within the NSC system is currently done within a regional or country context, and there are also operational reasons for NSC expertise of this sort—as discussed earlier, the President needs timely and reliable information in support of his personal diplomatic relationships with foreign leaders. Unfortunately, the NSC has too often mirrored the vices of State in this area as well, and accorded too much importance and autonomy to staffers with these responsibilities. Generally speaking, a disproportionate number of NSC staff members have been assigned to regional clusters, and these clusters have tended to operate in an overly compartmented manner, without the measure of integration that is imposed even on State's regional bureaus by the Under Secretary for Political Affairs. Reducing the number of such staffers, and improving their control and coordination, could only enhance their authority and general effectiveness.

Accordingly, in addition to a Special Assistant for Political Affairs who would have overall responsibility for its management, the Political Affairs group should have as a rule no more than one or two staffers for each of the following functions: (1) Soviet and East European affairs, (2) West European affairs, (3) East Asia and Pacific affairs, (4) Western Hemisphere affairs, (5) Middle East and South Asia affairs, (6) African affairs, (7) United Nations and global affairs, and (8) public diplomacy.

This division of the world's nations generally follows that of the State Department, with the very important exception that it creates a separate position for Soviet and East European Affairs that cuts across conventional regional divisions. The United Nations and global affairs position would correspond to the activities of State's bureaus of International Organizations and Human Rights and Humanitarian Affairs (and of the semiautonomous U.S. Mission to the United Nations). Finally, public diplomacy is included in this group (contrary to what has recently been the practice) in recognition of the need for tighter links between information and policy in both the formulation and execution of U.S. foreign policy.[5]

Defense Policy

In the defense area, a particularly good argument can be made for maintaining maximum flexibility in the NSC structure in order to be able to concentrate staff resources on particular issues and areas as they arise. Major defense procurement issues or foreign military sales can generate intense interest in the Congress and impose particularly heavy requirements on the NSC for intragovernmental coordination as well as congressional liaison. On the other hand, there are certain basic defense functions which probably require the permanent full-time involvement of at least one relatively senior NSC staffer. The Defense Policy group should be headed by a Special Assistant who ought to be a senior academic figure or other civilian with extensive experience in military affairs and knowledge of the Defense Department bureaucracy. A division of the group's functions along the following lines would seem to make sense: (1) strategic forces, (2) theater forces, (3) naval forces, special forces, and strategic mobility, (4) command, control, and communications, (5) space policy, (6) mobilization and emergency planning, (7) defense resources, and (8) defense information.

There should be little question concerning the need for a strong NSC staff effort in the area of strategic nuclear forces, a key element of the U.S. defense posture and one that has invariably been politically controversial. With President Reagan's Strategic Defense Initiative, the area of strategic defense has assumed a similar importance. Integration of strategic offensive and defensive programs and strategies, historically difficult because of Army-Air Force rivalries, will be a critical task facing American planners over the next decade, and one that stands in particular need of aggressive White House leadership.

Improvements in strategic command, control, and communications (C^3) have also been a centerpiece of the Reagan strategic modernization program. C^3 is centrally important for every aspect of U.S. military power, yet has always lacked the visibility and status to assure adequate support of it either within the military itself or in the Congress; this is a compelling reason for special NSC-level attention to the issue. In addition, however, the NSC staffer assigned to this area should have policy and operational oversight responsibilities for all C^3 issues relating directly to the presidential office. As discussed earlier, this includes the U.S.–Soviet "Hotline" as well as military communications systems and procedures.

There is inevitable arbitrariness in devising a few categories to cover the diverse aspects of U.S. nonnuclear military power. The categories suggested here are intended to correspond to distinct missions more than specific forces, and reflect the broad division of U.S. military responsibilities between major land theaters of operations (Europe, Korea, and the Persian Gulf) on the one hand, and the forces required to project and sustain U.S. power globally on the other.

Emergency preparedness and mobilization should cover a wide range of activities, including defense manpower issues, industrial mobilization, civil defense, defense of military assets and civilian administrative facilities against sabotage and special operations, continuity of government, and other aspects of national emergency planning for crises and wartime. None of these functions clearly falls within the purview of a single government agency, and all have been neglected in varying degrees in the past; strong NSC leadership is essential if they are to be performed effectively. It may be added that this position should also have assigned to it (perhaps in conjunction with the Crisis Management Center) policy and operational oversight responsibilities relating to the role of the presidential office and the NSC staff in crisis and wartime.

In the past, space policy at the NSC has been handled within the intelligence group, usually by an Air Force colonel with a background in technical intelligence collection systems. The time would seem to have come to recognize the growing importance of space for a variety of military functions (not least strategic defense) as well as for national strategy in the broadest sense. Although a case can be made for associating the space policy function at NSC with intelligence or with science and technology policy, the Defense Policy group would appear its most satisfactory home. At the same time, it may be well to reconsider the tradition of assigning an Air Force officer to deal with it (particularly a relatively junior officer on active duty), if only because of the Air Force role as a bureaucratic player in what is often a highly contentious area. The NSC Director of Space Policy should ideally be a senior civilian with Defense Department experience; or, if a military officer, he should be of one or two star rank and retired or in his final tour.

Given the complexity and political salience of defense budget issues, it is almost certainly desirable to assign an NSC staffer full time responsibility for following them on a day-to-day basis. The staffer responsible for resource planning within the Planning Group would have a broader mandate and a longer-term focus.

Finally, a good case can be made that the handling of public information relating to military affairs is a strategic function of sufficient importance to warrant full-time NSC staff attention. An NSC Director of Defense Information could be responsible for, among other things, formulating national policies concerning the declassification of defense-related intelligence, coordinating the U.S. response to Soviet propaganda and active measures campaigns on key defense issues (such as the Strategic Defense Initiative), reviewing and coordinating the production of major defense-related publications of the government (such as *Soviet Military Power,* the annual Defense Department posture statements, and relevant State Department and USIA publications), and developing national policies and procedures for managing the relationship between U.S. military forces and the media in crises and wartime.

Political-Military Affairs

When Frank Carlucci took over the reins at NSC, one of his first acts was to disband the so-called Political-Military Affairs office that had served as the base of operations for Lt. Col. Oliver North. Yet whatever North's sins in the Iran-Contra affair, an excellent case can be made for retaining an NSC office that deals in a comprehensive and integrated fashion with the policy areas that were in his portfolio. While it is true that many of the issues handled throughout the NSC can be characterized broadly as "political-military" in nature, it seems useful nonetheless to designate a separate NSC staff element under this or a similar name with specific responsibilities in the areas of low intensity conflict and alliance management. Such a group would have four principal functions: (1) low intensity warfare policy, (2) counterterrorism policy, (3) security assistance, and (4) alliance security policy.

At first glance, it might seem that these functions are ill-assorted and could just as easily be dispersed among other staff elements. Yet there is an underlying logic that unites them. Many of the problems the United States has experienced in the past in dealing effectively with insurgent and terrorist movements in the Third World have derived from a neglect of the political strategy of such movements and the political context in which they operate. The tendency has been to deal with hostile armed groups on a purely military basis, with insufficient attention both to the political objectives these groups pursue and to the political-military requirements of the states and organizations the United States is trying to help or whose cooperation it needs. Especially in a post-Vietnam era when the likelihood of extended involvement of U.S. combat forces in a Third World conflict remains relatively remote, the center of gravity of U.S. policy toward these conflicts is to be found in its relationships with friendly states and organizations. The political and military advice and assistance the United States can provide, whether to governments (as in El Salvador) or to rebel movements (as in Nicaragua), and not the direct application of American military force, is what is truly critical here. Yet little effort has been made to develop coherent national-level doctrine, policy, and strategy in an area that continues to suffer from severe bureaucratic warfare and an absence of consistent leadership at the top.

An NSC Director of Low Intensity Warfare Policy should have overall responsibility for developing doctrine, policy, and strategies for U.S. involvement in combatting or supporting revolutionary insurgencies in the Third World. He would necessarily work closely with staffers in the Political Affairs group with responsibilities for particular regions or countries as well as with the special warfare specialist in the Defense Policy group. But his primary function would be to develop and maintain a coherent approach to the general problem of low intensity conflict. It need hardly be added that he should not be expected to carry out operational coordination of U.S. policy in specific cases. (The critically important question of operational coordination of U.S. involvement in low intensity conflicts will be discussed later on.)

The counterterrorism function properly conceived is closely linked both with U.S. policy toward revolutionary movements and with U.S. alliance relationships. What is at issue here is not merely the U.S. military or paramilitary response to terrorist incidents or threats, but also the broader political context of alliance cooperation against terrorists and the states that aid and abet them.

Security assistance is a vitally important (and all too often mishandled and neglected) aspect of U.S. involvement in low intensity conflict situations. But it is also a critical aspect of U.S. relations with certain of its major allies, such as Israel, Egypt, and Turkey, and one that has traditionally been highly controversial in the Congress. Dedicating an NSC staff position to this function would help gain greater recognition for its role as a vital strategic instrument of U.S. national security policy.

Perhaps because most of our alliances are such fixtures on the international scene, Americans tend to take them for granted. Yet the U.S. alliance structure is a vital and integral part of this country's defense posture, as well as the foundation of America's political influence in many regions of the globe. Strange though it may seem, the U.S. government has never had an institutional focus for the development of general policy and strategy with respect to its alliance relationships. This is owing in part to the regional focus which has characterized the State Department's approach to alliance issues, and in part to perennial difficulties in the relationship between State and Defense in this area. An excellent case can be made for assigning a single NSC officer overall responsibility for monitoring the U.S. security relationship with its formal and informal allies around the world and bringing greater coherence to U.S. policy in this critical area. Ideally, such a function should extend beyond the purely military dimension of U.S. alliance relations to security-related areas such as strategic economic cooperation and intelligence sharing as well as to broader political questions. While the NATO alliance would inevitably be the central focus of such an effort, perhaps its chief merit would be to draw more concentrated attention to second- or third-order relationships such as ANZUS (currently under severe threat as a result of the anti-nuclear policies of the government of New Zealand), the U.S.–Japanese alliance, or U.S. bilateral security ties with key states in the Middle East.

Arms Control

In part reflecting the Reagan administration's doctrinal view of its role in U.S. national security policy, arms control at the NSC was, until the Carlucci reorganization, formally subordinated to the Defense Policy group. While it is certainly appropriate to emphasize the importance of fully integrating arms control with defense policy generally, as a practical matter there is a good deal to be said for establishing a separate NSC arms control staff headed by a senior officer of substantial independent stature. The very considerable strategic importance of arms control, in terms of its impact on U.S. and NATO military capabilities, and the scope and complexity of current arms control issues are argument enough for assigning a senior NSC officer to this area. At the same time, the growing centrality of arms control in the relationship between the United States and its NATO allies (not to speak of the Soviet Union itself) give it a very high political content, and greatly complicate the bureaucratic problems involved in handling it. As pointed out earlier, arms control was one of the most contentious and intractable areas of interagency dispute under the Reagan administration, and the divergent perspectives of the foreign affairs and defense bureaucracies virtually guarantee that it will remain so under foreseeable circumstances. Only a strong NSC can exercise the kind of discipline that appears to be required if the U.S. government is to act effectively in this area.

In addition to a Special Assistant for Arms Control of the appropriate stature and seniority, an Arms Control group should have staffers assigned in the following areas: (1) strategic forces and space, (2) theater and conventional forces, (3) multilateral affairs, and (4) verification and compliance. The first three categories reflect the differing interlocutors for different sorts of arms control negotiations—respectively, the United States and the Soviet Union, NATO and the Warsaw Pact, and the United Nations.

The fourth function, verification and compliance, merits some additional remarks. In recognition of the severe and long-standing difficulties the U.S. government has faced both in devising effectively verifiable arms control agreements and in securing compliance with agreements in force, the Reagan administration moved in 1983 to create an interagency Verification Committee under the chairmanship of the National Security Adviser himself to address these issues in a coherent and vigorous manner. Unfortunately, little progress was made, and the committee itself soon fell into disuse, once it became clear that the NSC staff had neither the resources nor the authority to follow up effectively on the tasks that the committee had been set. The vital importance of the verification and compliance issue, together with the strong disincentives existing in the major agencies to deal with it seriously, make this a prime candidate for active and continuous NSC leadership.

Economic, Scientific, and Technological Affairs

The NSC has always paid some attention to international economic policy, though its involvement and influence in this area have fluctuated sharply over time. In certain areas, such as technology transfer, a leading NSC role has been virtually unavoidable given the sharp divergence of perspective between the national security agencies on the one hand and agencies with a primarily domestic orientation such as Treasury, Commerce, or Agriculture on the other. In other areas, the very proliferation of government actors and the political salience of the issues make an NSC coordinating role highly desirable, while at the same time introducing unique complications and constraints on the NSC's ability to perform this role effectively.

In large part because of the existence of a separate office in the White House dealing with scientific and technical matters (the Office of Science and Technology Policy, headed by the President's Science Advisor), the NSC has tended to involve itself in this area only at the margins. In the larger perspective of national strategy, however, there are a number of scientific or technology-related issues that have very considerable importance and need to be integrated as closely as possible with other aspects of U.S. national security policy. Regardless of the precise functions of the Science Advisor's office and its relationship to the NSC and the President, a good argument can be made for an increased attention to such issues within the NSC itself. Given the very substantial commercial and economic dimension of strategic technologies, it would seem to make sense to combine the economic and scientific-technological functions in a single NSC group.

The Economic, Scientific, and Technological Affairs group should probably cover at least the following areas: (1) international trade, (2) international monetary affairs and financial security, (3) development aid, (4) energy and resource security, (5) strategic technologies, (6) telecommunications and data processing.

It is worth emphasizing, in view of the little-known history of Soviet manipulation of financial processes, the strategic importance of maintaining the integrity of the international banking system.

The other international economic functions are traditional and self-explanatory. The primary responsibility of a Director of Strategic Technologies would lie in the area of technology transfer policy. However, it would be useful to establish a broader mandate for such a position, to include long-term forecasting relative to emerging technologies, intelligence and counterintelligence issues relating to strategic technologies, and similar questions. Telecommunications and data processing technologies, in addition to their very considerable and growing commercial importance for the United States and its allies, have significant strategic and foreign policy aspects, and national policy in this area could benefit substantially from an enhanced NSC role.

Intelligence

Until very recently, little attention has been paid to the NSC role, actual or potential, in the area of intelligence; and recent attention has focused almost exclusively on the involvement of NSC staffers in covert operations. Yet, as indicated earlier, there are excellent reasons for maintaining and even strengthening NSC involvement in a number of aspects of the intelligence business. That a Director of Strategic Intelligence should be established within an NSC Planning group was suggested a moment ago; this position could as easily be located within the Intelligence group, though perhaps with some loss in the integration of intelligence and (especially) long-range planning. In addition, the Intelligence group should include the following staff positions: (1) current intelligence, (2) intelligence policy and resources, (3) special activities, and (4) counterintelligence and strategic security.

The Director of Current Intelligence (who might serve concurrently in a senior position in the Crisis Management Center, which has assumed a major role in this area on behalf of the NSC) should have primary responsibility for monitoring current intelligence issues and overseeing the flow of intelligence to the NSC staff, the National Security Adviser, and the President. The Director of Intelligence Policy and Resources should have responsibility for overseeing general administration policy relating to intelligence, the formulation of intelligence requirements by the policy agencies and the NSC as a whole, intelligence resource planning based on those requirements, and the management of technical intelligence collection systems. The need for a staffer in the area of "special activities" (the legal term for covert action) should be self-evident given the importance and sensitivity of these activities. It should not be necessary to add that this officer need not and should not be involved in the operational dimension of covert action. He will have more than enough to do in handling coordination of covert action programs across the intelligence, defense, and foreign policy communities as well as between the executive branch and the intelligence committees of the Congress. Equally critical is the position of Director for Counterintelligence and Strategic Security, whose responsibilities should encompass not only counterintelligence in the traditional sense but a range of related areas such as communications security, security clearance issues, and domestic security.

PROCEDURES

Some further remarks are in order on the subject of the procedures governing the operations of the NSC staff. No matter how perfect the NSC organizational chart, it is inevitable that there will be many overlapping responsibilities and a strong requirement for continuous intrastaff communication and coordination. To some extent, individual staffers can be counted on to have the common sense to perform these functions in the absence of formal procedures. But this is rarely enough. As remarked earlier, there are many pressures that combine to fragment the work of the staff. Security requirements are a powerful reason to limit the flow of information within the staff; individual staffers have reasons of their own to control the information available to them and attempt to maximize their own freedom of action; and the volume and pace of work make it difficult for staffers to keep in view the overall picture of national policy and maintain a proper sense of priorities. If the NSC is to perform what is arguably its central function, however, the staff *must* have a good understanding of the larger strategic picture and of the strategic and political priorities of the President.

It is therefore essential that the NSC leadership create artificial mechanisms that act in a direction opposite to the natural tendency of things. In the first instance, and most importantly, the separate NSC groups and the senior staff in charge of them must be counted on to perform a strong and continuous integrating role. Staff meetings are another such mechanism, and these have been a regular practice under most NSC regimes. Another is a formal system of concurrences on internal memoranda. Finally, a variety of written reports by individual staff members can perform a useful function, by allowing management to keep better track of the staff's activities and thinking. Unfortunately, unless carefully managed from the top, some of these mechanisms have a tendency to become routinized and lose their value, while certain of them can prove counterproductive.

The creation of subgroups or clusters within the NSC staff has often been regarded merely as a matter of administrative convenience, instead of what it should be—a mechanism for the genuine coordination and integration of a range of related functions. Although it is essential for staff members to have specialized areas of responsibility of the sort discussed above, the small size of the NSC staff and the impossibility of clean compartmentalization of its functions suggest the importance of encouraging a broad familiarity with current policy issues directly or indirectly related to a staffer's main interests. Group directors can foster this familiarity through simple measures such as regular staff meetings and the routine circulation of important documents in various stages of their preparation. As mentioned earlier, the NSC sector that would be most radically affected by more integrated management of this sort is the one dealing with regional and political affairs. Currently, and at most times in the past, NSC regional offices have been headed by relatively senior figures operating in semiautonomous fashion and reporting directly to the Adviser. While it is important that all staffers have regular and relatively easy access to the Adviser himself, this practice has only served to reinforce the astrategic and client-oriented approach to foreign policy characteristic of the State Department. Instead, the NSC needs to make a deliberate and unremitting effort to counter this perennial bias at State and to insist on an integrated and cross-regional approach to foreign policy decision making. In other areas too, however, NSC groups should be structured and managed so as to cut across and counterbalance the institutional biases of the bureaucracies to which they correspond.

Weekly meetings of the entire staff, which were a fixture at NSC under the Reagan administration, are generally of very limited utility except as a way of communicating important messages from the top. Sensitive matters cannot be discussed in a group of this sort, and few other issues require or can benefit from an airing before more than a handful of staffers. Much more useful are regular meetings of senior staff, especially under an organizational arrangement of the sort proposed above, in which a small number (six to eight) of senior officers have line authority over the rest of the staff. Such a group should be capable of dealing discreetly with most sensitive issues, and is small enough to permit genuine discussion.

A system of concurrences of some sort is probably necessary, though it can also be crippling if not intelligently conceived and applied. Since the need for such a system results in large part from compartmentalization of information, increasing the exposure of staffers to wider information wherever feasible can help to reduce reliance on what can easily become a cumbersome and mechanical process. One alternative is to require formal concurrences only on particularly important types of memoranda (for example, those prepared in connection with a major policy document for presidential signature). In any case, ensuring appropriate coordination of this sort should be regarded as a vital function of the NSC management and receive extensive and continuous attention. In the last several years, the revived office of Executive Secretary has proved highly useful for this purpose. But the involvement of senior staff on a regular basis is also necessary.

Confidential weekly reports are an important vehicle for staff members to communicate directly with the NSC front office, and particularly the National Security Adviser himself. These can be used for a wide variety of purposes—to flag emerging policy issues, personnel problems in the agencies, problems of interagency or intrastaff coordination, and the like. Other sorts of reports or analyses for circulation within NSC can be very useful, although this has been less commonly done in the past. For example, each staff member can be asked to prepare a year-end assessment of the status of his policy area, together with a proposed strategy for proceeding in the coming year.

In general, it seems fair to say that NSC management has been less than successful over the years in devising and implementing effective procedures for intrastaff coordination. Extreme compartmentalization of information and responsibilities has been generally seen as the lesser evil given the pervasive threat of leaks of even the most sensitive information, and is in any case the path of least resistance. While the concern over leaks is certainly well-founded, it can be questioned whether too high a price has not been paid for this approach to managing the staff. As indicated above, it defeats much of the fundamental rationale for the NSC as an organization uniquely devoted to the strategic perspective of the presidential office. An eminently reasonable alternative would be much tighter security controls over NSC staff personnel, including the polygraphing of all staff members on a routine basis and strict disciplining of offenders.

Perhaps the most troublesome area has to do with staff access to presidential decision documents. At the NSC as well as throughout the bureaucracy, access to National Security Decision Directives (NSDDs)—the primary vehicle for presidential decisions on fundamental national security issues—has been tightly controlled, and increasingly so in recent years. Unfortunately, the result is too often that NSC staffers are unaware of or unfamiliar with presidential decisions that have a significant bearing on their own areas of activity. Needless to say, this can be a crippling liability, not only because it affects the quality of their work but also by undermining their credibility and standing with the bureaucracy.

RELATIONSHIPS

Surprisingly little attention has been paid over the years to the question of the NSC's role within the White House bureaucracy. As has been seen, uncertain or antagonistic relations between the National Security Adviser and senior White House officials played a major role in the turbulent history of the NSC under the Reagan administration. In addition, however, the NSC must deal on a regular or occasional basis with a variety of offices within the White House and the Executive Office of the President. Chief among these are the Office of Management and Budget and the White House directors of Communications and Legislative Affairs. But also of potential importance are NSC relations with the Office of Science and Technology Policy, the Office of Presidential Personnel, the President's Foreign Intelligence Advisory Board, the Intelligence Oversight Board, the White House Military Office, the White House Legal Counsel, and the domestic and economic policy staffs (the Office of Policy Development and Council of Economic Advisers). Finally, of course, and closely connected with its relationships within the White House, is the question of the NSC's relationship with the Congress. In most if not all of these cases, the current situation is characterized by the absence of formal mechanisms or procedures, ad hoc informal contacts, and an overall relationship which is less than satisfactory in meeting NSC's institutional requirements.

The fundamental problem in the relationship between the NSC and the White House, to repeat what was said earlier, is the short-term and political orientation characteristic of the immediate presidential office and those who staff it. White House officials, beginning with the Chief of Staff and extending to virtually all senior figures, are commonly chosen for their political skills or political connections, and rarely have more than a passing familiarity with foreign policy and national security issues. Frequently, they are inclined to see such questions as an unwelcome distraction from the business of maintaining the President's political standing and popularity, rather than as a central area of presidential responsibility.

It is tempting to leave it at saying that the National Security Adviser should have direct and unimpeded access to the President so as to be in a position to make the best case possible for a genuinely strategic approach to national security questions. Unfortunately, given natural presidential proclivities, this approach could well have the effect of submerging the national security dimension of White House policy making in a tide of domestic and tactical political considerations. The fact of the matter is that national security and domestic questions are rarely cleanly separable. The National Security Adviser must therefore cultivate personal and institutional relationships within the White House that can help to maximize the national security input into broad policy and political deliberations, as well as ensuring that national security issues will themselves be considered in a predominantly strategic perspective.

The best approach to countering the inevitable bias of senior White House staff is to strengthen the institutional presence of the NSC within the White House structure. The size and location of the National Security Adviser's office, trivial though it may seem, is a by no means negligible aspect of this institutional presence; so are the various White House privileges accorded or denied members of his staff. More important, however, are institutional mechanisms for ensuring that the National Security Adviser and the NSC staff are fully integrated into the overall apparatus of White House decision making.

This is true above all in the case of those White House offices and committees that operate at a more strategic level. The offices are, as a rule (though not necessarily or to the same degree), the Office of Management and Budget (OMB), the White House Chief of Staff and Director of Legislative Affairs (who generally work closely together), and the White House Director of Communications. During the Reagan years, the OMB under David Stockman was for a period the principal instrument of the administration's overall strategy of governance; after Stockman's departure, power gravitated steadily toward the Chief of Staff. The White House Communications office aspired to a greater strategic role during the tenure of Pat Buchanan, but was for the most part unable to play it. The NSC enjoyed good working relations with none of these offices, with the partial exception of Buchanan's. The principal vehicles for intra-White House coordination of policy and political strategy in recent years were the Legislative Strategy Group and the Budget Review Board. The NSC did not enjoy a satisfactory relationship with either of them.

The dominance within the White House of legislative and budgetary perspectives is not remarkable, reflecting as it does the realities of power and the centrality of the legislative-executive relationship in the operation of the government as a whole. But it is equally obvious that this situation is not the best possible. It is certainly not optimal from the point of view of the NSC. One of the most important institutional steps that could be taken to enhance the NSC's role would be the creation of a coordinating mechanism that would force greater consideration of broad strategic and political issues by senior White House staff. To explore fully possible alternatives would take us too far afield, but what seems basically wanted is a committee chaired by the Chief of Staff and including at a minimum the NSC Adviser, the Director of OMB, the Director of the Office of Policy Development (OPD), and the directors of the White House Communications, Legislative Affairs, and Political Affairs offices. Meeting on a regular basis, such a committee (let us call it the White House Strategy Group) could monitor important political and congressional developments and chart overall guidelines for administration action. It could also adjudicate (or propose for presidential resolution) important substantive or bureaucratic conflicts between the various offices involved.

One may go a step further and suggest that such a committee is likely to function effectively only if it can call on dedicated staff support. As mentioned earlier, in the first Reagan term an Office of Planning and Evaluation (OPE) was created by Ed Meese with a mandate to undertake strategic planning at a political level. This office was never properly supported and eventually fell victim to intra-White House feuding, but the idea behind it was a sound one. A small staff of this sort could be used to monitor political developments on a continuous basis, to format and display relevant information, to prepare agendas for the committee's meetings, and to oversee and facilitate staff-level coordination. To perform these tasks effectively, of course, such an office would have to be, and be seen to be, nothing other than an extension of the White House Chief of Staff and the President.

The question of the NSC's relationship to White House legislative and legal officials is a critical and neglected one. As Congress has come to play an ever larger and more assertive role in national security policy over the last several decades, the NSC's area of responsibility has become increasingly hedged about with legal requirements and restrictions of various kinds. The Iran-Contra affair has highlighted the potential legal vulnerabilities of NSC staffers as they pursue particular interpretations of congressional intent, and in response to congressional concerns in this area the Carlucci regime has upgraded the status of the NSC legal adviser. But it remains unclear precisely where responsibility lies for developing administration legal policy relative to NSC's activities. This involves much more than the question of compliance with existing laws. It involves overall administration strategy in dealing with congressional restrictions on its prerogatives in the national security area. Questions such as the status of the War Powers Act or the meaning of the various Boland amendments restricting aid to the Nicaraguan Contras are fundamental to the administration's ability to plan and execute coherent and effective national security policies. Yet there is no mechanism for developing genuine legal or legislative strategies to deal with these questions.

The fact of the matter is that the legal advisory offices in the White House as well as in the agencies tend to approach all such issues cautiously, passively, and from a legalistic perspective, instead of treating them as the strategic and political issues they so emphatically are. At the same time, legislative affairs offices in the White House and the agencies tend to reflect in exaggerated and parochial fashion the momentary concerns of interested members of Congress, and tend to favor appeasement of those concerns. In the face of all this, it can be extremely difficult for the NSC to impose its own perspective within the administration's councils, or indeed to make itself heard at all.

What kind of institutional remedies are there for this? It is not clear that there are any very satisfactory solutions other than ad hoc ones. At the very least, the NSC should be permitted to participate routinely and as an equal player in the White House Legislative Strategy Group or its equivalent. In addition, it might be given a specific mandate to develop longer-term, more comprehensive strategies to deal with critical points of executive branch dissatisfaction with congressional behavior (such as the Boland amendments or the defense budget process).

Another important area of NSC interaction with the White House is speechwriting and public affairs. It is probably not possible to devise a single correct procedure for handling the preparation of presidential speeches, but it needs to be recognized that these are indeed strategic instruments of the presidency. All too often, such speeches are treated within the White House as mere collections of words rather than as what they are—presidential deeds. A variety of tactics is available to White House officials for retaining control of or influence over the preparation of important speeches, perhaps the chief one being simple delay. Accordingly, it is often difficult for the NSC to become involved in speech preparation at a sufficiently early stage to affect the overall concept of a speech or to ensure a close linkage between the speech and its policy context. The problem generally lies not with the presidential speechwriting staff itself, but with senior White House officials who are more interested in short-term public relations effects than in the strategic impact of a presidential speech.

Again, it is difficult to come up with convincing institutional remedies for this problem. It was proposed earlier that an NSC Director of Speechwriting be included within an NSC planning group. The function of this staffer should not be speechwriting as such (though he would inevitably do some of it), but rather the planning of speeches by the President and other senior cabinet officials on national security issues. This should involve systematic coordination of major speeches with policy, including both preparatory and follow-up work to ensure that a speech has maximum impact and supports administration strategic and political objectives. In order to be effective, such a staffer should be granted full and regular access to the White House Director of Communications and his speechwriters and should work closely with them. If the relationship is a successful one, it should help ensure that the strategic perspective of the NSC is brought to bear on important speeches from the very beginning.

In the area of public affairs, it is also vital that the NSC work closely with the White House. This relationship has been a reasonably successful one in recent years in terms of coordination of public positions on day-to-day national security issues. In 1982, a formal committee was created under the rubric of the Special Planning Group for Public Diplomacy, under the cochairmanship of the Deputy National Security Adviser and the White House Director of Communications, to improve the coordinated handling of national security issues of salience from a White House point of view. Certain ad hoc public affairs and public liaison activities on key national security issues have been supported with some consistency by the White House, notably (or notoriously) relating to Central America. On the whole, however, much more could be done to support a strategic approach to public affairs in the national security area. As in the case of legal and legislative affairs, those responsible for public affairs in the White House as well as the agencies tend to be cautious and reactive, very oriented to the short term, and overly responsive to their immediate constituency, the national media. To the extent that the NSC is accorded a greater structural role in public affairs decision making, it can bring at least a salutary counterweight to these tendencies. NSC directors for Public Diplomacy and Defense Information, as recommended above, would usefully supplement the traditional NSC public affairs officer by providing a greater strategic and long-term perspective on national security information issues and—equally important—by integrating international and domestic aspects of these issues. This should help mitigate at least to some extent the massive influence of the domestic media on the public presentation of national security matters.

The federal budget is another area where the NSC's role in White House decision making has been less than commensurate with its essential functions and responsibilities. Except for the abortive Defense Program Review Committee of the Nixon era, no formal mechanism has existed for White House–level integration of budgetary and policy considerations relating to national security. The effect of this has been to give considerable discretion to the Office of Management and Budget in setting priorities and directions for national security programs on behalf of the executive branch. There is little apparent reason why this needs to be the case. It is difficult to overestimate the tenacity with which the agencies attempt to maintain maximum control over spending levels and priorities in their particular fields, and OMB plays an essential role in imposing discipline on them in the name of a wider administration perspective. Yet the OMB perspective is not a strategic one except by default. What would seem required under these circumstances is something like a National Security Resources Board, under the chairmanship of the National Security Adviser, and including as members the Director of OMB, the Deputy Secretary of Defense, the Deputy Secretary of State, and the Director of Central Intelligence. This committee could have overall responsibility for establishing priorities and directions for government spending on all national security programs, including those of the State Department and the intelligence community as well as the Department of Defense, with authority to review agency budget submissions and make recommendations to the President concerning overall spending levels and breakdowns by major program category. The NSC Director of Economic and Resource Planning would be the principal NSC staff officer for the Board. Conflicts within the Board could be adjudicated by the White House Strategy Group proposed above, which would retain overall administration responsibility for resource allocation questions.

Finally, something further needs to be said about the perennially controversial question of the handling of international economic affairs within the White House. As indicated earlier, the economic area is one in which the NSC is inescapably involved, yet finds it particularly difficult to operate because of the close interconnection of foreign and domestic economic policy and the weight of the domestic policy agencies and the political constituencies with which they must deal. In the past, foreign economic policy has been handled within the White House in a variety of ways. A Council on International Economic Policy existed briefly under the Nixon administration, but proved unable to compete successfully for the President's attention. Foreign and domestic economic policy were subsequently handled together by a Council on Economic Policy and (under the Ford administration) an Economic Policy Board. During the Carter administration, an Economic Policy Group was co-chaired by the Secretary of the Treasury and the Chairman of the Council of Economic Advisers, but much of the work of coordinating international economic policy was undertaken informally by a senior NSC official (Henry Owen).

Under the first Reagan administration, foreign economic policy issues were handled either through "cabinet councils" dealing with various aspects of economic and domestic policy, or through a Senior Interdepartmental Group on International Economic Policy (SIG-IEP), established in 1982. This group, though formally reporting to the National Security Council, was actually a cabinet-level committee, with the Secretary of the Treasury as chairman, the Secretary of State as vice chairman, and a senior NSC official (Norman Bailey) acting as executive secretary. In 1985, the cabinet council system was abolished and replaced by an Economic Policy Council (EPC) and a Domestic Policy Council (DPC), chaired respectively by the Secretary of the Treasury and the Attorney General. In this reorganization, the EPC assumed the functions of the SIG-IEP as well as the relevant cabinet councils, but excluded State, the CIA, and the NSC from formal membership. And while it retained a White House base, the EPC secretariat reported to the White House Chief of Staff (former Treasury Secretary Donald Regan) rather than the National Security Adviser. The effect of all this was to sharply diminish the influence of the NSC and the national security agencies generally on foreign economic policy making.

It is not clear that there is a single optimal way of handling the development of international economic policy, but there can be little question that the present situation is unsatisfactory. Recent experience seems to show several things. A White House mechanism devoted solely to international economic policy (like the Nixon CIEP) is almost certainly unworkable; but a White House mechanism for the coordination of economic policy generally cannot be expected to give adequate weight to the national security and foreign policy dimension of economic issues without special institutional steps to ensure that this occurs. Probably the best solution is some combination of the two Reagan systems, with a lower level interagency group operating within the NSC system but reporting to a cabinet-level equivalent of the Economic Policy Council. Variants of the first group would include a SIG-IEP chaired by the NSC Special Assistant for Economic, Scientific, and Technological Affairs, or a higher level Economic Security Board chaired by the National Security Adviser (or perhaps his deputy) and including appropriate representation from other White House offices.

It is hardly necessary to emphasize the extent to which the Congress has become an integral part of the process of national security policy development within the executive branch. Some remarks have already been made concerning the need for a stronger NSC role in the formulation by the executive branch as a whole of strategies for dealing with Congressional involvement in national security issues. But it is necessary to raise the further question whether some effort should not be made to institutionalize the relationship between the NSC itself and the Congress. Several issues should be briefly addressed in this connection: whether the National Security Adviser should be subject to confirmation by the Senate; the extent to which the Adviser or the NSC staff should become involved in consultation and negotiation with congressmen or their staffs; and whether changes should be undertaken in the structure and procedures of Congress in the national security area in order to facilitate its interaction with the NSC.

The issue of possible confirmation of the NSC Adviser (on the analogy of the Director of OMB) was aired in congressional hearings in 1980 following a period of acute and public conflict between then NSC Adviser Zbigniew Brzezinski and Secretary of State Cyrus Vance. Some senators asked whether an NSC Adviser who is as authoritative a spokesman for the administration's foreign policy as the Secretary of State himself should not be made equally answerable to Congress. Although Brzezinski himself has pronounced in favor of such a step, it has found few other proponents. As observers at the time pointed out, it would most likely only legitimize and exacerbate the existing NSC-State rivalry. The more fundamental question, however, is how such a change would affect the existing balance of power between the executive and legislative branches. There can be little question but that, at least under present circumstances, confirmation of the Adviser would represent a serious blow to the already doubtful control the President exercises over national security policy development, and the recent inquiry of the Tower Commission appears to indicate that this remains a consensus view in Washington. Desirable as it may be to strengthen the institutional position of the Adviser within the White House, formalizing his position beyond a certain point would almost certainly be counterproductive and tempt presidents to devise alternative channels of confidential policy advice. Moreover, as a practical matter it is difficult to imagine how the Adviser could perform his very demanding job if constantly required to appear before committees of Congress and burdened with endless reporting requirements.

This is not to suggest that the Adviser can or should avoid any dealings with the Congress. There are times when the prestige of the Adviser can be essential in the task of persuading influential congressmen to support administration policy in critical areas of national security. Yet the President needs to recognize that the Adviser (like the President himself) is a strategic resource, to be deployed only on exceptional occasions when truly strategic interests of the administration are at stake. It would be a wise policy for the Adviser to restrict his informal contacts on Capitol Hill for the most part to the leadership and the ranking majority and minority members of the House and Senate foreign relations, armed services, and intelligence committees. The Adviser would also be well advised to craft general policies governing the nature of the interaction between his own staff and the Congress. One possibility might be to give NSC senior staff special responsibilities for dealing with Congress, while restricting or discouraging dealings between the working level of the NSC and members of Congress or their staffs. This would minimize opportunities for the Congress to fish for information at the NSC or to play off the NSC against other agencies.

Finally, the point needs to be made that, in terms of its own structure and procedures, Congress is very much a part of the problem rather than a part of the solution. The fragmentation of authority as between foreign relations, armed services, and intelligence committees (not to mention appropriations and budget committees) in both houses mirrors and exacerbates the fragmentation of decision-making authority within the executive branch in the national security area, and further complicates the coordinating and integrating role that the NSC should play within the government as a whole. Suffice it to say that it is unrealistic and unreasonable for Congress to expect to enjoy a close working relationship with the NSC and the National Security Adviser unless and until it takes steps to rationalize its own approach to national security. This could involve such measures as reducing the number of relevant committees (for example, as the Tower Commission has recommended, by creating a single joint intelligence committee for both houses), creating subcommittees with a strategic focus and overlapping committee membership, reducing the number of congressional staffers with access to sensitive national security information, restoring order to the congressional budget process, and the like. A serious effort in this direction would help to restore some measure of the mutual confidence and respect between the branches that is so necessary to the effective operation of the United States government as a whole, and is now so sorely lacking.

Chapter 6

National Security and Presidential Governance

In 1980, the National Academy of Public Administration issued an influential study of the presidency that spoke of a "crisis of public management" stemming from the increasing fragmentation of power within the American political system. While noting the perennial institutional tensions between the President and the Congress, the study argued that the truly critical problem lay not so much in the relationship between these branches as in the lack of organizational coherence within each of them.[1] The struggle between Ronald Reagan and an increasingly recalcitrant and partisan Congress has occupied the forefront of the Washington political scene in the intervening years, but the underlying bureaucratic problems—at both ends of Pennsylvania Avenue—have not only persisted, but in some respects have worsened significantly. A recent study of foreign policy decision making in the United States since the 1930s describes disunity in the executive branch as "one of the conspicuous hallmarks of American diplomacy" during the Reagan years, and exceeding any witnessed since World War II—a judgment echoed, as has been seen, by former National Security Advisers Brzezinski and Kissinger in the wake of the Reykjavik summit.[2] Only in the defense area has there been real progress in achieving fundamental reform of institutional structures and culture. Yet even the reform of the Joint Chiefs of Staff is very likely to prove barren of significant consequences if it is not sustained by a wider consensus on the need for fundamental change throughout the national security establishment—and above all, for substantial improvement in the way the national security establishment is managed by the President and by the presidency as an institution.

What is to be done? It is well beyond the scope of the present study to rehearse and evaluate the many proposals that have been made over the years for reform of the national security bureaucracy. As indicated earlier, many of these proposals have reflected serious misunderstandings of the nature of the federal bureaucracy generally and of the institutional character and culture of the national security agencies in particular. Rather, attention will be focused principally on the key steps that might be taken by the President to strengthen his own control over the national security agencies and to impart greater strategic coherence to national security policy. Only second-arily will some consideration be given to possible changes in the organization and bureaucratic culture of the agencies themselves.

That the President needs a personal staff with broad authority to manage the national security policy process has been the argument of the preceding chapters. The impossible demands of the modern presidency, and the inevitable divergence between the perspective of the President and the perspectives of the various national security agencies and the officials who run them, suggest the need for some-thing very like the NSC staff that serves him today. Yet the NSC is and always has been an imperfect instrument. Positioned as it is midway between a highly routinized bureaucracy and an intensely personal and political White House, the NSC shares the characteristics of both, but is fully integrated into neither. As a result, many presidents seem to have been uncertain about the NSC's proper role. At one extreme, it has been treated as a personal staff useful primarily for executing presidential policies independently of the bureaucracy; at the other, it has been treated in effect as simply another national security agency, with a voice but not necessarily a distinctive role in interagency policy deliberations. Most commonly, it has been seen as an administrative body responsible primarily for "coordina-tion" of the work of the various national security agencies. Rarely has it been used aggressively by a President to discipline the policy process and project the presidential perspective into the shaping of fundamental national security policy options.

What seems needed in the first instance is greater recognition on all sides of the critical institutional role that the NSC must play if the national security bureaucracy as a whole is to perform its tasks effectively. Strengthening the NSC as an institution obviously entails limiting the power of the bureaucracy; less obviously, it also requires certain constraints on the use of the NSC by the President.

As argued earlier, the NSC has a variety of legitimate or essential roles, but many of them have for the most part been neglected by recent presidents, while operational functions of questionable appropriateness have sometimes been favored. Presidents themselves need to understand that the presidential office is more than an extension of their own personalities, with certain structural requirements deriving from the Constitution, the characteristics of the current international environment, and the nature of executive leadership.

In the final analysis, however, the NSC is and must remain essentially a surrogate for the President. It cannot carry alone the burden of day-to-day management of the national security bureaucracy, and without constant validation of its authority by the President himself, it is doomed to ineffectiveness. This means that the NSC role cannot be properly discussed without considering the President's personal relationship with the political executives who control the national security agencies. The National Security Council as such, it must be remembered, is not a part of the bureaucracy so much as an advisory committee made up of the senior officials representing the most important national security agencies. In theory, the President is perfectly entitled to ignore the individual or collective advice of these individuals in making fundamental decisions affecting their departments. In practice, however, this is difficult or impossible, and the President's manner of dealing with his cabinet is a critical dimension of his management of national security affairs.

Put another way, no matter how institutionally strong the NSC is and how well armed with the presidential mandate, it can accomplish only so much if faced with a sullen and resentful bureaucracy and by political executives who have chosen to throw in their lot with it. The President cannot afford to rely wholly on the NSC while neglecting the line authority he formally possesses over the national security agencies themselves. At the same time, the President cannot leave it at the appointment of loyal henchmen to a few top positions in these agencies. For the reasons outlined earlier, there can be little assurance that his senior appointees will prove able or willing to impose the President's perspective and policy views on their respective bureaucracies. It is therefore incumbent on a President to take additional measures to ensure that senior political executives maintain more than nominal control of their agencies, and are in a position to resist pressures to identify themselves with the institutional perspectives and interests of those agencies.

THE NSC AND THE INTERAGENCY SYSTEM

It was argued earlier that the NSC has an important role to play not only in the development but also in the implementation of presidential policy. Generally speaking, the NSC, together with the interagency committees existing under the aegis of the National Security Council, have been viewed principally as a tool of policy development, while policy implementation has been seen as the responsibility of the individual agencies. In fact, however, the need for interagency coordination exists at the tactical and operational as well as the strategic level. Not surprisingly, the requirement for a vigorous NSC role in tactical or operational matters can become even more pressing where policy guidance at the strategic level is weak, delayed, or confused. To return to an earlier example, feuding among State, Defense, the CIA, and the White House over Central American policy in the first Reagan term undoubtedly gave the initial impetus to the NSC's operational involvement in the region. Even where strategic-level policy is fully adequate, however, there remain problems in implementation that arguably require, if not an active NSC role, at least a revamping of existing organizational and procedural arrangements. This is especially true outside of Washington. Indeed, as suggested earlier, problems of operational coordination among U.S. government agencies in the field remain an underappreciated but very significant factor in U.S. national security policy failures. The Moscow embassy scandal is a conspicuous recent example.

In the area of policy development, three general issues need to be addressed: the structure of the interagency committee system, the management of that system, and the management of the presidential decision process.

It is necessary at the outset to raise some fundamental questions concerning the composition of the National Security Council itself and its relationship to the larger community of national security agencies. Current legislation establishes as members of the National Security Council the President, Vice President, Secretary of State, and Secretary of Defense, while the Chairman of the Joint Chiefs of Staff, the Director of Central Intelligence (DCI), and the Director of the Arms Control and Disarmament Agency (ACDA) are designated as statutory advisers. Although the composition of the Council has never generated much political controversy, there have been occasional complaints concerning the special weight accorded to the military and intelligence establishments,[3] and suggestions for additional members—especially the Secretary of the Treasury, the Attorney General, and the Director of the United States Information Agency (USIA). In fact, although the Chairman of the JCS and the DCI are formally designated as advisers to the Council, the distinction does not seem to have made much difference in practice, and these officials—particularly under the Reagan administration—have tended to participate on a more or less equal footing. This was particularly true of the DCI, since Director William Casey was accorded cabinet rank and came to play an independent role as foreign policy adviser to the President. Some versions of the JCS reform legislation circulating in Congress in recent years would have made the JCS Chairman a full statutory member of the Council. Although this change was not enacted, it is symptomatic of the extent to which the policy role of senior military and intelligence officials has come to be taken for granted.

Because the Council altogether is an advisory body, not a decision-making one, the precise legal status of its members is of limited significance. Moreover, the President is perfectly entitled to invite other officials in his administration to participate in the Council's deliberations on issues of concern to them. At the same time, however, it has to be admitted that the existing arrangement creates a political reality, and one with significant effects on the operation of the interagency policy process. The key question has to do with the role of the JCS. The position of the Chairman of the JCS as a named participant in National Security Council deliberations has had the effect of sanctioning the participation of JCS representatives as independent players in interagency committees of all types and levels, including those dealing with fundamental foreign and defense policy. What is worrisome in all this is not so much that it gives the Defense Department two votes in such meetings, but rather that it often creates unnecessary delays (owing to the need for clearance through the cumbersome JCS system), takes capable JCS officers away from the professional military functions that should be their primary concern, and blurs the responsibilities of JCS (and the uniformed military generally) relative to the Office of the Secretary of Defense (OSD) (and civilian authority generally). An excellent case can be made for allowing OSD alone to represent the Defense Department in interagency policy deliberations on political-military and foreign policy issues. Doing so would, among other things, undoubtedly improve JCS-OSD cooperation in some important areas, and lessen concerns that a strengthened joint staff operation might eventually threaten civilian control of the military (the so-called Prussian General Staff syndrome). In the event of fundamental disagreement between these agencies, the JCS Chairman could always elevate the issue to the National Security Council or, in his capacity as senior military adviser to the commander-in-chief, directly to the President.

As discussed earlier, the fundamental structure of the interagency system of the Reagan administration was laid out in National Security Decision Directive (NSDD) 2, issued in early 1982. This directive established three Senior Interdepartmental Groups (SIGs) covering foreign policy, defense policy, and intelligence, chaired respectively by the Deputy Secretary of State, the Deputy Secretary of Defense, and the Director of Central Intelligence; subordinate Interdepartmental Groups (IGs) reporting to them were also mandated in specific areas. Predictably, this system was stillborn. It only imitated the fragmentation of the national security bureaucracy rather than attempting to come to grips with it. Agency heads and their subordinates had few if any incentives to convene meetings of these committees or, if forced to do so, to manage them in an impartial fashion. All three SIGs remained essentially dead letters, and the secretariats assigned to them under NSDD 2 were never created. In the defense and intelligence areas, there was little activity at any level; in the foreign policy field, individual SIGs and IGs were established at different times in ad hoc fashion to deal with particular countries (such as Poland) and particular functional issues (such as strategic arms control and summit planning), but the regional IGs mandated by NSDD 2 to provide a more institutionalized framework for policy development were for the most part never created. In the absence of SIG secretariats or an effective planning staff, the work of these groups has not been adequately coordinated or integrated. Moreover, their function has generally been seen as the adjudication of agency positions and the development of a consensus view, rather than analysis of genuine strategic and policy options.

The key structural reform needed to remedy these problems is, to repeat the point made earlier, to vest NSC with chairmanship of the SIGs and other high-level interagency committees and clear authority to manage them. Beyond that, the number of such committees should be expanded, and their relationship to one another and to lower-level committees more clearly defined.

It will be well at this point simply to propose a comprehensive roster of senior interagency committees, with identification of the NSC official who would chair each of them. The following committees, to begin with, should be chaired by the National Security Adviser himself or (to the extent feasible) his deputy, with representation at the level of Deputy Secretary of State or DCI:

National Security Resources Board

Policy Review Group

Crisis Pre-Planning Group

Special Activities Review Group

The following committees should be chaired by the appropriate NSC Special Assistant (SA):

Interagency Planning Group (SA/Planning)

Operations Coordinating Group (SA/Political Affairs)

SIG for Policy Development (SA/Political Affairs)

SIG for Low Intensity Conflict (SA/Political-Military Affairs)

SIG for Arms Control (SA/Arms Control)

SIG for Defense Policy (SA/Defense Policy)

SIG for Emergency Preparedness (SA/Defense Policy)

SIG for Space Policy (SA/Defense Policy)

SIG for International Economic Policy (SA/Economic, Scientific and Technological Affairs)

SIG for Intelligence (SA/Intelligence)

This scheme represents a kind of synthesis of the simplified system put in place by Frank Carlucci with the preexisting SIG arrangement; yet in critical respects it differs significantly from both. It disestablishes the SIG for Foreign Policy, replacing it with a new SIG for Policy Development as well as an Operations Coordinating Group (OCG)—essentially a version of the Eisenhower-era Operations Coordinating Board. These groups, both chaired by the NSC Special Assistant for Political Affairs, would have responsibility for the development and implementation of policy on the broad spectrum of political-military and foreign policy issues. The SIG for Policy Development would work closely with the Interagency Planning Group, which would be charged with longer-range (beyond one year) planning on national security issues generally. The OCG would work closely with the Crisis Pre-Planning Group (CPPG), which would retain operational as well as policy responsibilities for specific crisis situations, and with regionally and functionally oriented Interdepartmental Groups (IGs). The CPPG, the Special Activities Review Group (for covert action), and perhaps the Interagency Planning Group would report to the National Security Planning Group (NSPG).[4] The other SIG-level committees would report to the National Security Council, where necessary through the Policy Review Group.

It should not be necessary to discuss at length the higher-level committees mentioned above, which (with the exception of a National Security Resources Board) are currently in existence in some form. The Policy Review Group (PRG), a creation of the Carlucci NSC, is a useful mechanism for dealing with contentious issues of all kinds that cannot be resolved at the SIG level. This group can also serve as the locus for what was described earlier as short-term planning—that is, for handling pressing issues of a noncrisis character that require quick resolution at a high level. These would include various congressional actions, declaratory or public diplomacy approaches to unanticipated international events (such as the Daniloff episode, the Korean Air Lines shootdown, and the like), and certain kinds of arms control issues.[5]

One of the key defining features of the individual SIGs proposed here is their differing memberships. The SIG for Policy Development would include representatives only of State (the Under Secretary of State for Political Affairs), OSD (the Under Secretary of Defense for Policy), and NSC. The Interagency Planning Group would include representatives from a wider range of agencies, including JCS and (probably) Treasury. The operationally oriented CPPG and OCG would frequently function at the Assistant (rather than Under) Secretary level, and hence would tend to vary in membership according to the issues involved. The SIG for Low Intensity Conflict, while primarily policy-oriented, will inevitably become heavily involved in the sorting out of bureaucratic disputes, and should therefore almost certainly include JCS as well as OSD, State, and CIA; smaller agencies such as AID and USIA should probably be represented as well. The SIG for Defense Policy would include OSD, JCS, and NSC (though not State), and where appropriate OMB. The SIG for Arms Control would include OSD (but not JCS), State, and ACDA. The SIGs for Space Policy, International Economic Policy, Emergency Preparedness, and Intelligence would each include agencies not otherwise normally involved in the NSC system.

To elaborate in detail the structure of the interagency system at lower levels is not necessary and would take us too far afield. But several points should be made. First, it is essential that the SIG-level committees discussed above be supported by active IGs with well-defined mandates and real institutional continuity. Second, IGs need not be chaired by the NSC in all or even most cases, but NSC chairmanship should always be an option in areas of particular contentiousness or policy sensitivity.[6] Third, IGs should be understood to have a critical role in the implementation of policy. This is particularly true in the case of regionally oriented IGs. These IGs, though reporting both to the SIG for Policy Development and the Operations Coordinating Group, should be seen primarily as a mechanism for the planning, coordination, and implementation of policy at the operational level, and not as a vehicle for the development of strategic-level policy, as has generally been the case in the past. It is also important to emphasize again the importance of ensuring that such groups bring a genuine regional focus to policy, rather than serving merely as forums for the handling of policy issues narrowly focused on one or a few individual countries.

Some further remarks may be in order regarding the SIG for Defense Policy. There can be no doubt that the Pentagon's lack of enthusiasm for the defense SIG established by NSDD 2 had much to do with the role this document assigned the State Department and the intelligence community in the development of defense policy. In fact, to the extent that the NSC is recognized as the institutional guardian of national strategy in the largest sense, there is little need for participation in such a committee by State Department representatives, and no justification at all for a role for the DCI. The real utility of a SIG for Defense Policy is that it provides a mechanism for the orderly handling of fundamental questions of defense resources and strategy that today are too frequently addressed haphazardly and without adequate national-level review. There should probably be at least two standing IGs reporting to this committee: one for defense resources, chaired by NSC and including OMB representation, and one for strategy, chaired by NSC or OSD. The IG for strategy could have responsibility, among other things, for reviewing major defense programs from a strategic perspective, for reviewing and developing new strategic concepts or approaches (for example, the Navy's "Maritime Strategy"), and for reviewing annual defense policy guidelines and public and congressional presentations of strategic issues.

Regarding the proper management of the interagency system, the first and most fundamental point, to repeat what was said earlier, is that the NSC must have general authority over the structure and operating procedures of the NSC system as a whole. Specifically, it must have the right to establish and disestablish SIGs and IGs, to designate chairmen of these committees, to control representation by the agencies, and to control the dissemination of information relating to committee deliberations. It must also be empowered to ensure that the committees act as a vehicle for the development of policy options for presidential decision, not as a forum for agency horse-trading and bureaucratic consensus formation. Policy documents prepared by the interagency committees should be structured to reflect the nature of the issue under consideration and the requirements for higher-level decision; they should not simply report agency positions. Where agency representatives prove unwilling or unable to prepare papers fairly representing the issues, the NSC should be understood to have the prerogative to recast them so as to include missing options or rationales.

If the search for interagency consensus is a danger to the policy development process, it is fatal in the area of policy implementation. Much of the paralysis that has recently afflicted the U.S. government in contentious areas such as arms control reflects the extension of the requirement for consensus to the operational and even tactical levels of bureaucratic activity. This is something that is particularly apt to happen in a system marked by ambiguous, inconsistent, or shifting policy at the strategic level; yet it is an ever-present danger where agencies have persistent differences of outlook and a lack of familiarity or trust among working-level personnel. In addition, the impulse toward consensus in implementation also reflects the bureaucratic (and perhaps also peculiarly American) tendency to avoid the assigning of clear personal responsibility for failure. A good case can be made for greatly increasing the responsibility and accountability of specific individuals and agencies for the implementation of national security policy generally. Operationally oriented NSC committees such as the OCG and the CPPG could be used as vehicles for moving the system as a whole in this direction.

Finally, some remarks may be made concerning the management of the presidential decision process. The President has available to him a number of vehicles for the formulation and dissemination of administration decisions on national security issues. At one extreme, presidential decisions can be conveyed orally and informally to a few key advisers; at the other, they can be embodied in formal documents that serve as authoritative statements of national policy and as guides to bureaucratic action over a period of months, years, or even decades. Little systematic analysis seems to have been devoted to the question of the character of presidential decision documents on national security issues and their handling. This is certainly owing in part to the fact that most such documents are classified and closely held; yet enough have been released to the public (or their general contents divulged) to permit certain judgments to be formed about them.

At the present time as in the past, there is essentially only one vehicle for the formal dissemination of presidential policy decisions on national security issues, the National Security Decision Directive (NSDD).[7] No comprehensive list of Reagan administration NSDDs is available, but they number in the hundreds, and cover all of the major areas of national security policy. Although many deal with strategic issues of prime national importance, such as national military strategy (NSDD 32) or the Strategic Defense Initiative (NSDD 85 and others), some appear to be devoted to relatively minor issues or matters of transitory concern, such as the KAL shootdown (NSDD 102).[8] Generally speaking, there is little evidence of consistency in the occasion, the purpose, the format, or the specificity of NSDDs. As noted earlier, recent practice has been to compartmentalize the production and dissemination of NSDDs to a very high degree. This runs the considerable risk of creating uncertainty in the bureaucracy as to the weight of particular NSDDs and forfeiting much of the strategic perspective which should lend authoritativeness to these presidential documents. Together with the lack of attention to the implementation of NSDDs that has always been a key problem in the management of the interagency system, the result has arguably been to devalue the NSDD system generally and lessen its utility.

It would make sense to consider whether a wider range of documents ought to be available to the President for the dissemination of decisions of different types and levels of specificity and classification, with more rigorously defined formats to improve integration of presidential decision making and facilitate implementation. This seems particularly desirable in view of the possibilities only recently opened up by the computerization of information management at the White House. While a full discussion cannot be attempted here, a few suggestions may be offered. A simple yet potentially very beneficial reform might involve creating a new type of document and associated procedures for the enunciation of fundamental national policy, as distinct from more routine, limited, short-term or operationally oriented policies. The Strategic Defense Initiative is a clear example of such a policy; others might include the Maritime Strategy, a comprehensive counterterrorism policy, a space strategy for the next several decades, and the like. This document (let us call it a National Security Policy Directive) could be produced at different classification levels for dissemination to different audiences both within and outside the executive branch, so as to maximize its educational effect as well as its impact on actual policy. And it could be accompanied by a set of implementing directives that would deal comprehensively with such matters as public affairs or public diplomacy implications, intelligence requirements, supporting organizational changes, and procedures for handling and review. Under an arrangement of this sort, NSDDs could then be reserved for more routine or short-term matters requiring presidential decision. Where highly operational presidential involvement is required, as in crisis situations, yet another (probably more standardized) decision format might be developed.

COORDINATION AT THE OPERATIONAL LEVEL

Let us move to the question of interagency coordination at the operational and tactical levels. As noted earlier, this has been one of the most neglected aspects of the national security policy process, yet it is one whose importance can hardly be overestimated. What has perhaps been most neglected is the impact on national-level decision making of the institutional fragmentation and lack of communication that characterizes the national security bureaucracy outside of Washington. For to the extent that issues cannot be resolved (or new complications for policy are created) by the absence of good working relations between agencies in the field, the burdens on top-level officials in Washington—and ultimately the President—are increased. Not only that, but pressures are generated for operational intervention by the President's own staff or, especially in crisis situations, by the President himself. That the President should reserve the right to violate the bureaucratic chain of command under certain circumstances is difficult to dispute. Yet the real issue is whether it is necessary or desirable to force the President to do so simply because responsible U.S. officials in the field cannot talk to one another without checking with their superiors in Washington.

In a theoretical sense, interagency coordination in the field is effected by U.S. ambassadors in particular countries, under what has come to be known as the "country team" concept. Ambassadors, because they hold their appointment directly from the President, are supposed to be viewed as agents of the U.S. government in their country, not merely of the State Department. In practice, however, even ambassadors who are political appointees are rarely able to assert their authority effectively over representatives of agencies other than the State Department, especially the uniformed military and the intelligence community. Nor, for that matter, is it clear that it makes sense to put ambassadors in the position of taking responsibility for U.S. officials who may be engaged in sensitive activities in their countries. In any event, as noted earlier, career foreign service ambassadors tend to lack sympathy for the missions assigned to military and intelligence personnel, and frequently regard their presence as little more than an encumbrance to good relations with the host government.

Beyond this, however, is the larger and more serious problem of coordination among foreign service, military, and intelligence personnel within particular regions. There are no established mechanisms for coordination even among ambassadors within particular regions (for example, Latin America) or subregions (for example, Central America), and there is no official below Assistant or Deputy Assistant Secretary of State capable of playing the coordinating role. Worse still, there is no mechanism for coordination between State Department representatives in a region and the theater commanders of U.S. military forces. The CINCs must deal directly with the appropriate Assistant Secretary of State regarding region-wide political-military issues. Unfortunately, however, there is a considerable mismatch between the State Department's division of the world into regional bureaus and the geographical boundaries of the U.S. theater commands.

Two fundamental reforms are needed to improve the present situation. The first is to adjust the relationship between State's regional bureaus and the U.S. theater commands. The second is to create a new type of ambassador with special responsibilities for regional coordination.

With the major exception of its European bureau, which should be split in any case into separate bureaus for Western Europe and for the Soviet Union and Eastern Europe, State's regional divisions are adequate for practical purposes.[9] The unified theater commands, on the other hand, are exposed to criticism on a number of fronts, not least of which is that they are essentially wartime organizations which take little account of the peacetime diplomatic context and of the political-military issues that in practice occupy much of the attention of the CINC and his staff. Two changes in the structure of these commands would greatly facilitate operational interaction with the State Department: transfer of responsibility for the Caribbean from the Atlantic Command to Southern Command (which would then become the counterpart to State's Latin American bureau), and expansion of Central Command to include all of Africa, the Middle East, and South Asia (thus covering the areas assigned to State's African and Near East bureaus).[10]

As mentioned earlier, the State Department and the White House have long been at odds over the proper use of the presidential appointment power for ambassadors. Presidents have consistently asserted their constitutional authority in this area to award ambassadorships to persons outside the Foreign Service for essentially political reasons, while State has pushed to limit such appointments to the extent possible. More generally, State tends to contest the very notion that ambassadors are agents of the President in more than a nominal sense. It views ambassadors simply as employees of the Secretary of State who exercise their theoretical right of direct access to the President only at their own peril.

That there is merit in both sides of this argument can hardly be denied. Inexperienced political appointees in key ambassadorial slots can cause serious embarrassment if not irreparable damage to American diplomacy, and lack of clarity in an ambassador's reporting relationship to Washington can create practical problems, and on occasion an intolerable conflict of loyalties. On the other hand, as noted earlier, there is no reason in principle why political appointees cannot perform as capably as career officers, and in fact they not infrequently bring deeper knowledge and a broader perspective to the job. In addition, lacking the career orientation and loyalties of the Foreign Service, they are in a better position to rise above bureaucratic disputes or to adjudicate them on an impartial basis. Such ambassadors can serve, then, as operational counterparts to the President's immediate staff, representing a national-level perspective that transcends parochial agency concerns.

The solution to this dilemma would appear to lie in the creation of a new dual-track system for ambassadorial appointments.[11] Under such a scheme, all but perhaps ten to twenty ambassadorships would become appointments of the Secretary of State, losing their current executive-level status, and would normally go to Foreign Service officers. The remainder would be presidentially appointed, and would enjoy special status and a recognized reporting relationship to the

President and the National Security Adviser as well as the State Department. Of course, nothing would prevent a President from using these appointments to reward political associates, as in the past. But a President conscious of the need to strengthen his own role in the implementation of national security policy could use these few appointments to better advantage than the many now available to him, by targeting key countries (or international negotiations) and choosing appropriate and well-qualified individuals. Perhaps the most important use to which they might be put is to serve as a cadre of ambassadors with special regional or subregional coordinating responsibilities.

Where possible, to begin with, it would make sense to assign an ambassador of this sort to act as liaison with U.S. theater commanders, with broad responsibility for coordination of political-military issues affecting the theater as a whole. Thus, for example, U.S. ambassadors to Panama and to NATO would routinely enjoy presidential status, while the U.S. ambassador to the Republic of Korea might perform a similar role in the Pacific. In addition, subregional coordinating roles might be undertaken by presidential ambassadors in countries such as Mexico, Brazil, South Africa, Nigeria, Egypt, Poland, India, and Australia.[12] Other presidential ambassadors could be assigned to countries simply because of their general importance, especially the major West European countries, the Soviet Union, Japan, and the People's Republic of China.

Effecting operational coordination of U.S. involvement in insurgency and counterinsurgency warfare in the Third World is almost certainly the single most difficult task facing American ambassadors and military and intelligence personnel abroad. Confused agency relationships and reporting channels were a notorious problem during the years of U.S. involvement in Southeast Asia, and little fundamental progress seems to have been made in handling the current conflict in Central America. It is not clear how or whether the new unified Special Operations Command will function in low intensity conflict situations or what its relationship to the existing theater commands will be. In any event, the critical difficulties are to be found less in the military chain of command than in the relationship between U.S. military and civilian organizations both in the theater and in Washington. Technical and operational incompatibilities between agency communications systems remain a major if infrequently discussed problem. Intelligence collection and analysis in support of the operational requirements of U.S. theater commanders is another problem area, though one that has seen major improvement in recent years.[13] The truly critical area, however, is that of political-military planning and operations generally—integrating regional diplomatic and alliance considerations with military ones, coordinating security assistance and economic aid programs, and encouraging allied governments or insurgent groups to combine military efforts with effective political and civic action. Here, the absence of well established mechanisms, practices, or doctrines for operational coordination between the military, the State Department, and smaller agencies such as USIA or AID remains a serious stumbling block, and one that is generally overcome (if it is overcome at all) only through ad hoc arrangements and personal relationships.[14]

It is not evident that any single organizational reform could correct this complex of problems. But significant improvement would almost certainly result if presidential ambassadors were utilized under such circumstances with a special mandate and overall responsibility for the management of U.S. involvement in a particular country or group of countries constituting the immediate theater of conflict. If the military component of the U.S. presence were relatively extensive, such an ambassador might appropriately be drawn from the ranks of retired military officers. In any event, he would work closely with the White House as well as the State Department, and specifically with the NSC Special Assistant for Political-Military Affairs, thus ensuring timely and high-level resolution of important interagency disputes through the mechanism of the SIG for Low Intensity Conflict. It might prove desirable to establish a special working group under the SIG to provide operational guidance to the ambassador on a continuing basis; or such guidance could be provided through the normal channel of the Operations Coordinating Group and the appropriate regional IG, depending on the pace and complexity of events in the region.

AGENCY ORGANIZATION AND CULTURE

At the forefront of public discussion of the problem of presidential management of national security in recent years has been the question of the relationship between the NSC and the State Department. Unfortunately, much journalistic and academic writing on the national security policy process has badly misconceived the issue by posing a simple choice between NSC and State Department primacy in policy development.[15] At the root of this error, as argued at length above, is a failure to distinguish adequately between the strategic and operational levels of policy. Properly understood, the roles of State and NSC need not conflict, but rather should complement one another. The NSC should have primacy in—though by no means sole custody of—policy development at the strategic level; State should have primacy in policy development at the operational level in those areas falling clearly within its domain. And, needless to say, State should have a virtual monopoly on policy implementation at the level of the actual conduct of diplomacy. The real question is how both NSC and State should function so as to make the strategy-operations faultline as frictionless as possible.

One of the foremost current students of the national security policy process, though assigning to State a central role in that process that is unrealistic and undesirable, has nevertheless correctly stressed the need for substantial reform of the State Department so as to make it more responsive to presidential direction, arguing in particular that the President needs to create "centers of strength" at different levels of the State hierarchy in order to ensure greater operational effectiveness of the department in the carrying out of his policies.[16] It will be well to spell out briefly the ways in which State could be reformed so as to support the presidentially centered NSC system that is proposed in the present study.

There can be little doubt, to begin with, that much of the reason for the State Department's notorious recalcitrance to presidential direction over many years has to do with the shallow and tenuous nature of the control exercised over the department by presidential appointees. Foreign Service Officers have regularly occupied most key positions in the department below the level of Deputy Secretary, including the Under Secretary for Political Affairs, the Under Secretary for Management, the regional Assistant and Deputy Assistant Secretaries, and the Executive Secretary, who controls the flow of paper to the Secretary of State. Where such jobs have gone to political appointees, these outsiders have frequently found themselves cut out of important decisions, starved for staff and office space, and subjected to other forms of psychological warfare by the Foreign Service establishment. There is every justification for a President to attempt to impose a level of political control on State that is taken for granted in most other government agencies. In particular, the Secretary of State should be strongly urged to accept loyal presidential appointees in the key "seventh floor" positions—above all, the Under Secretaries for Political Affairs and Management, and most if not all of the regional Assistant Secretaries. More Deputy Assistant positions in critical areas could also be reserved for political appointees than has generally been the case in the past.

As far as the organization of the State Department is concerned, there are three key changes that would be relatively easy to effect and would make a large difference in the functioning of the department and in the prospects for political control of it. These are: (1) expansion of the Executive Secretariat into a Policy Coordination Staff under the Under Secretary for Political Affairs, (2) creation of new Under Secretary positions for Political-Military Affairs and Economic, Scientific, and Technological Affairs, and (3) strengthening of the staffs and line authority of the Under Secretaries.

The Under Secretaries of the State Department are notorious for their lack of authority, ill-defined responsibilities, and frequent underemployment. In general, Assistant Secretaries of at least the more important bureaus are more powerful figures, with direct access to the Secretary and the White House. Paradoxically, the Under Secretaries often play a more operational role than Assistant Secretaries, representing the department or the government on high-level diplomatic missions abroad rather than playing a central role in the development of broad national policy. It would seem to make eminent sense to reverse this relationship. The Under Secretaries should be integral to the line organization of the department, and should have special responsibility for the functional integration of policy within the department as well as for representing State in SIG-level NSC committees in their policy area. By contrast, as suggested earlier, the Assistant Secretaries should devote themselves primarily to operational planning and implementation of nationally approved policies within their respective regions.

The principal motive for all of the changes suggested here would be to strengthen policy integration at top levels of the department, in support of a stronger strategic planning effort at the national level. Perhaps the most important single measure toward this end is the amalgamation of the Executive Secretariat and the staff of the Under Secretary for Political Affairs into a single unit that would function within the State Department in some respects the way the NSC staff functions with respect to the bureaucracy as a whole.[17] In virtue of this office's day-to-day control of the mechanisms of intradepartmental coordination, it would be a potent instrument for ensuring genuine political control of the department by the Secretary as well as for countering the centrifugal tendencies of the regional bureaus and enhancing policy integration. The Policy Coordination Staff could be headed by a Deputy Under Secretary for Political Affairs. Another Deputy Under Secretary for Political Affairs could manage the Policy Planning Staff. Such an arrangement would have the great merit of establishing clear organizational relationships among all key players on State's seventh floor, and of linking policy development and policy planning in a fashion parallel to the NSC staff. The director of the Policy Planning Staff would serve as principal staff officer to the Under Secretary for the Interagency Planning Group proposed earlier; the director of the Policy Coordination Staff would serve as his principal staff officer for the SIG for Policy Development, and could also act as State's representative to the interagency Operations Coordinating Group.[18]

However the Under Secretary role is defined, there can be little doubt that the current responsibilities assigned these positions need readjustment. At a minimum, the current Under Secretaries for Economic Affairs and for Security Assistance, Science, and Technology should be replaced by an Under Secretary for Economic, Scientific, and Technological Affairs and an Under Secretary for Political-Military Affairs. The Under Secretary for Political-Military Affairs would have roughly the same core area of responsibility as the NSC Special Assistant for Political-Military Affairs—low intensity conflict, security assistance, and alliance management. In addition, he might be given the leading role within State in the development of arms control policy.

Other organizational changes at State would require the creation of new presidential-level positions and thus congressional approval. One such change has been mentioned already—the splitting up of the current European bureau (EUR) into a bureau for West European Affairs and one for Soviet and East European Affairs. This would reduce the disproportionate influence of EUR within the department, while at the same time facilitating a more global approach to dealing with the Soviet imperium.

Other major reforms might involve a redefinition of the relationship between State and the smaller foreign affairs agencies, especially ACDA and USIA. A full discussion of this complex topic cannot be attempted here. For political reasons, it would no doubt be extremely difficult if not impossible to abolish the Arms Control and Disarmament Agency or to alter in significant ways its bureaucratic charter. Yet few feel this agency can or should play a leading role in interagency deliberations on arms control, and there is little evidence that it has done so in the past. Instead, it simply compounds the difficulty of formulating and coordinating government-wide policies in this sensitive and contentious area. In the event of the creation of an Under Secretary for Political-Military Affairs who had overall responsibility for arms control policy at State, it might make sense to consider altering ACDA's relationship to State so as to give it a more clearly secondary or operational role—for example, for the preparation and conduct of international negotiations on arms control, or for verification and compliance issues.[19]

As regards USIA, a strong argument can certainly be made for reintegration of much or all of that agency with the State Department, and doing so might be politically feasible. As was indicated earlier, the main argument in favor of an independent USIA is the lack of interest the State Department has traditionally shown in the public diplomacy mission. Yet the penalty that is paid for relegating public diplomacy to second-class status institutionally has proven a severe one, and it is by no means evident that, given sufficient organizational and personal incentives, State could not be induced to do the job. An approach that would seem to make sense would involve the creation of a new Under Secretary of State for Public Diplomacy, with authority over State's existing bureaus of Public Affairs, International Communications and Information Policy, Human Rights and Humanitarian Affairs, and a new bureau of International Programs, which would have policy responsibilities in the areas of international information, international political affairs, and educational and cultural affairs. The Voice of America, though nominally a bureau of USIA, is in fact virtually autonomous, and could easily be made a separate agency. USIA (together with its overseas counterpart, the United States Information Service) would then become essentially an operational arm of the State Department for the administration of the various programs currently under its control.[20]

Some brief remarks may be added about the organization of the Defense Department. It is much too soon to assess the impact of the recent legislation reforming the JCS, or to speculate about the likely evolution of the relationship between the JCS and OSD in the coming years. In particular, it is not clear whether or to what extent the JCS will develop greater competence and organizational capability in dealing with fundamental issues of military strategy, and hence to what extent OSD should try to compete with the JCS in this area. But it is probably safe to say that any serious effort to improve the quality of strategic thinking in the Defense Department will require the active collaboration of the JCS and OSD, and some institutional adjustments in the way both of these organizations operate.

OSD's organizational weaknesses in the area of political-military policy broadly understood are similar in important respects to those of State. The Under Secretary of Defense for Policy is a key figure in the Pentagon hierarchy and one with a vast range of responsibilities, yet little clearly defined line authority or personal staff support; in practice, the Assistant Secretaries for International Security Affairs (regional political-military issues) and International Security Programs (technology transfer, nuclear forces, and arms control) have tended to dominate policy in their areas. At the same time, the organizational elements most concerned with broader strategic planning—the offices of Net Assessment and Program Analysis and Evaluation—tend to exist on the bureaucratic margins, without a clear role or mandate.

One possible solution might lie in a division of the responsibilities of the Under Secretary of Defense for Policy among two new positions—an Under Secretary for Policy and Planning and an Under Secretary for Political-Military Affairs. The Under Secretary for Policy and Planning would have overall responsibility for the development of joint military strategy and its integration with U.S. national security strategy generally. Like the Under Secretary of State for Political Affairs, he could be supported by two Deputy Under Secretaries, one for longer-range strategy and planning and the other for current policy issues. The Deputy Under Secretary for Planning would have a planning staff of his own (perhaps building on the existing Defense Guidance Staff), as well as overall responsibility in the areas of intelligence, net assessment and program analysis. The Deputy Under Secretary for Policy would have broad responsibilities for current strategic and theater force issues, arms control, space policy, and emergency planning. The Under Secretary for Policy and Planning would represent the Defense Department in the SIGs for Defense Policy, Arms Control, Space, Emergency Preparedness, and Intelligence, as well as in the Interagency Planning Group.

The Under Secretary of Defense for Political-Military Affairs would be the counterpart to the NSC Special Assistant for Political-Military Affairs and the Under Secretary of State for Political-Military Affairs, but would have a wider responsibility for regional security issues generally. The Assistant Secretaries for Low Intensity Conflict and

International Security Affairs would report to him. He would represent the Defense Department in the SIGs for Policy Development and Low Intensity Conflict as well as in the Crisis Pre-Planning Group, and would have overall DOD responsibility for crisis management. A Deputy Under Secretary might also be created with operational responsibility for crisis management and policy implementation generally; this official could represent the Defense Department on the interagency Operations Coordinating Group.

It may be well to repeat here the cautionary note that was sounded at the outset of this study concerning the limited effectiveness of organizational tinkering by itself. The culture of the national security bureaucracy is as important in its behavioral impact as organization in a narrow sense. For the changes suggested here to be fully effective, then, they must be supported by a larger reform effort geared to more fundamental changes in the education, training, and career patterns of the managers of the national security agencies.

To detail such changes is beyond the scope of the present study, but it may be helpful to indicate where they are likely to prove most fruitful. Clearly, much could be done by improvement in the institutions that provide basic education and mid-career training to officers in the armed forces and to civil servants in important positions throughout the national security establishment. The nation's four war colleges should be in the forefront of education in strategic and political-military studies; in reality, they are for the most part sadly inadequate to this task.[21] Much the same, if not worse, can be said for the Defense Intelligence College and the Foreign Service Institute. In addition, though, much more could be done to educate both career and political officials on the job. The lack of institutional memory throughout the national security agencies as well as at the White House is a widely observed and lamented problem, but not one that should lead us to despair. A serious effort needs to be made to develop national-level as well as agency-specific doctrines and operating procedures that can help make up for the virtually inevitable deficiencies in educational background and cultural outlook of newcomers to the bureaucracy—and not least, political appointees.

Personnel policy is a highly complex and politically hazardous area, but one of the most promising in terms of its potential for effecting major changes in bureaucratic culture. It must suffice for present purposes simply to mention two reforms in federal personnel policy that would have a radical effect on current practices, though there is little prospect of realizing such sweeping changes. The first would be to reverse the Wriston reforms of 1954, which incorporated civil service personnel employed by the State Department into the Foreign Service. The second would be to create a new career service for senior civil servants throughout the national security agencies. The combined effect of these changes would be to weaken greatly the exclusive institutional cultures of the defense, intelligence, and foreign affairs bureaucracies and to foster a common and broader intellectual outlook among officials of these bureaucracies. In particular, by restricting the Foreign Service primarily to overseas assignments, it would reduce to more reasonable proportions the policy role of the Foreign Service within the State Department.

RETHINKING PRESIDENTIAL GOVERNANCE

One of the principal lines of argument developed in this study is that presidential management of national security affairs can and should be strengthened by a variety of institutional means. In the final analysis, however, the institution of the presidency is a fragile vehicle, and one that is highly dependent for its successful employment on the individual who occupies the office at a given moment. As noted earlier, even the best NSC structure cannot be expected to operate effectively for long if the President reveals in word or deed a lack of concern for the prerogatives of his office in the national security area or a lack of support for those in the White House who are empowered to speak in his name. A President who is determined to reorder the relationship between the White House and the bureaucracy must be prepared to do two things. The first is to establish clear ground rules affecting his relationship to his cabinet and other senior officials in the national security agencies, and to enforce those rules. The second is to assure himself of the continuing loyalty and effectiveness of his own staff, especially the National Security Adviser and the NSC.

To begin with the latter point, there is little need in the aftermath of the Iran-Contra affair to stress the potential the NSC has for causing political difficulties for the President if not properly handled. The NSC is the President's own staff, not a separate agency, and its activities reflect directly on him in a way those of other agencies do not. Presidents would be well advised to develop personal working relations not only with the National Security Adviser and his Deputy, but with NSC senior staff members as well (something that does not seem to have happened since the Kennedy administration). By the same token, they should insist on accountability for performance from the senior staff, and be prepared to dismiss these officials for incompetence or disloyalty. Failure to enforce accountability on the part of the President himself necessarily undermines the efforts of senior officials to do so throughout the bureaucracy as a whole.

Critical to the President's ability to ensure the effectiveness of his NSC is maintenance of the confidentiality of NSC operations. As argued earlier, the coherent strategic focus that is essential to the NSC's proper functioning tends to be lost in an NSC environment that is highly compartmentalized and secretive. Past experience has shown, however, that ensuring confidentiality in the White House is no easy matter; and the incentives for leaking can be expected to become increasingly strong to the extent that power shifts toward the NSC and greater emphasis is placed on national-level strategy and planning. All of this suggests that an extraordinary presidential effort would probably be required to protect the NSC staff and system from congressional and public inquiry, on the one hand, and on the other, to prevent unauthorized disclosure of sensitive information by the NSC itself.

There can be little question but that the failure of the Reagan White House to assert executive privilege relative to sensitive NSC and even presidential records during the Iran-Contra investigation was a fundamental and damaging error. Far from ensuring (as many administration critics claimed) that the airing of this material would prevent the irregular and secretive handling of sensitive policy questions by the NSC in the future, it virtually guaranteed more of the same. If Congress is serious about improving policy deliberations within the executive branch, it might begin by undertaking a full-scale review of existing legislation (especially the Freedom of Information Act) as it applies to public and congressional access to national-level documents relating to national security, with a view to restoring some measure of assured confidentiality at least at the highest levels and for the most sensitive information. Failing congressional cooperation in this endeavor, the President himself should consider developing a unilateral executive branch strategy in this area that includes avowed noncompliance with selected existing laws or with future congressional inquiries—and joining the issue at the level of constitutional confrontation.

Congressional critics who have recently attempted to blame the administration for the bulk of press leaks on national security matters seem to have forgotten that it was the Congress itself that stymied an effort by the White House in 1983 to tighten up security within the executive branch through an aggressive use of polygraphing and other measures. Even in the absence of a tough government-wide effort to crack down on leaking, however, the President himself could certainly take special steps with respect to his immediate office to discourage unauthorized disclosure of national security information. Such steps might include a strict policy of no NSC contact with media representatives except with written permission in advance from the National Security Adviser or his Deputy; polygraphing on suspicion, or perhaps routinely; and, all else failing, more drastic measures such as selective wiretapping of White House telephones. Needless to say, all such measures should be within existing legal constraints and fully advertised, with agreement to submit to them considered a condition of employment on the NSC staff.

Let us move to the question of the President's relationship to his senior national security officials. The argument was made earlier that the members of a President's cabinet cannot automatically be relied upon to make implementation of the President's agenda their first priority, and therefore that "cabinet government" is in the last analysis a fatally flawed approach to presidential governance. On the other hand, the President's senior cabinet officers in the national security area—the secretaries of State and Defense—are by tradition major political figures in any administration, enjoy high visibility not only in Washington but throughout the world, and therefore cannot be disciplined or dismissed without causing major political turmoil with potential international complications. This means that the President cannot afford the appearance or the reality of circumventing these officials, either in policy or operational matters, by having recourse to his National Security Adviser. Even a National Security Adviser whose status had been enhanced through congressional confirmation could not realistically be expected to hold his own in the face of persisting sharp disagreement and noncooperation from either Secretary. Rather, the President should see his National Security Adviser as an essential check on the autonomy of his two senior advisers and an instrument for mediating their differences on the basis of agreed national policy.

The triangular relationship between the secretaries of State and Defense and the National Security Adviser is perhaps the critical element in any NSC system, one of which the President must be conscious at all times and be prepared to adjust as circumstances require. As suggested earlier, it is almost certainly desirable for the President to accord his National Security Adviser the equivalent of cabinet rank, so as to make him a truly credible interlocutor with senior national security officials, and in particular with the secretaries of State and Defense. Yet the Adviser's status as surrogate for the President can be pressed too far. It is probably inappropriate for the Adviser to chair meetings (other than informal ones) that include the two senior secretaries, as was done during the Carter administration. At the same time, though, the Adviser should clearly take precedence over the Director of Central Intelligence and the Chairman of the Joint Chiefs. To the extent that these officials have discharged policy responsibilities within the National Security Council, they have arguably done so in response to the fundamental failure of the nation's political leadership to develop a national strategic perspective and a coherent set of policies deriving from it. To the extent that the National Security Adviser is successful in maintaining the primacy of the strategic perspective at the White House, there should be less reason for the involvement of military and intelligence professionals in its policy deliberations.

It was suggested earlier that the National Security Adviser and his staff could assume a greater role than they have had in the past in monitoring the implementation of policy and the performance of individual officials within the bureaucracy. Obviously, such a role is not likely to come to much without the President's insistence—from the very beginning of his administration—that it be tolerated by the secretaries of State and Defense. By the same token, the President should under no circumstances forego his prerogatives regarding the appointment of officials at subcabinet level, and should give all reasonable support to the White House Office of Personnel in its screening of potential candidates. In general, the President should insist on a greater degree of accountability by political appointees at both cabinet and subcabinet level than has been the case in the past. It is unrealistic to expect a cabinet member or other senior official to resign, or for the President to fire him, over every policy disagreement or failure of implementation. At a certain point, however, the visible prospering of officials who are disloyal or incompetent or both begins to be seen as a sign of administration weakness and lack of seriousness. Presidents need to be more sensitive to this dimension of presidential management of the national security policy process than they have been in the past, particularly the recent past.

Finally, to repeat another point discussed earlier, the President should lay down clear ground rules regarding the NSC and White House role in the planning and drafting of major speeches by cabinet and subcabinet officials. No effort at a restoration of presidential discipline over the bureaucracy can hope to succeed if senior officials are permitted to make pronouncements that do not conform to agreed-on national policy or to engage in public arguments with one another over fundamental policy questions. Ideally, a President should seek to develop a general understanding with his secretaries of State and Defense concerning the preferred type and nature of public appearances by these officials as well as by the President himself. It must be recognized that all such appearances are by their nature if not by choice an integral part of an administration's political impact, and should be guided by coherent public affairs or public diplomacy strategies. Here again, the President should map out a clear role for the National Security Adviser insofar as he acts as guardian of the administration's overall strategic account of itself.

Something should be said finally about the President's relationship to the Vice President with respect to national security matters. It has recently been argued that a plausible alternative to strengthening the role and authority of the NSC Adviser might be to give the Vice President a quasi-institutional responsibility for overseeing administration activities in the national security area.[22] It will be recalled that under the Reagan administration the Vice President was assigned responsibility for chairing the senior interagency crisis management committee. The apparent obsolescence of this arrangement is suggestive of one problem with any such scheme: if a matter is important enough to involve the Vice President, it is likely to be important enough to involve the President, thus making the Vice President's role superfluous. The more fundamental problem, though, is the subtle but inevitable rivalry that exists between the President and the Vice President, as indicated in the traditional reluctance of presidents to give their vice presidents any significant substantive role in their administration. This problem can be expected to be especially acute in the national security area, given the potentially dramatic political impact of international events. It seems unlikely that any President would want to commit himself in advance to carving out a role for the Vice President that might result in a diminution or constraint on his own authority and ability to make decisions.

Having said all this, it may be added that there are a number of responsibilities that might usefully be considered for the Vice President. Perhaps the most important is liaison and negotiation with the Congress. It is certainly conceivable that the President might want to take advantage of the Vice President's stature and his senatorial position to employ him as an emissary to Capitol Hill, thus enabling the President at once to signal the administration's seriousness and to avoid a commitment of his personal prestige. Secondly, the Vice President might be given some role in managing internal staff operations within the White House. Particularly if he were given a watching brief for congressional relations, it might make sense to use the Vice President to organize and chair the White House Strategy Group sketched earlier.

But perhaps the most useful role the Vice President might play lies in the area of personnel and administration. The Vice President might be given a general mandate by the President to oversee White House relations with the bureaucracy and to act as troubleshooter in the event of problems of policy discipline or personnel. Such a role could prove particularly valuable in the national security area. In delicate disputes between the National Security Adviser and the secretaries of State or Defense or other agency heads, the Vice President might be able to act as an impartial arbiter or negotiator of compromise. He might also be given a similar role in adjudicating disagreements between the White House and the agencies over presidential appointments.

Under the impact of the Iran-Contra revelations, there has been much talk of the need for "hands on" presidential management, and facile assumptions concerning the proper scope of presidential cognizance and decision have found wide acceptance. The fact of the matter is that it is totally unrealistic to expect a President to involve himself in all decisions that qualify in some sense as U.S. "policy." It is a truism among Washington insiders that foreign policy is made in State Department cables ostensibly devoted to the details of policy implementation. But it would be foolish for the President or his staff to join battle with the bureaucracy on the bureaucracy's terms. Policy devolves to the operational level only through a failure to capture it at the level of strategy. The capture of policy by strategy requires two things: the conceptualization of strategy in a form that is practically useful, and a sustained effort at giving it operational reality through monitoring its implementation and imposing penalties for failure. It is a sobering reflection that this eminently sensible management style more closely describes the Soviet than the contemporary American approach.[23] That it is not entirely alien to American practice appears from the Eisenhower and Kennedy-Johnson presidencies (although it could perhaps be said that the first of these had strategy without discipline, while the second had discipline without strategy). At all events, the alternative is not one that should affront American sensibilities, if undertaken with due regard and preparation for the resistance it is bound to encounter. There is every reason to believe that the American people will welcome a presidency that treats its constitutional responsibilities for national security with the seriousness that is warranted by the position of this nation in today's world.

Notes

Introduction

1. See *The Tower Commission Report* (New York: Bantam Books and Times Books, 1987), p. 2. The members of the Commission were former Senator John Tower, former National Security Adviser Brent Scowcroft, and former Senator and Secretary of State Edmund Muskie.

2. For a general assessment of the achievements of the Reagan administration in these respects see Lester M. Salamon and Michael S. Lund, eds., *The Reagan Presidency and the Governing of America* (Washington, DC: The Urban Institute Press, 1984).

3. A recent classified study carried out by a blue-ribbon panel under the chairmanship of former Secretary of Defense Melvin Laird described conditions at the Moscow embassy (and at the U.S. consulate in Leningrad) as a "national disgrace." Joan Mower, "Embassy Report Hit Officials," *Washington Post,* February 26, 1988.

4. Zbigniew Brzezinski, "Reagan Is Leaving an Ominous Legacy in Foreign Policy," *Washington Post,* October 5, 1986.

5. Henry A. Kissinger, "Danger at the Summit," *Newsweek,* October 13, 1986, p. 41.

6. See especially Hugh Heclo, *A Government of Strangers: Executive Politics in Washington* (Washington, DC: The Brookings Institution, 1977), and Hugh Heclo and Lester M. Salamon, eds., *The Illusion of Presidential Government* (Boulder, CO: Westview Press, 1981).

7. For a general analysis see James W. Ceaser, "The Theory of Governance of the Reagan Administration," in Salamon and Lund, *The Reagan Presidency and the Governing of America,* pp. 56–87.

8. National security has been at least as much a casualty as domestic policy, at least in recent years. See, for example, Richard Haass, *Congressional Power: Implications for American Security Policy,* Adelphi Paper

153 (London: International Institute for Strategic Studies, 1979); David M. Abshire and Ralph D. Nurnberger, eds., *The Growing Power of Congress* (Washington, DC: Georgetown Center for Strategic and International Studies, 1981); Robert J. Art, "Congress and the Defense Budget: Enhancing Policy Oversight," *Political Science Quarterly* 100 (Summer 1985), pp. 227–48; Staff Report to the Committee on Armed Services, U.S. Senate, *Defense Organization: The Need for Change* (Washington, DC: USGPO, 1985), pp. 569–611.

9. On this general issue see Morton H. Halperin, *Bureaucratic Politics and Foreign Policy* (Washington, DC: The Brookings Institution, 1974), pp. 173–95, and more recently, Martin Linsky, *Impact: How the Press Affects Federal Policy-Making* (New York: Norton, 1986). An excellent brief discussion is Michael Ledeen, "Secrets," *The National Interest* (Winter 1987/88), pp. 48–55.

10. Consider the critical remarks of I. M. Destler, *Presidents, Bureaucrats, and Foreign Policy* (Princeton: Princeton University Press, 1972), pp. 16–51. A useful comparative perspective is provided by Ezra N. Suleiman, ed., *Bureaucrats and Policy Making* (New York: Holmes and Meier, 1984).

11. A good general discussion of the importance and difficulty of organizational questions may be found in *Report of the Commission on the Organization of the Government for the Conduct of Foreign Policy,* Appendices, Vol. 4 (Washington, DC: USGPO, 1975), pp. 8–12.

12. On the President's lack of effective control of federal personnel policy see Heclo, *A Government of Strangers,* pp. 19–33, and G. Calvin Mackenzie, "The Paradox of Presidential Personnel Management," in Heclo and Salamon, *The Illusion of Presidential Government,* pp. 113–46.

13. For a general treatment see Donald J. Devine, *The Political Culture of the United States* (Boston: Little, Brown, 1972).

14. For an extended comparison of U.S. and Soviet national strategic styles or cultures see Colin S. Gray, *Nuclear Strategy and National Style* (Lanham, MD: Hamilton Press, 1986), pp. 33–96, as well as Carnes Lord, "American Strategic Culture," *Comparative Strategy* 5 (1985), pp. 269–93.

Chapter 1. The Presidency and the Problem of Bureaucracy

1. For a general account of the legislative, administrative, and budgetary functions of the contemporary presidency, see Richard M. Pious, *The American Presidency* (New York: Basic Books, 1979), pp. 176–292. For the historical and political significance of the rise of presidential as distinct from congressional governance in the United States, see Theodore J. Lowi, *The Personal President* (Ithaca and London: Cornell University Press, 1985).

2. See, for example, Louis C. Gawthrop, *Bureaucratic Behavior in the Executive Branch* (New York: The Free Press, 1969), pp. 249–60.

3. See generally Louis Fisher, "Congress and the President in the Administrative Process," in Hugh Heclo and Lester M. Salamon, eds., *The Illusion of Presidential Government* (Boulder, CO: Westview Press, 1981), pp. 21–43.

4. A good general discussion of the notion of organizational essence and its application to the national security agencies may be found in Morton H. Halperin, *Bureaucratic Politics and Foreign Policy* (Washington, DC: The Brookings Institution, 1974), pp. 28–40.

5. The point is made, for example, by Halperin, *Bureaucratic Politics and Foreign Policy,* pp. 51–54.

6. Compare the analysis of W. W. Rostow, *The United States in the World Arena* (New York: Harper and Row, 1960), pp. 497–500.

7. See, for example, Gawthrop, *Bureaucratic Behavior in the Executive Branch,* pp. 214–67, and I. M. Destler, *Presidents, Bureaucrats, and Foreign Policy* (Princeton: Princeton University Press, 1972), pp. 75–78.

8. The growing politicization of the bureaucracy and its implications are well discussed by Hugh Heclo, *A Government of Strangers: Executive Politics in Washington* (Washington, DC: The Brookings Institution, 1977), pp. 34–82.

9. This term is also borrowed from Halperin (*Bureaucratic Politics and Foreign Policy,* pp. 54–56).

10. For some pertinent remarks on this and related deficiencies in professional development in the national security agencies, see Michael Ledeen, *Grave New World* (New York: Oxford University Press, 1985), pp. 92–101, and Edward N. Luttwak, *The Pentagon and the Art of War* (New York: Simon and Schuster, 1984), pp. 157–203.

11. For what follows see especially Heclo, *A Government of Strangers,* and Laurence E. Lynn, Jr., "The Reagan Administration and the Renitent Bureaucracy," in Lester M. Salamon and Michael S. Lund, eds., *The Reagan Presidency and the Governing of America* (Washington, DC: The Urban Institute, 1984), pp. 339–79.

12. On this subject see the classic study of Richard Fenno, Jr., *The President's Cabinet* (Cambridge: Harvard University Press, 1959).

13. Dawes, the first director of the Bureau of the Budget, was interested in making a relatively limited point: "cabinet members are vice-presidents in charge of spending, and as such they are the natural enemies of the president" (quoted in Richard Neustadt, *Presidential Power* [New York: John Wiley and Son, 1961], p. 39).

14. The original Reagan DCI, William Casey, though closely associated with the President politically, also had a background in intelligence work stemming from World War II. Casey's attempt in 1981 to appoint Max Hugel, a political associate lacking any experience in intelligence, as CIA

Deputy Director for Operations was widely criticized, and foundered when questions were raised (possibly with assistance from elements in the CIA itself) about Hugel's business activities. On this episode and the question of Reagan administration control over the intelligence community, see Morton Kondracke, "Casey's CIA," *The New Republic,* November 28, 1983, pp. 13–18. It should be noted that Casey's tenure began with a rejection of the radical reforms of the CIA urged by the presidential transition team. See generally John Ranelagh, *The Agency: The Rise and Decline of the CIA* (New York: Simon and Schuster, 1986), pp. 656–75.

15. Haig's view of the Foreign Service and of the role of the State Department in national security policy are apparent in his memoir *Caveat: Realism, Reagan, and Foreign Policy* (New York: Macmillan, 1984), pp. 57–63. Conservative unhappiness with the performance of the State Department in the Reagan era set in quickly; see, for example, James T. Hackett, "Regaining Control of the State Department," in Stuart M. Butler, Michael Sanera, and W. Bruce Weinrod, eds., *Mandate for Leadership II: Continuing the Conservative Revolution* (Washington, DC: The Heritage Foundation, 1984), pp. 449–52. On the Defense Department see, for example, the (somewhat caricatured) account of Strobe Talbott, *Deadly Gambits* (New York: Alfred A. Knopf, 1984), pp. 15–18.

16. See John Helmer, "The Presidential Office: Velvet Fist in an Iron Glove," in Heclo and Salamon, *The Illusion of Presidential Government,* pp. 45–81.

17. See James W. Ceaser, "The Theory of Governance of the Reagan Administration," in Salamon and Lund, *The Reagan Presidency and the Governing of America,* pp. 61–63; Erwin C. Hargrove and Michael Nelson, *Presidents, Politics, and Policy* (Baltimore: The Johns Hopkins University Press, 1984), pp. 87–127; and Paul J. Quirk, "Presidential Competence," in Michael Nelson, ed., *The Presidency and the Political System* (Washington, DC: Congressional Quarterly Press, 1984), pp. 133–55.

18. A good analysis is available in the report on presidential management of a panel of the National Academy of Public Administration, *A Presidency for the 1980s,* in Heclo and Salamon, *The Illusion of Presidential Government,* pp. 299–345.

19. See the account of Chester A. Newland, "Executive Office Policy Apparatus: Enforcing the Reagan Agenda," in Salamon and Lund, *The Reagan Presidency and the Governing of America,* pp. 135–80.

20. Richard Neustadt's *Presidential Power* (originally published in 1961) is the classic statement of the now conventional approach. Noteworthy examples of the newer approach are Pious, *The American Presidency,* and Hargrove and Nelson, *Presidents, Politics, and Policy.* Of particular interest for its argument concerning the preeminence of presidential power in national security affairs is Jeffrey Tulis, "The Two Constitutional Presiden-

cies," in Michael Nelson, ed., *The Presidency and the Political System* (Washington, DC: Congressional Quarterly Press, 1984), pp. 59–86.

21. Harvey C. Mansfield, Jr., "The Ambivalence of Executive Power," in Joseph M. Bessette and Jeffrey Tulis, eds., *The Presidency in the Constitutional Order* (Baton Rouge: Louisiana State University Press, 1981), pp. 314–33.

22. Edie N. Goldenberg, "The Permanent Government in an Era of Retrenchment and Redirection," in Salamon and Lund, *The Reagan Presidency and the Governing of America,* pp. 381–413.

23. See, for example, Henry A. Kissinger, *The Necessity for Choice* (New York: Harper and Row, 1960), pp. 169–75.

24. That the practice of management by consensus *within* agencies has proven a recipe for stalemate and paralysis is a commonplace of the literature dealing with the State Department.

25. The notion of presidential strategy is conspicuous by its absence in the literature on the presidency. An unusual analysis of the political leadership of recent presidents in terms of an overall strategic concept is provided by Hargrove and Nelson, *Presidents, Politics, and Policy,* pp. 87–127.

Chapter 2. National Security and the National Security Agencies

1. Exceptions include Keith C. Clark and Laurence J. Legere, eds., *The President and the Management of National Security* (New York: Praeger, 1969), pp. 132–38, and Philip Odeen, "National Security Policy Integration:" Report of a Study Requested by the President under the Auspices of the Presidential Reorganization Project—September, 1979, in *The National Security Adviser: Role and Accountability,* Hearings before the Committee on Foreign Relations, U.S. Senate, 96th Cong., 2d Sess. (Washington, DC: USGPO, 1980), pp. 106–28.

2. Gen. Paul F. Gorman, former commander-in-chief of the U.S. Southern Command, has been reported as saying that he does not believe the CIA was capable of mounting or supporting a successful insurgency. See James LeMoyne, "Before the Latest Contra Setback, U.S., in Review, Found the Outlook Poor," *New York Times,* December 15, 1986, as well as Gorman's testimony on this question in *National Security Strategy,* Hearings before the Committee on Armed Services, U.S. Senate, 100th Cong., 1st Sess. (Washington, DC: USGPO, 1987), pp. 783–88.

3. For the struggle between State and the White House over Central American policy in the first Reagan term, see Barry Rubin, *Secrets of State* (New York/Oxford: Oxford University Press, 1985), pp. 218–31. For the problems in interagency coordination, see Gen. Paul F. Gorman, "Command, Control, Communications and Intelligence: USCINCSO's Perspective, 1983–85," paper delivered at a conference at the National Defense University, June 25, 1986.

4. See Gordon Humphrey and Jack Kemp, "Pivotal Post in Pakistan," *Washington Times,* March 2, 1987, and John Walcott and Tim Carrington, "CIA Resisted Proposal to Give Afghan Rebels U.S. Stinger Missiles," *Wall Street Journal,* February 16, 1988.

5. "Report on Terror Calls U.S. Unready," *New York Times,* September 29, 1986. See Joint Low Intensity Conflict Project Final Report, Vol. I, *Analytical Review of Low Intensity Conflict,* United States Army Training and Doctrine Command, Fort Monroe, Virginia, 1 August 1986, as well as Department of Defense, *Proceedings of the Low Intensity Warfare Conference,* mimeo, January 14–15, 1986.

6. *Discriminate Deterrence: Report of the Commission on Integrated Long-Term Strategy* (Washington, DC: USGPO, January 1988), pp. 13–22.

7. On U.S. special operations forces generally see Frank R. Barnett, B. Hugh Tovar, and Richard H. Shultz, *Special Operations in US Strategy* (Washington, DC: National Defense University Press, 1984), and John M. Collins, *U.S. and Soviet Special Operations,* Congressional Research Service, Library of Congress, December 23, 1986.

8. See Conference Report on S. 2638, "National Defense Authorization Act for FY 1987," in *Congressional Record—House,* October 14, 1986, pp. 10193–94. The amendment defines special operations activities as including direct action, strategic reconnaissance, unconventional warfare, foreign internal defense (i.e., counterinsurgency), civil affairs, psychological operations, counterterrorism, humanitarian assistance, search and rescue, and other activities as directed by the President or the Secretary of Defense. See also "Special Forces: Can They Do the Job?" *U.S. News and World Report,* November 3, 1986, pp. 36–42.

9. For the continuing struggle over implementation of the new legislation see, for example, James M. Dorsey, "President Expected to Settle Rift on Key Defense Position," *Washington Times,* April 16, 1987, and Stephen Engleberg, "Tug and Pull over a Vacant Chart," *New York Times,* December 31, 1987.

10. See especially Harry G. Summers, Jr., *On Strategy: A Critical Analysis of the Vietnam War* (Novato, CA: Presidio Press, 1982); Robert W. Komer, *Bureaucracy at War: U.S. Performance in the Vietnam Conflict* (Boulder, CO/London: Westview Press, 1986); and Andrew F. Krepinevich, Jr., *The Army and Vietnam* (Baltimore/London: The Johns Hopkins University Press, 1986). Major Krepinovich's important book persuasively documents the Army's inability or unwillingness to develop an effective operational approach to counterinsurgency. See Alvin H. Bernstein, "Vietnam: A Military Post-Mortem," *The National Interest* (Winter 1987/8), pp. 79–86.

11. For a critical review of Grenada and other recent operations, see Richard A. Gabriel, *Military Incompetence: Why the American Military Doesn't Win* (New York: Hill and Wang, 1985).

12. See *Report of the DOD Commission on Beirut International Airport Terrorist Act* ("Long Report"), December 20, 1983. For the intra-administration dispute over the use of force see, for example, "Shultz vs. Weinberger— When to Use U.S. Power," *U.S. News and World Report,* December 24, 1984, pp. 20–21.

13. See, for example, the remarks of Gen. Paul F. Gorman, "Low Intensity Conflict: American Dilemma," in *Proceedings of the Low Intensity Warfare Conference,* pp. 26–29. Gorman stresses the value for Third World military establishments of such rudimentary items as durable boot soles and canned rations, as well as inexpensive capabilities such as transport aircraft adapted for easy maintenance and use under rugged conditions.

14. See especially Strobe Talbott, *Deadly Gambits: The Reagan Administration and the Stalemate in Nuclear Arms Control* (New York: Alfred A. Knopf, 1984).

15. See, for example, Walter Pincus and Don Oberdorfer, "More SALT II Struggles Looming," *Washington Post,* April 27, 1986; Leslie H. Gelb, "The Resurgent Shultz: How a Comeback Is Made," *New York Times,* July 21, 1986; and David Ignatius, "Maneuvering to Legalize SDI Tests," *Washington Post,* February 6, 1987.

16. See the account of John Newhouse, *Cold Dawn: The Story of SALT* (New York: Holt, Rinehart and Winston, 1973), as well as James E. Dougherty, *JCS Reorganization and U.S. Arms Control Policy,* National Security Paper 5 (Cambridge, MA/Washington, DC: Institute for Foreign Policy Analysis, 1986).

17. Particularly instructive is the contrast between the unconditional JCS endorsement of the treaty on intermediate-range nuclear forces (INF) signed in December 1987 and its highly conditional endorsement of SALT I. John H. Cushman, "Pentagon Asks No New Weapons in Return for Backing Arms Pact," *New York Times,* January 24, 1988.

18. A thorough, authoritative, and critical account of the Reykjavik summit and the events surrounding it is available in *The Reykjavik Process: Preparation for and Conduct of the Iceland Summit and Its Implications for Arms Control Policy,* Report of the Defense Policy Panel, U.S. House of Representatives, Committee on Armed Services, December 15, 1986. Among the report's conclusions: "The arms control process has been captured by a small group of people not representative of the interagency community. From the drafting of the July 25 letter through the Vienna follow-up to Reykjavik, all aspects of arms control have been monopolized by a group which has excluded the military, and often the Secretary of Defense and the Arms Control and Disarmament Agency, from real decision-making. Evidence includes the exclusive committee which drafted the July letter, the makeup of the Reykjavik delegation which consisted of sixty-seven State Department officials and two Defense Department representa-

tives, and the composition of the inner working group in Reykjavik which included the civilian DOD representative but not the military. . . . When the JCS finally had a chance after the mini-summit to consider the implications of all that had been proposed, the Administration ignored their warnings and went ahead with negotiating instructions to Geneva. A thorough JCS study was commissioned after Reykjavik, but final results are not expected until early 1987—a full three months after the proposals were tabled" (pp. 19–20).

19. See Goldwater-Nichols Department of Defense Reorganization Act of 1986—Conference Report, *Congressional Record—Senate,* September 16, 1986, pp. S12651–60; *Defense Organization: The Need for Change,* Staff Report to the Committee on Armed Services, U.S. Senate (Washington, DC: USGPO, 1985); and *Armed Forces Journal,* October 1985 (Extra), which reprints the executive summary of the committee staff report together with the text of six speeches delivered in the Senate on these issues by Senators Sam Nunn and Barry Goldwater. See also *A Quest for Excellence,* Final Report by the President's Blue Ribbon Commission on Defense Management (Washington, DC: USGPO, June 1986).

20. Representative of this literature are Richard A. Gabriel and Paul L. Savage, *Crisis in Command: Mismanagement in the Army* (New York: Hill and Wang, 1978); Summers, *On Strategy: A Critical Analysis of the Vietnam War;* Asa A. Clark IV, Peter W. Chiarelli, Jeffrey S. McKittrick, and James W. Reed, eds., *The Defense Reform Debate: Issues and Analysis* (Baltimore/London: The Johns Hopkins University Press, 1984); Edward N. Luttwak, *The Pentagon and the Art of War* (New York: Simon and Schuster; 1984); and Arthur T. Hadley, *The Straw Giant* (New York: Random House, 1986).

21. The CINCs are the operational commanders of U.S. military forces. There are currently eight unified commands and two specified commands: Atlantic Command, Pacific Command, European Command, Southern Command (Latin America), Central Command (Middle East), Special Operations Command, Space Command, Transportation Command, Strategic Air Command, and Forces Command. In the past, each command has tended to be dominated by a particular service; the creation over the last several years of new unified commands for special operations, space, and transportation represents a movement away from this tradition.

22. See particularly the remarks of Senators Nunn and Goldwater in *Armed Forces Journal,* October 1985 (Extra), pp. 24–27. Other critical accounts of the OSD role may be found in Victor H. Krulak, *Organization for National Security* (Washington, DC: United States Strategic Institute, 1983), pp. 53–102, and Archie D. Barrett, *Reappraising Defense Organization* (Washington, DC: National Defense University Press, 1983), pp. 191–239. The Goldwater-Nichols bill mandates a series of studies of the OSD

role and internal organization with a view to preparing additional legislation to support the current reforms.

23. Samuel P. Huntington, *The Soldier and the State: The Theory and Politics of Civil-Military Relations* (Cambridge, MA/London: The Belknap Press, 1957), pp. 80–97 and passim.

24. Two of the four directors of the State Department's bureau of Political-Military Affairs during the Reagan administration have been serving military officers. Active duty military officers of senior rank have headed the NSC defense policy group through much of the administration, two Navy admirals and an Army general have served as NSC deputy, and two of these officers (Admiral John Poindexter and General Colin Powell) as National Security Adviser. The recent nomination of an Army general as Director of the Arms Control and Disarmament Agency has caused some unhappiness in Congress on both sides of the aisle.

25. Consider, for example, the remarks of Philip A. Odeen, "Organizing for National Security," *International Security* 5 (Summer 1980), pp. 118–21.

26. See, for example, Huntington, *The Soldier and the State,* pp. 315–44.

27. For a recent overview of the foreign policy establishment, see Andrew L. Steigman, *The Foreign Service of the United States: First Line of Defense* (Boulder, CO: Westview Press, 1985). A sharply critical account from a liberal perspective may be found in John Franklin Campbell, *The Foreign Affairs Fudge Factory* (New York: Basic Books, 1971). See also Smith Simpson, *Anatomy of the State Department* (Boston: Houghton Mifflin, 1967); I. M. Destler, *Presidents, Bureaucrats, and Foreign Policy* (Princeton: Princeton University Press, 1972), pp. 154–90; Donald P. Warwick, *A Theory of Public Bureaucracy: Politics, Personality, and Organization in the State Department* (Cambridge: Harvard University Press, 1975); *Report of the Commission on the Organization of the Government for Foreign Policy* (Washington, DC: USGPO, 1975), pp. 39–51 and passim; and Martin Weil, *A Pretty Good Club* (New York: Norton, 1978).

28. See, for example, James L. McCamy, *Conduct of the New Diplomacy* (New York: Harper and Row, 1964), and Andrew M. Scott, *The Revolution in Statecraft: Intervention in an Age of Interdependence* (Durham, NC: Duke Press Policy Studies Paperback, 1982; originally published 1965).

29. See, for example, Roger Morris, "Rooting for the Other Team: Clientism in the Foreign Service," *Washington Monthly,* November 1973, pp. 37–45.

30. Consider the complaints of William I. Bacchus, *Staffing for Foreign Affairs* (Princeton: Princeton University Press, 1985), pp. 58–68, as well as Michael Ledeen, *Grave New World* (New York: Oxford University Press,

1985), pp. 92–101. Insufficient attention has been given to analyzing the bureaucratic culture or ideology of the State Department. Still relevant is Andrew M. Scott, "The Department of State: Formal Organization and Informal Culture," *International Studies Quarterly* 13 (March 1969), pp. 1–18.

31. For an elaboration of this argument, see Richard Pipes, *Survival Is Not Enough* (New York: Simon and Schuster, 1984), pp. 273–77.

32. Much of the relevant material is now available in Brian D. Dailey and Patrick J. Parker, eds., *Soviet Strategic Deception* (Lexington, MA/Toronto: Lexington Books, 1987).

33. Perhaps the most egregious example is the history of the new U.S. embassy in Moscow; see, for example, David B. Ottaway, "Moscow Embassy's Leaks, Gaps and Bugs," *Washington Post,* October 21, 1986. For State's resistance to a greater FBI role in controlling the foreign intelligence presence in the United States, see Bill Gertz, "Bickering Finally Ends with Naming of Nolan," *Washington Times,* July 21, 1986.

34. These aspects of the Foreign Service have become a target of conservative reformers in the last several years. See James T. Hackett, "Regaining Control of the State Department," in *Mandate for Leadership II* (Washington, DC: The Heritage Foundation, 1984), pp. 447–50.

35. A good discussion of these issues may be found in Laurence H. Silberman, "Toward Presidential Control of the State Department," *Foreign Affairs* 57 (Spring 1979), pp. 872–93.

36. Recent treatments of this subject are Richard F. Staar, ed., *Public Diplomacy: USA Versus USSR* (Stanford: Hoover Institution Press, 1986), and Carnes Lord, "In Defense of Public Diplomacy," *Commentary* (April 1984), pp. 42–50.

37. For a recent discussion of the history and role of U.S. international broadcasting, see James L. Tyson, *U.S. International Broadcasting and National Security* (New York: National Strategy Information Center, 1983).

38. See, for example, Joshua Muravchik, "Exporting Democracy: A Progress Report," *The American Spectator* (November 1985), pp. 19–21.

39. See especially Gifford D. Malone, "Functioning of Diplomatic Organs," in Staar, *Public Diplomacy,* pp. 124–41.

40. On the origins of the CIA and the history of the agency generally, see John Ranelagh, *The Agency: The Rise and Decline of the CIA* (New York: Simon and Schuster, 1986).

41. A comprehensive overview is available in Jeffrey T. Richelson, *The U.S. Intelligence Community* (Cambridge, MA: Ballinger, 1985).

42. See especially Roy Godson, ed., *Intelligence Requirements for the 1980's: Analysis and Estimates* (Washington, DC: National Strategy Informa-

tion Center, 1980), pp. 1–8, 49–82, and John Prados, *The Soviet Estimate: U.S. Intelligence and Russian Military Strength* (New York: Dial Press, 1982).

43. That this disposition has continued to exist under the Reagan administration is apparent from Michael R. Gordon, "C.I.A., Evaluating Soviet Threat, Often Is Not So Grim as Pentagon," *New York Times,* July 16, 1986.

44. The comment is by Leo Cherne, former chairman of the President's Foreign Intelligence Advisory Board, in Roy Godson, ed., *Intelligence Requirements for the 1980's: Intelligence and Policy* (Lexington, MA/Toronto: Lexington Books, 1986), p. 34.

45. On the intelligence-policy relationship see particularly Godson, *Intelligence Requirements for the 1980's: Analysis and Estimates,* pp. 11–45; Hans Heymann, "Intelligence/Policy Relationships," in Alfred C. Maurer, Marion B. Tunstall, and James M. Keagle, eds., *Intelligence: Policy and Process* (Boulder, CO/London: Westview Press, 1985), pp. 57–66; and Godson, *Intelligence Requirements for the 1980's: Intelligence and Policy,* pp. 1–40.

46. See Roy Godson, ed., *Intelligence Requirements for the 1980's: Clandestine Collection* (Washington, DC: National Strategy Information Center, 1982), especially pp. 101–26, 161–95.

47. See especially Roy Godson, ed., *Intelligence Requirements for the 1980's: Counterintelligence* (Washington, DC: National Strategy Information Center, 1980). For recent efforts that have been undertaken by Congress and by the National Security Council staff to improve counterintelligence, see *Congressional Record—Senate,* September 24, 1986, pp. S13568–70.

48. See Godson, *Intelligence Requirements for the 1980's: Analysis and Estimates,* pp. 123–59, and Dailey and Parker, *Soviet Strategic Deception,* especially pp. xvi–xvii.

49. *National Security Planning and Budgeting,* Report of the President's Blue Ribbon Commission on Defense Management (Washington, DC: USGPO, June 1986), pp. 12–13.

50. For a general account (with particular emphasis on food and trade issues) see I. M. Destler, *Making Foreign Economic Policy* (Washington, DC: The Brookings Institution, 1980).

51. See Roger W. Robinson, Jr., "Soviet Cash and Western Banks," *The National Interest* (Summer 1986), pp. 37–44, and "East-West Financial Security," *Global Affairs* (Fall 1987), pp. 86–103.

52. See especially Central Intelligence Agency, *Soviet Acquisition of Western Technology: An Update* (Washington, DC, September 1985).

53. See, for example, Roderick L. Vawter, *Industrial Mobilization: The Relevant History* (Washington, DC: National Defense University Press,

1983); Hardy L. Merritt and Luther F. Carter, eds., *Mobilization and the National Defense* (Washington, DC: National Defense University Press, 1985); Comptroller General of the United States, *Continuity of the Federal Government in a Critical National Emergency—A Neglected Necessity,* Report to the Congress, Washington, DC, June 1978; and Federal Emergency Management Agency, *Report for the Senate and House Committees on Armed Services on the National Civil Defense Program,* Washington, DC, July 1986.

54. Recent assessments of the bureaucratic state of play within the U.S. space program may be found in Philip M. Boffey, "Rebuilt NASA 'on Way Back' as an Array of Doubts Persist," *New York Times,* December 29, 1986; John Noble Wilford, "Threat to Nation's Lead in Space Is Seen in Lack of Guiding Policy," *New York Times,* December 30, 1986; Kathy Sawyer, "U.S. Faces Self-Doubt, Competition in Space," *Washington Post,* January 27, 1987; "White House Accused of Failing to Give NASA Sense of Mission," *Washington Post,* August 17, 1987.

55. Craig Covault, "President Signs Space Policy Backing Lunar, Mars Course," *Aviation Week and Space Technology,* January 18, 1988, pp. 14–16.

Chapter 3. The NSC and the NSC System

1. *The National Security Act of 1947,* P.L. 253, July 26, 1947 and amendments of 1949, 1953, 1958 (Washington, DC: USGPO, various years). The Director of the since defunct Office of Civil and Defense Mobilization was also a statutory member of the original NSC; this domestic emphasis has since been largely though not entirely lost. The Chairman of the Joint Chiefs of Staff and the Director of Central Intelligence (a position elevated to cabinet status under the Reagan administration) are formally designated as advisers to the NSC, but in practice they are virtually full members. Since 1975, the Director of the Arms Control and Disarmament Agency has also been a statutory adviser.

2. Some representative recent treatments are I. M. Destler, "A Job That Doesn't Work," *Foreign Policy* (Spring 1980), pp. 80–88; Alexander L. George, *Presidential Decision-Making in Foreign Policy: The Effective Use of Information and Advice* (Boulder, CO: Westview Press, 1980), pp. 191–208; *The National Security Adviser: Role and Accountability,* Hearing Before the Committee on Foreign Relations, U.S. Senate, 96th Congress, 2d session (Washington, DC: USGPO, 1980), pp. 106–28.

3. On this history see especially Paul Y. Hammond, "The National Security Council: An Interpretation and Appraisal," *American Political Science Review* 54 (December 1960), pp. 899–910 (reprinted in Alan A. Altshuler, ed., *The Politics of the Federal Bureaucracy* [New York: Dodd, Mead, 1968], pp. 140–56), and *Organization for Defense: The American Military Estab-*

lishment in the Twentieth Century (Princeton: Princeton University Press, 1961).

4. On the Truman NSC see especially the comments of Adm. Sydney W. Souers, the original Executive Secretary of the NSC, "The National Security Council under President Truman," in Sen. Henry M. Jackson, ed., *The National Security Council: Jackson Subcommittee Papers on Policy-Making at the Presidential Level* (New York: Praeger, 1965), pp. 99–110. On NSC-68 see Paul Y. Hammond, "NSC-68: Prologue to Rearmament," in Warner Schilling et al., *Strategy, Politics and Defense Budgets* (New York: Columbia University Press, 1962).

5. See Robert Cutler, "The National Security Council under President Eisenhower," in *Jackson Subcommittee Papers*, pp. 111–39, and more generally Anna Kasten Nelson, "National Security I: Inventing a Process (1945–60)," in Hugh Heclo and Lester M. Salamon, eds., *The Illusion of Presidential Government* (Boulder, CO: Westview Press, 1981), pp. 229–62.

6. The chief vehicle of this criticism was the hearings and staff reports of the Jackson subcommittee: U.S. Senate, Committee on Government Operations, Subcommittee on National Policy Machinery, *Organizing for National Security,* 3 vols. (Washington, DC: USGPO, 1961); see the selections in *Jackson Subcommittee Papers,* especially pp. 3–42. On the politics surrounding this effort see Gary W. Reichard, "The Domestic Politics of National Security," in Norman A. Graebner, ed., *The National Security: Its Theory and Practice, 1945–1960* (New York: Oxford University Press, 1986), pp. 264–66.

7. The Eisenhower presidency as a whole has been the beneficiary of a revisionist interpretation which bears directly on Eisenhower's management of national security affairs. See Fred I. Greenstein, *The Hidden-Hand Presidency: Eisenhower as Leader* (New York: Basic Books, 1982), and for the NSC in particular, Anna Kasten Nelson, "The 'Top of Policy Hill': President Eisenhower and the National Security Council," *Diplomatic History* 7 (Fall 1983), pp. 307–26, and Phillip G. Henderson, "Advice and Decision: The Eisenhower National Security Council Reappraised," in R. Gordon Hoxie, ed., *The Presidency and National Security Policy* (New York: Center for the Study of the Presidency, 1984), pp. 153–84.

8. Dwight D. Eisenhower, "The Central Role of the President in the Conduct of Security Affairs," in Amos O. Jordan, ed., *Issues of National Security in the 1970s* (New York: Praeger, 1967), pp. 206–19. It is also clear that many of the key national security decisions of the Eisenhower years were made by informal and relatively ad hoc groups. See Douglas Kinnard, *President Eisenhower and Strategic Management* (Lexington: University Press of Kentucky, 1977), and I. M. Destler, "The Presidency and National Security Organization," in Graebner, *The National Security: Its Theory and Practice, 1945–1960,* pp. 226–42.

9. Nelson A. Rockefeller, "The Executive Office of the President," in *Jackson Subcommittee Papers*, pp. 167–90 (Eisenhower's view is conveyed on p. 179).

10. McGeorge Bundy, "The National Security Council in the 1960's," in *Jackson Subcommittee Papers*, p. 278.

11. On the Kennedy-Johnson era see I. M. Destler, *Presidents, Bureaucrats, and Foreign Policy* (Princeton: Princeton University Press, 1972), pp. 95–118, and "National Security II: The Rise of the Assistant (1961–81)," in Heclo and Salamon, *The Illusion of Presidential Government*, pp. 263–85; and Richard M. Moose, "The White House National Security Council Staffs Since 1947," in Keith C. Clark and Laurence J. Legere, eds., *The President and the Management of National Security* (New York: Praeger, 1969), pp. 70–98.

12. These remarks were made in a campaign speech (reported in *New York Times*, October 25, 1968).

13. On the Nixon-Kissinger NSC see Henry A. Kissinger, *White House Years* (Boston: Little, Brown, 1979), pp. 38–48; Destler, *Presidents, Bureaucrats, and Foreign Policy*, pp. 118–53; John Leacacos, "Kissinger's Apparat," *Foreign Policy* (Winter 1971–72), pp. 3–27; and Chester Crocker, "The Nixon-Kissinger National Security Council System, 1969–1972: A Study in Foreign Policy Management," *Report of the Commission on the Organization of the Government for the Conduct of Foreign Policy*, Appendix O (Vol. 6) (Washington, DC: USGPO, 1975), pp. 79–99.

14. Norman Bailey and Stefan A. Halper, "National Security for Whom?" *The Washington Quarterly* 9 (Winter 1986), pp. 188–89.

15. See Zbigniew Brzezinski, *Power and Principle* (New York: Farrar, Straus and Giroux, 1983), pp. 10–11, 57–63, and "The Best National Security System: A Conversation with Zbigniew Brzezinski," *The Washington Quarterly* 5 (Winter 1982), pp. 71–82.

16. Zbigniew Brzezinski, "Deciding Who Makes Foreign Policy," *New York Times Magazine*, September 18, 1983, pp. 56 ff.

17. As Reagan is reported to have told Haig, "I won't have a repeat of the Kissinger-Rogers situation. . . . I will look to you": Alexander M. Haig, *Caveat: Realism, Reagan, and Foreign Policy* (New York: Macmillan, 1984), pp. 12–13. Reagan agreed that the NSC Adviser and his staff would have no independent contact with the press or with foreign visitors (*ibid.*, p. 58).

18. See, for example, Bernard Gwertzman, "Haig Opposes Plan for New Bush Role but Reagan Moves," *New York Times*, March 25, 1981. A general account of State-NSC infighting from early 1981 through 1983 (with particular emphasis on Central America and the Middle East) is given by Barry Rubin, *Secrets of State: The State Department and the Struggle over U.S. Foreign Policy* (New York: Oxford University Press, 1985), pp. 203–31;

see also I. M. Destler, "The Evolution of Reagan Foreign Policy," in Fred I. Greenstein, ed., *The Reagan Administration: An Early Assessment* (Baltimore: The Johns Hopkins University Press, 1983), pp. 117–58.

19. For Haig's expectations of the Foreign Service, see *Caveat,* p. 63. For some contemporary assessments of the original Reagan NSC operation, see Michael Getler, "Scaled-Down National Security Adviser Still a White House Pillar," *Washington Post,* April 7, 1981; Leslie Gelb, "Foreign Policy System Criticized by U.S. Aides," *New York Times,* October 19, 1981; and Dick Kirschten, "His NSC Days May Be Numbered, but Allen Is Known for Bouncing Back," *National Journal,* November 28, 1981, pp. 2114–17.

20. A text of NSDD 2 as well as of Carter administration directives relating to the NSC system may be found in Robert E. Hunter, *Presidential Control of Foreign Policy: Management or Mishap?* The Washington Papers No. 91 (New York: Praeger/The Center for Strategic and International Studies, 1982), pp. 103–15.

21. See Ronald H. Hinckley, "National Security in the Information Age," *The Washington Quarterly* 9 (Spring 1986), pp. 125–39.

22. According to Leslie Gelb, the membership of the NSPG in 1981 consisted of the President, the Vice President, the Secretary of State, the Secretary of Defense, the Director of Central Intelligence, and the three senior members of the White House staff ("Foreign Policy System Criticized by U.S. Aides").

23. On the interagency arms control struggles of the first Reagan term see Strobe Talbott, *Deadly Gambits: The Reagan Administration and the Stalemate in Nuclear Arms Control* (New York: Alfred A. Knopf, 1984).

24. See the collection of articles in *Conservative Digest,* February 1982, as well as Steven R. Weisman, "The Influence of William Clark," *New York Times Magazine,* August 14, 1983, pp. 17 ff.

25. A text of the relevant presidential directive (NSDD 77) is available in Richard F. Staar, ed., *Public Diplomacy: USA Versus USSR* (Stanford: Hoover Institution Press, 1986), pp. 297–99.

26. William P. Clark, "National Security Strategy," speech delivered at the Center for Strategic and International Studies, Georgetown University, May 21, 1982.

27. See Haig, *Caveat,* pp. 303–16.

28. Weisman, "The Influence of William Clark," p. 20, and Rubin, *Secrets of State,* pp. 224–28.

29. See particularly Destler, "The Evolution of Reagan Foreign Policy," pp. 145–51.

30. See Dick Kirschten, "Insider Clark Decides Now Is the Time to Go Public on NSC Policy Issues," *National Journal,* June 11, 1983, pp. 1217–20.

31. Rowland Evans and Robert Novak, "Baker's Bid for Security Adviser," *Washington Post,* October 21, 1983.

32. See, for example, David Ignatius, "Foreign Policy Rows Make McFarlane's Job Unusually Tough One," *Wall Street Journal,* August 10, 1984; "Family Feud," *The New Republic,* October 14, 1985, p. 15; Suzanne Garment, "McFarlane Leaves the Rudderless Policy Ship," *Wall Street Journal,* December 6, 1985.

33. Norman Bailey and Stefan A. Halper, "National Security for Whom?" *The Washington Quarterly* 9 (Spring 1986), pp. 187–92. According to Bailey and Halper, this collaboration went so far under McFarlane that new NSC staff appointments were subject to clearance by State.

34. See, for example, Lou Cannon and David Hoffman, "Reagan Adviser Poindexter Under Criticism by Colleagues," *Washington Post,* June 24, 1986, and "That Shy Fellow on the Firing Line," *Time,* July 28, 1986, p. 15.

35. Roger Fontaine, " 'Irrelevant' NSC Lightning Rod for Partisan Thunder," *Washington Times,* August 6, 1986, and "Poindexter's Penchant for Work Matches Passion for Anonymity," *Washington Times,* August 7, 1986.

36. See Michael R. Gordon, "NSC Being Restructured to Give More Focus to Coordinating Policy," *New York Times,* December 22, 1986; "Under Carlucci the Word Is 'Process'," *New York Times,* March 30, 1987; and Dick Kirschten, "Competent Manager," *National Journal,* February 28, 1987, pp. 468–79.

37. Thus also Henry A. Kissinger, "Not Its Power, But Its Weakness," *Washington Post,* December 21, 1986.

38. Michael R. Gordon, "At Foreign Policy Helm: Shultz vs. White House," *New York Times,* August 26, 1987.

39. Richard Halloran, "Case of the Reluctant General," *New York Times,* October 5, 1987, and Lou Cannon, "Powell Well-Regarded in Difficult Post," *Washington Post,* November 5, 1987.

Chapter 4. Rethinking the NSC Role

1. An influential early statement of this idea may be found in Richard Neustadt, *Presidential Power* (New York: John Wiley and Sons, 1961), Ch. 7.

2. On the various levels of military art see especially Edward N. Luttwak, *Strategy: The Logic of War and Peace* (New York: Simon and Schuster, 1987), pp. 69–189.

3. This argument has been well developed by former NSC Director of Intelligence Programs Kenneth deGraffenreid in Roy Godson, ed., *Intelligence Requirements for the 1980's: Intelligence and Policy* (Lexington, MA: Lexington Books, 1986), pp. 9–31.

4. Improved net assessment of U.S. military capabilities, as noted earlier, has been urged recently by the Packard Commission, *National Security Planning and Budgeting* (Washington, DC: USGPO, June 1986), pp. 12–13.

5. For an overview of current U.S. national security planning and its deficiencies, see John M. Collins, *U.S. Defense Planning: A Critique* (Boulder, CO: Westview Press, 1982).

6. The scope and seriousness of Soviet national security planning is underappreciated in the West, especially in the little-discussed area of long-range planning. See Jan Sejna and Joseph D. Douglass, Jr., *Decision-Making in Communist Countries: An Inside View* (Washington, DC: Pergamon-Brassey's, 1986).

7. The National Strategy Act, sponsored in the Senate by Senators Nunn and Warner and in the House by Representatives McEwen and Cheney, became law in October 1986, as an amendment to the Department of Defense Authorization Bill. The first annual report under the act was compiled by the NSC staff and submitted to Congress in early 1987: The White House, *National Security Strategy of the United States* (Washington, DC: USGPO, January 1987). At about the same time, the Secretary of Defense announced the creation of a bipartisan Commission on Integrated Long-Term Strategy to chart broad guidelines for military strategy and the development of defense technology over the next fifteen to twenty years, with particular attention to the relationship of strategic offensive and defensive systems and to technology for low intensity warfare. See John H. Cushman, Jr., "Applying Military Brain to Military Brawn, Again," *New York Times,* December 17, 1986. Whether these encouraging efforts will have a significant impact very much remains to be seen.

8. Robert C. McFarlane, "The National Security Council: Organization for Policy Making," in R. Gordon Hoxie, ed., *The Presidency and National Security Policy* (New York: Center for the Study of the Presidency, 1984), p. 272.

9. Under the Carlucci regime, the CMC was reduced substantially in size, amalgamated with the Situation Room staff, and subordinated to the NSC Executive Secretary, partly in an effort to integrate the CMC more completely with the work of the NSC staff.

10. Deficiencies in policy implementation and the need to devise mechanisms to correct them are important themes of I. M. Destler's *Presidents, Bureaucrats, and Foreign Policy* (Princeton: Princeton University Press, 1972), as well as the *Report of the Commission on the Organization of the Government for the Conduct of Foreign Policy* (Washington, DC: USGPO, 1975) (see especially Appendix K, pp. 6–7, 43–46).

11. Henry A. Kissinger, *White House Years* (Boston: Little, Brown, 1979), p. 30. Cf. I. M. Destler, "A Job That Doesn't Work," *Foreign Policy* (Spring 1980), pp. 86–87.

12. See the authoritative account of Ronald H. Hinckley, "National Security in the Information Age," *The Washington Quarterly* (Spring 1986), pp. 125–39.

13. Consider the remarks of McFarlane, "The National Security Council: Organization for Policy Making," pp. 268–69.

14. The United States has never formally disclosed the circumstances and content of past U.S.–Soviet Hotline exchanges; however, participating U.S. officials have revealed that it was used during the Arab-Israeli wars of 1967 and 1973 and the Indo-Pakistani war of 1971. Recurrent suggestions to upgrade the Hotline to voice and video capability have been—rightly—rejected by the U.S. government, most recently by Secretary of Defense Caspar W. Weinberger, *Report to the Congress on Direct Communications Links and Other Measures to Enhance Stability* (Washington, DC, April 11, 1983).

15. See Bill Gulley, *Breaking Cover* (New York: Warner Books, 1980), pp. 213–32.

16. See particularly Bruce G. Blair, *Strategic Command and Control: Redefining the Nuclear Threat* (Washington, DC: The Brookings Institution, 1985), pp. 65–78 and passim.

Chapter 5. The NSC as an Organization

1. In many cases, the primary incentive for remaining in career service has probably been salary level. The NSC budget should be given sufficient flexibility to deal with this problem.

2. The tightening of hierarchical relationships under Carlucci came primarily in response to the perceived irregularity of the direct reporting channel between North and Poindexter.

3. Under the Carlucci regime, strategic planning was the responsibility of a single senior staffer (Peter Rodman, former director of the State Department's Policy Planning Staff). A planning group was created early in the first Reagan term, but enjoyed little clear responsibility and less authority; a more serious planning effort was organized by Deputy Adviser Don Fortier during the McFarlane era.

4. In the 1983 reorganization, NSC staffers were for the first time given formal titles and grades. Some eight to ten senior staff are designated Special Assistant to the President for National Security Affairs; these have generally (though not always) been reserved for the heads of staff subunits, and bring supergrade rank as well as certain privileges within the White House. Other staffers are designated Director or Deputy Director of a particular area. This system has come in for some criticism as being pompous and somewhat misleading. But whatever the precise titles used, a good case

can be made for differentiation of rank within the staff along essentially these lines.

5. Prior to the Reagan administration there was no dedicated NSC staff position in the field of public diplomacy. In 1983, a separate public diplomacy group was formed within the NSC under a special assistant. This was abolished by Carlucci and the function assigned to one staffer in a newly created group concerned with technology transfer and a miscellany of global issues. While there is an important technical dimension to public diplomacy, the primary bureaucratic problem that needs redressing is the looseness of the information-policy relationship.

Chapter 6. National Security and Presidential Governance

1. *A Presidency for the 1980s,* A Report on Presidential Management by a Panel of the National Academy of Public Administration, November 1980; reprinted in Hugh Heclo and Lester M. Salamon, eds., *The Illusion of Presidential Government* (Boulder, CO: Westview Press, 1981), pp. 299–345.

2. Cecil V. Crabb, Jr. and Kevin V. Mulcahy, *Presidents and Foreign Policy Making: From FDR to Reagan* (Baton Rouge/London: Louisiana State University Press, 1986), pp. 2, 8.

3. See, for example, John Franklin Campbell, *The Foreign Affairs Fudge Factory* (New York: Basic Books, 1971), pp. 268–72.

4. Under existing arrangements, the CPPG reports to a Special Situation Group (SSG) chaired by the Vice President. The SSG does not seem to have been utilized since the Grenada operation of 1983, however, and it is far from evident that there is a need for a group at this level which does not include the President. A Planning and Coordinating Group under the chairmanship of the Deputy National Security Adviser was created in response to the criticisms of the Tower Commission to review existing covert action findings and ensure their coordination with policy; given political realities, such a committee is likely to persist in some form. It is almost certainly beneficial to have some interagency forum for the consideration of covert action operations below the level of the NSPG, especially given the informality and principals-only character of this body. It would be even more helpful, though, if the Planning and Coordinating Group or its equivalent could be given some responsibility for ensuring operational coordination of covert activities.

5. The combination of a standing arms control SIG and ad hoc involvement in pressing arms control issues by the PRG would seem decidedly superior to the existing arrangement, where integration of IG-level work on different arms control issues occurs only in a Senior Arms Control Group chaired by the National Security Adviser himself. The arrangement suggested here presupposes, however, greater interagency consensus on

basic arms control questions than existed during most of the Reagan administration.

6. A good case can be made, for example, for NSC chairmanship of IGs or their equivalent in the areas of public diplomacy, technology transfer, counterintelligence, and counterterrorism.

7. This excludes Executive Orders, which are documents implementing existing legislation on national security as well as domestic and administrative matters, and covert action "findings" as required under the Intelligence Oversight Act.

8. Seymour M. Hersh, *"The Target Is Destroyed"* (New York: Random House, 1987), p. 161. On NSDD 85 see, for example, Paul B. Stares, *The Militarization of Space: U.S. Policy, 1945–84* (Ithaca: Cornell University Press, 1985), pp. 226–29.

9. A respectable argument can also be made for splitting up State's bureau of Near East and South Asian affairs (NEA) into two separate bureaus dealing with North Africa/Middle East and Southwest/South Asia.

10. It is not clear to what extent unity of command throughout the Atlantic would be necessary in wartime, but in any case there could be prior agreement that responsibility for the Caribbean (and South Atlantic) would revert to Atlantic Command on the outbreak of general war. On the other hand, an argument can certainly be made that expanding the Central Command (CENTCOM) area of responsibility makes strategic and operational sense in purely military terms. European Command has a clearly defined and overriding mission, the defense of Western Europe, and should be relieved of responsibility for the Eastern Mediterranean (where the lengthened chain of command evidently caused problems during the U.S. intervention in Beirut) as well as the bulk of Africa. An expanded CENTCOM might eventually be given more substantial dedicated naval forces to deal with Persian Gulf as well as Eastern Mediterranean contingencies. It would also seem to make sense to assign Southern Command responsibility for U.S. naval forces on station off the coast of Nicaragua.

11. This argument is developed in Laurence H. Silberman, "Toward Presidential Control of the State Department," *Foreign Affairs* (Spring 1979), pp. 872–93.

12. Parallel arrangements might also be considered for CIA Chiefs of Station.

13. In 1983, a Central America Joint Intelligence Team was created under the Defense Intelligence Agency and located in the Pentagon following a JCS decision to "echelon back" to Washington major elements of the forces assigned to Southern Command; this organization proved an unqualified success. See the discussion of this and related matters in Paul F. Gorman, "Command, Control, Communications and Intelligence: USCINCSO's Per-

spective, 1983–1985," paper delivered at a conference at the National Defense University, June 25, 1986. Also see Gorman's remarks concerning the need for a "National Command Communications System" in *National Security Strategy,* Hearings Before the Committee on Armed Services, U.S. Senate, 100th Cong., 1st Sess. (Washington, DC: USGPO, 1987), p. 771.

14. Pertinent observations may also be found in (former CINCSO) Wallace Nutting, "Organizing for Low-Intensity Warfare," *Global Affairs* (Summer 1987), pp. 92–105.

15. A noteworthy recent exception is Duncan L. Clarke, "Why State Can't Lead," *Foreign Policy* (Spring 1987), pp. 128–42.

16. I. M. Destler, *Presidents, Bureaucrats, and Foreign Policy* (Princeton: Princeton University Press, 1972), Chs. 4 and 9, and "State: A Department or 'Something More'?" in Duncan L. Clarke, ed., *Public Policy and Political Institutions: United States Defense and Foreign Policy—Policy Coordination and Integration* (Greenwich, CT: JAI Press, 1985).

17. This suggestion is not wholly new. See Keith C. Clark and Laurence J. Legere, eds., *The President and the Management of National Security* (New York: Praeger, 1969), pp. 164–65, and Destler, *Presidents, Bureaucrats, and Foreign Policy,* pp. 271–74.

18. Another change that should be considered in this connection is abolition of State's Bureau of Intelligence and Research (INR) and transfer of its key functions to a new Deputy Under Secretary for Information Management under the Under Secretary for Political Affairs. At present, State performs too much independent intelligence analysis, while being sadly inadequate in the management of all-source data as well as of its own reporting assets.

19. In a theoretical sense, it is difficult to justify the existence of an agency whose organizational essence is limited to the conclusion of arms control agreements. In fact, however, the charge that ACDA has been an institutional partisan of arms control divorced from a larger strategic framework is hardly a fair one, at least in more recent years; on the contrary, ACDA has on the whole been less dovish than at least some elements of the State Department under recent administrations. The problem is rather that of a plethora of cooks for the arms control broth. On the other hand, it should be noted that one ACDA component, the Bureau of Verification and Intelligence, performs a unique and exceedingly important bureaucratic function.

20. One possibility might be to amalgamate VOA and USIA's television service in a new U.S. Overseas Broadcasting Agency, formally reporting to the Secretary of State on the model of the Agency for International Development. Although there will always be a danger in too close a relationship between VOA and State, the case for such a relationship would be much stronger if State itself were to adopt a more serious and strategically coherent

approach to public diplomacy. It has sometimes been suggested that VOA should be established as a separate agency under the presidentially appointed Board for International Broadcasting (BIB). It would seem preferable, though, not to blur the difference between VOA and the semiofficial surrogate radios that come under the jurisdiction of the BIB. Indeed, Radio Marti should be removed from VOA at the earliest opportunity and made an autonomous entity reporting to the BIB.

21. See Williamson Murray, "Grading the War Colleges," *The National Interest* (Winter 1986/7), pp. 12–19.

22. Crabb and Mulcahy, *Presidents and Foreign Policy Making,* pp. 337–40.

23. See especially Charles H. Fairbanks, Jr., "Bureaucratic Politics in the Soviet Union and in the Ottoman Empire," *Comparative Strategy* 6 (1987), pp. 333–62.

Index